THE ARTS ENTWINED
MUSIC AND PAINTING
IN THE NINETEENTH CENTURY

EDITED BY
MARSHA L. MORTON AND PETER L. SCHMUNK

GARLAND PUBLISHING, INC.
A MEMBER OF THE TAYLOR & FRANCIS GROUP
NEW YORK & LONDON
2000

Published in 2000 by
Garland Publishing, Inc.
A member of the Taylor & Francis Group
19 Union Square West
New York, NY 10003

10 9 8 7 6 5 4 3 2 1

Library of Congress Cataloging-in-Publication Data

The arts entwined : music and painting in the nineteenth century /
    edited by Marsha L. Morton and Peter L. Schmunk.
        p.   cm. — (Garland reference library of the humanities ;
    v. 2099. Critical and cultural musicology ; v. 2)
        Includes index.
        ISBN 0-8153-3156-8 (alk. paper)
        1. Art and music.   2. Music—19th century—History and criticism.
    3. Painting, Modern—19th century.   I. Morton, Marsha.
    II. Schmunk, Peter L.   III. Series: Garland reference library of the
    humanities ; v. 2099.   IV. Series: Garland reference library of the
    humanities. Critical and cultural musicology ; v. 2.
    ML3849.A78 1999
    700'.9'034—dc21   99-34397
                                                                      CIP

Cover: Detail of Henri Fantin-Latour, *Around the Piano,* 1885, oil on canvas,
160 × 222 cm. Musée d'Orsay, Paris. Used by permission.

Printed on acid-free, 250-year-life paper
Manufactured in the United States of America

Contents

Critical and Cultural Musicology

MARTHA FELDMAN

Musicology has undergone a sea change in recent years. Where once the discipline knew its limits, today its boundaries seem all but limitless. Its subjects have expanded from the great composers, patronage, manuscripts, and genre formations to include race, sexuality, jazz, and rock; its methods from textual criticism, formal analysis, paleography, narrative history, and archival studies to deconstruction, narrativity, postcolonial analysis, phenomenology, and performance studies. These categories point to deeper shifts in the discipline that have led musicologists to explore phenomena that previously had little or no place in musicology. Such shifts have changed our principles of evidence while urging new understandings of existing ones. They have transformed prevailing notions of musical texts, created new analytic strategies, recast our sense of subjectivity, and produced new archives of data. In the process, they have also destabilized canons of scholarly value.

The implications of these changes remain challenging in a field whose intellectual ground has shifted so quickly. In response to them, this series offers essay collections that give thematic focus to new critical and cultural perspectives in musicology. Most of the essays contained herein pursue their projects through sustained research on specific musical practices and contexts. They aim to put strategies of scholarship that have developed recently in the discipline into meaningful exchanges with one another while also helping to construct fresh approaches. At the same time they try to reconcile these new approaches with older methods, building on the traditional achievements of musicology in helping to forge new disciplinary idioms. In both ventures, volumes in this series also attempt to press new associations among fields outside of musicology, making aspects of what has often seemed an inaccessible field intelligible to scholars in other disciplines.

In keeping with this agenda, topics treated in the series include music and the cultures of print; music, art, and synesthesia in nineteenth-century Europe; music in the African diaspora; relations between opera and cinema; Marxism and music; and music in the cultural sensorium. Through enterprises like these, the series hopes to facilitate new disciplinary directions and dialogues, challenging the boundaries of musicology and helping to refine its critical and cultural methods.

THE ARTS ENTWINED

CHAPTER 1

"From the Other Side"
An Introduction

MARSHA L. MORTON

There is only one Art; painting and music are
only different fields, part of this general Art;
one must know the boundaries, but also how it
looks from the other side; yes, the painter who
is musical, just as the composer who paints,
these are the true, genuine artists. . . .[1]
—CARL FRIEDRICH ZELTER

When Carl Friedrich Zelter made these remarks during a conversation in 1783, few would have imagined their prescience. By the turn of the next century synesthetic beliefs were to nurture a truly symbiotic relationship between music and painting, with artists from Debussy to Gauguin enriching and reformulating their art through mutual exchange. While this direction culminated in twentieth-century abstraction and the creation of musical compositions inspired by paintings or incorporating visual elements, the nineteenth century represented the critical period of gestation when music "came of age" and painting approached the threshold leading into nonobjective realms. As Charles Baudelaire observed, the arts aspired to a condition "in which they len[t] each other new powers."[2]

Through selected topics, the essays included in this volume explore specific details of this interchange. Some provide new information for familiar figures; others discuss individuals (Saint-Saëns, Monet, Van Gogh) who have been infrequently mentioned in this context. Although considerable interest has been shown in this subject during the previous decade, primarily among German scholars, few publications have

1

appeared in English. Our book is intended to address this omission and to stimulate further investigations.[3]

Music's meteoric ascent among the arts in the nineteenth century, rising beyond its more humble status in the eighteenth century, is a well-known fact. *Ut pictura poesis* was succeeded by *ut pictura musica,* and painters, seemingly ever the runners-up, shifted their sights to a new model. It is therefore not surprising that more painters were inspired by music, and in more fundamental structural ways—music leading to radical developments in abstraction—than composers were inspired by the visual arts. As Wolfgang Dömling and Karl Schawelka have recently argued, the notion of "musicality" in painting is not matched by a corresponding doctrine of "painterliness" in music which is equally compelling.[4] Additionally, efforts to pinpoint influence from the visual arts in music are muddied by the fact that those influences are often entangled with literary sources (characterization in music, for example, does not reflect a uniquely pictorial quality but a narrative one that could also be found in a written text) and with general vision (musical evocations of nature do not distinguish between "real" landscapes and their painted versions). The varied range of musical inspiration is demonstrated by Thomas Grey in Chapter 4 where he argues that the *Hebrides* Overture references Mendelssohn's trip to Fingal's Cave, depictions of the site, and paintings and poems of the mythic Ossian legend. In all cases, however, the composer is crossing borders in an attempt to expand the range of his art to things extramusical.

The essays in this book deal with visualization in music in the broader meaning of images seen as well as the more specific one of paintings viewed. Considered from this perspective, the reciprocal influence between music and the visual arts becomes central to discourses on the very nature and identity of both mediums: absolute versus program music (and tone painting), and narrative representational styles versus abstracting symbolic ones in painting. Encoded in these options are ideological choices regarding artistic meaning and the determining role of content and/or form, issues that are at the heart of discussions about nineteenth-century art.

Throughout the previous century roles had been reversed, with composers seeking to incorporate elements from the visual arts and literature. Judged according to traditional classical standards of imitation, music was at the bottom of the hierarchical heap, struggling to maintain a ranking as a "fine" art. It did so by copying nature, either externally (through its sounds) or internally (emotions). Musical compositions that evoked auditory images were referred to as tone paintings. Jean-Jacques Rousseau, an enthusiast, described the genre in terms of the verbal and visual arts: "Imitative music, using lively, accented, and, as it were, speaking inflections, expresses all the passions, paints every picture, renders every object, submits the whole of nature to its ingenious imitations, and by this means conveys to the human heart those sentiments proper for moving it."[5] The position of tone (or word) painting in the early nineteenth century is discussed further by Stephanie Campbell in Chapter 3 through her comparison of the role played by visualization in Zelter's compositional practises and in Goethe's conception of music.

Music's mimetic and linguistic capacities were obviously limited, however, and in the opinion of many, its borrowings from the other arts only served to underscore its inadequacies. Music was customarily perceived as an agreeable entertainment whose "sentiments" did not compensate for failures in the realms of cognition and reasoned thought. Kant dismissed music as "least amongst the fine arts, because it plays merely with emotions" and "communicates by means of mere sensations without concepts." In comparison to the representative arts it was seriously deficient. They "greatly excel it, for they freely stimulate the play of the imagination in a way that is suited to the intellect" and "create lasting impressions."[6]

When Kant published these remarks in 1790 reevaluations about music were already underway in England and Germany in writings by Charles Avison, Adam Smith, Johann Gottfried Herder, and Wilhelm Heinse. Nascent melomania was predicated on changes in aesthetic thought found especially in theories of the sublime, on developments within music itself, and on the new public concert venues. In the Romantic doctrine articulated by Wilhelm Wackenroder, Ludwig Tieck, the brothers Schlegel, and E.T.A. Hoffmann, music was now valued for its vague indeterminate content, previously regarded as its greatest weakness. Through its nonreferential suggestive forms, music was perceived as evoking an ineffable essence more metaphysically profound than anything communicated through language or sight. Music offered a glimpse of the absolute by way of the infinite or the inner soul.[7] Significantly, this transformation was inextricably linked to new forms of instrumental music (symphonic and keyboard), still in their infancy, coupled with a rejection of music that was imitative or accompanied by a text. In his essay "Symphonies" Tieck described music as an abstract structure that explores inner realms located beyond empirical reality. Painters throughout the nineteenth century would embrace and emulate this model:

> Art is independent and free in instrumental music; it prescribes its own
> rules all by itself . . . it completely follows its dark drives and ex-
> presses with its triflings what is deepest and most wonderful. . . .
> [the]sounds which art has miraculously discovered and pursues along
> the greatest variety of paths . . . do not imitate and do not beautify;
> rather, they constitute a separate world for themselves.[8]

The most indefatigable proselytizer of instrumental music was Hoffmann, whose 1810 review of Beethoven's Fifth Symphony, considered to
be the quintessential document of Romantic theory, was itself a polemic
for the supremacy of instrumental over vocal music:

> Beethoven's music presses the levers of terror, of fear, of dread, of
> pain, and awakens the endless longing that is the nature of romanti-
> cism. Beethoven is a purely romantic composer (and precisely because
> of that, a truly musical one,) which may explain why he is less success-
> ful with vocal music, which does not permit indefinite longing. . . .[9]

Such adjectives of passion were foreign to the world of Baroque music
and accompanied changes in composition introduced during the classical
period of Haydn, Mozart, and Beethoven. New technical improvements
during the late eighteenth and early nineteenth centuries, including piano
pedals, brass instrument valves, and improved fingering on wind instruments enabled composers, beginning with Beethoven, to broaden the expressive range and drama of orchestral sound by elevating tone color and
enhancing textural and timbral variety. As Charles Rosen has observed,
sound and orchestral color became fundamental to musical structure in a
more determining way.[10]

The development of instrumental music was also facilitated by the
growth of the public concert. Composers, no longer subject to the re-
quirements of court and church, were freed from the necessities of text
and occasion/function, while listeners became observers rather than
participants. Within the concert hall, standards for audience behavior
changed under the impact of the new Romantic veneration of music.
Eighteenth-century practices, where listening was combined with social
interaction during performances, could hardly be maintained if the audience was to experience a moment of spiritual transcendence.[11] Accordingly, lights were dimmed and silence maintained. This new attitude of
contemplation, akin to states of religious devotion, has been identified by
Schawelka as essential to the concept of the "musical" in painting. He

has argued that artists sought to evoke through their work responses similar to those elicited by music in which the enraptured listener absorbs the sounds as if in a dream state.[12] Certainly, museums would come to resemble concert halls in their imposed tone of hushed reverence. Wackenroder described the "correct" way to listen as an immersion in a "current of emotion" in which "all destructive thoughts" are banished.[13] Central to the process was the disengagement of the conscious mind: comprehension would destroy the magical power and irrational mystery of the experience. This attitude was reflected later in Thomas Carlyle's ecstatic remarks: "Who is there that, in logical words, can express the effect music has on us? A kind of inarticulate, unfathomable speech, which leads us to the edge of the Infinite, and lets us for a moment gaze into that !"[14] In a similar vein Mme. de Staël had proclaimed that "the delightful reverie into which it [music] throws us annhilates all thoughts which may be expressed by words; . . . music awaken[s] in us the sentiment of infinity. . . ."[15]

No greater indication of change in the status of music can be found than by comparing the remarks on concerts and instrumental music by the eighteenth-century aesthetician Johann Georg Sulzer with those of Arthur Schopenhauer. In 1793 Sulzer wrote: "In the last [lowest in artistic ranking] position we place the application of music to concerts, which are presented merely as entertainments, and perhaps for practice in playing. To this category belong concertos, symphonies, sonatas, and solos, which generally present a lively and not unpleasant noise, or a civil and entertaining chatter, but not one that engages the heart."[16] Thirty years later Schopenhauer observed that "a man who gives himself up entirely to the impression of a symphony experiences the metaphysical."[17]

Through Schopenhauer's writings music became a superstar as it emerged from Kant's earlier banishment to occupy an elite position within a philosophical system. Schopenhauer provided a theoretical explanation and justification for Romantic intuitions about music's unique nature. He maintained that objects of the phenomenal world, which are also those depicted in paintings and described in language, are merely indirect representations of the will through "Ideas," while music, in its complete independence from empirical reality, objectifies the will:

> Therefore music is by no means like the other arts, namely a copy of the Ideas, but a *copy of the will itself,* the objectivity of which are the Ideas. For this reason the effect of music is so very much more powerful and penetrating than is that of the other arts, for these others speak only of the shadow, but music of the essence.[18]

Given this belief, it is not surprising that Schopenhauer strongly opposed any form of interchange among the arts, which would only end by weakening music's ability to express the will. Visual imaging in instrumental music—he mentioned Haydn's *Seasons* and *Creation*—was to be completely rejected, and audiences were warned against the temptation to "see pictures" mentally while they listened to symphonies.[19] Implicitly, Schopenhauer would seem to suggest that any attempt on the part of artists to craft a "musical" style of painting, while understandable, is doomed to failure. Far from discouraging painters, however, Schopenhauer's conception of music—especially as interpreted by his followers Wagner and Nietzsche—acted as a beacon.

Schopenhauer severed further the connections between music and the conscious mind, theorizing that the act of composing was an "inspiration" imperfectly understood by the individual who mentally hears and "transcribes" the notes through a process inaccessible to the rational mind. He wrote: "The composer reveals the innermost nature of the world, and expresses the profoundest wisdom in a language that his reasoning faculty does not understand, just as a magnetic somnambulist gives information about things of which she has no conception when she is awake."[20] This perceived divorce from cognitive thought and language served to unite music with painting in some of the earliest comparisons between the arts. While Leonardo da Vinci had considered music and painting to be "sister arts" and Poussin had linked color schemes to musical modes, the Romantics consistently paired them on the basis of their shared nonverbal nature. From Sulzer to Wackenroder, Novalis, and Friedrich Schlegel, music and painting were the arts of "soul" and "spirit." Mme. de Staël, echoed later by Delacroix, proclaimed them "superior to thought: their language is colour, forms or sounds."[21] Painting and music were not only verbally inarticulate but also acted more directly on the senses through the heart or nervous system (an association later developed by Baudelaire), rather than the mind.

Despite projected unifications of the arts and early expressions of synesthesia, the Romantic doctrine was based on an ideal of music as an abstract instrumental form. Tone painting was disparaged, with Beethoven pointedly remarking that the *Pastoral Symphony*, seemingly an exception, was based on his feelings rather than on a painting.[22] The Romantic view did not go unchallenged, however, and at mid-century was opposed from two directions: by champions of program music and by formalist theorists of absolute music.[23] It was under the banner of program music that the first composition based on a painting *(La Sposalizio)* was written by Franz Liszt in 1839. Composers from Berlioz to Mendelssohn, Liszt, and Wagner began to doubt the unqualified merits of a purely abstract identity for music. Partly in reponse to Hegel, who predicted that music which "free[d] itself from an actual text as well as from the expression of any specific subject matter" would remain "empty and meaningless" (his own tastes ran to Rossini), composers began exploring ways to give music a "power of speech," one more precise than romantic "hieroglyphs" and capable of conveying ideas and concrete images.[24] As Dahlhaus has succinctly stated, program music replaced indefinite feelings with definite ideas.[25] Liszt, who aggressively sought to elevate the intellectual status of music through borrowings from other arts, provided the best explanation of program music's agenda in a discussion of the Wagnerian technique, the *leitmotiv:*

> Using a method which he applies in an entirely original manner, Wagner succeeds in extending the empire and the territorial rights of music. Not content with the power which she wields over the heart by awakening there the whole range of human feelings, he makes it possible for her to prompt our ideas, to address herself to our thought, to appeal to our reflective powers; he endows her with a moral and intellectual sense. . . . By forcing our memory and our power of meditation to so constant an exercise [in following the recurrent melodies], if in no other way, Wagner snatches the action of music from the domain of vague emotionalism, and adds to its charms some of the pleasures of the mind.[26]

Composers interjected content and "meaning" into their work by using literature and the visual arts as programmatic texts. Through devices such as Berlioz's *idée fixe,* Liszt's "motivic transformations," and Wagner's *leitmotiv*, instrumental music was able to suggest characterization, narration, and representation. Symphonic and piano music (and not just *Lieder* and opera) were now capable of conveying images and ideas in a more sophisticated and complex way than their ancestor, the tone painting. Contemporary advocates Franz Brendel and Adolf Bernhard Marx described program music in Darwinian terms as a progressive evolution from picturesque imitations to philosophical ideas. The popularity of program music, which began with Berlioz's *Symphonie Fantastique* of 1830 and flourished through the 1860s, also reflected consumer preferences for more substantive content in music, either visual or literary. This position has been persuasively argued by Thomas Grey in his discussion of the cultural isolation of absolute music, and Leon Botstein, who has chronicled audience demand for explanatory texts. Botstein writes that: "the inexpressible became intolerable. Specificity in linguistic terms was demanded from music, which became understandable insofar as it could be translated explicitly, in either narrative or poetic terms . . . and to a less extent, [in] painting."[27] Confirmation of this tendency can be found in Schopenhauer's caution to listeners against visualizing music (cited above) and in Hegel's observation that "Laymen like most in music . . . the intelligible expression of feelings and ideas, something tangible, a topic."[28] Schawelka has suggested that synesthetic visions experienced in concerts resulted from the indeterminacy of absolute instrumental music.[29]

Berlioz and Wagner, despite the latter's creation of the multimedia *Gesamtkunstwerk*, never composed music based on specific paintings and indeed confessed to an indifference to viewing the fine arts (remaining strangers to museums and exhibitions). Nonetheless their works are filled with visual imagery and were especially attractive to painters. This is perhaps ironic given Berlioz's arrogant assertion that "painting . . . cannot encroach on the domain of music; but music can by its own means act upon the imagination in such a way as to engender sensations analogous to those produced by graphic arts."[30] Debussy attributed Berlioz's appeal to the central role of color and narration in his music, while Liszt described Berlioz and himself as "malende Symphoniste."[31] Berlioz equated instrumentation in music with color in painting and, in his influential treatise on instrumentation, described symphonic music through pictorial metaphors of nature.[32] Wagner also assumed a patronizing air towards the visual arts. In his essay on Beethoven, Wagner approvingly quoted the earlier composer's contention that music would only be diminished if it sought to reproduce the effects of painting, defined as the "pleasing appearance of beautiful forms."[33] This view of painting, which for Beethoven was no doubt associated with Lessing and eighteenth-century neoclassical theory, acquires more superficial resonances when considered in conjunction with Wagner's favorite artist, Hans Makart.

It was Liszt, as mentioned, who created the first musical composition based directly on a pictorial source. His piano piece *La Sposalizio* was inspired by a Raphael painting of the same title seen during his travels in Italy. He soon followed it with *Il Pensieroso*, after Michelangelo's sculpture of Guiliano de Medici, in which he also incorporated rhythms borrowed from Beethoven to demonstrate affinities he perceived between the two masters.[34] Liszt's fusion of music and the visual arts succeeded earlier works based on poetry and led to his symphonic poems of the 1850s. They manifested his belief that the arts, when merged, produced synergistic effects. These he later maximized by combining auditory and visual experiences: together with another pianist he performed *Hunnenschlacht* in front of the Wilhelm von Kaulbach painting which had inspired his piece. (Kaulbach, it is interesting to note, was not impressed.) Similarly, he planned to commission from Bonaventura Genelli a series of paintings for his Dante Symphony, which would be projected as dioramas accompanying the music. Liszt's pioneering efforts were continued later in the century through Saint-Saëns who, as discussed in Chapter 6 by Carlo Caballero, altered and enhanced the symphonic poem's capabilities of conveying visual and sensual, rather than verbal, associations.

Liszt's compositions after paintings reveal conservative tastes (the Italian Renaissance and German academic art), in accordance with the preferences of his painter friends who included Friedrich Preller d. Ä. and Jean-Auguste-Dominique Ingres, his tour guide to the Sistine Chapel. Regarding subject matter, his selections were typical of sources used by other nineteenth-century composers, identified by Monike Fink as themes from religious, historical, mythological, or allegorical paintings.[35] Liszt's compositions attempted to translate either the mood, narrative elements, or specific images of the visual source; he represented, for example, the illuminated cross in Kaulbach's *Hunnenschlacht* with the Gregorian choral melody "Crux fidelis." He did not, however, create formal structures that paralleled those of the pictorial source, as Debussy was to invent for his musical transcriptions of paintings by Botticelli and Watteau.[36] Indeed, the painterly quality of pictures (color and texture), so inspirational to Debussy through Turner and Whistler, seems to have been of minimal interest to Liszt who composed *Hunnenschlacht* from a graphic reproduction.

The vogue for painterly-musical fusion was also evidenced through several articles published on the topic at mid-century by Julius Becker, Brendel, and Louis Viardot.[37] Previous writings, notably Johann Jakob Engel's "Ueber die musikalische Malerei" from 1780, had addressed tone painting, while nineteenth-century authors explored the possibilities of actual union.[38] This was especially true of Becker, who theorized mergers on the basis of synesthesia and on technical correlations between color and sound (seven colors in the rainbow and tones in the scale, triadic chords and primary colors, etc.).[39] Significantly, his guiding muses were Goethe and Zelter, whose writings were quoted at the beginning of this chapter. Philippe Junod, in Chapter 2, surveys and evaluates the various terms and structural models employed to rank and compare the two art forms during the nineteenth century.

In musical circles support for program music was hardly unanimous, with heated debates raging over the intrinsic nature of music and its content. The opposition was led by Eduard Hanslick whose book *Vom Musikalisch-Schönen* (1854) engaged in polemical differences with Wagner's publications. These arguments were to continue and intensify over the next few decades between supporters of Brahms and Wagner. Hanslick not only disapproved of musical forays into domains of the other arts, he also rejected Romantic interpretations of musical content as expressions of the soul, promising listeners an "escape from the dark realm of feeling."[40] Hanslick, building on the foundations of J. F. Herbart, preached a formalist doctrine advocating absolute music purged of metaphysics and poetry. The content and object of music, he maintained, "consists of forms set in motion by sounding."[41] Music is therefore unique among the other arts because of "the indivisibility of form and content." "In music," he wrote, "content and form, the material and its shaping by the composer, image and idea form a mysterious and inextricable unity."[42]

Hanslick believed that each art possessed individual characteristics based on different materials and techniques which precluded any blendings. Nonetheless, he offered compelling metaphors linking music with painting. Music is visualized, for example, as a "kaleidoscope of sounds" and a "moving" arabesque, "an organic design" described as "a pattern of lines first gently falling and then boldly rising, meeting and separating, forming large and small curves balancing each other. . . ."[43] Four decades later, Jugendstil designers Hermann Obrist and August von Endell would formulate theories of abstraction in the visual arts based on the non-mimetic musically expressive patterns of the decorative arts. Hanslick provided a model for judging beauty in music through abstract forms which would soon be echoed by Conrad Fiedler and Adolf Hildebrand. He wrote that the nature of beauty in music "lies entirely in musical sounds and their artistic arrangement, something independent of any exterior content," and proceeded to apply these standards to the visual arts: "a higher analogy with beauty in music can be found in architecture, in the human body, or in landscape—all of which present a fundamental beauty of outlines and colours, quite apart from any spiritual expression. . . ."[44] Here Hanslick suggests formal means of comparison very different from emotive Baudelairian correspondences.

Contemporary painters showed remarkably little awareness of or reponse to these controversies, remaining fixated on the talisman of "abstract" expressive music. Like the Romantics, they believed paradoxically in the possibility of a *Gesamtkunstwerk* and an ideal of "pure" music uncontaminated by the visual or literary arts. Their commitment to this ideal, which remained constant throughout the century, was substantially reinvigorated, on the one hand, by the formal analyses of Hanslick and, on the other, by Wagnerian theory and music. Merging (implausibly) Schopenhauer with program music, Wagner produced music dramas whose chromaticism and structural fluidity (the "musical prose" and "endless melody"), perceived as indeterminate and suggestive, were the apogée of Romanticism and the standard-bearer, to many, of modernism. The tremendous popularity and influence of Wagner in France is traced by Lisa Norris in Chapter 7 through her discussion of Henri Fantin-Latour and his circle of friends. Baudelaire reported that the chief characteristic of Wagner's music was "its nervous intensity, its violence in passion and in purpose. . . . It expresses all the deepest hidden secrets of the human heart."[45] The association between music and qualities of wordless profundity was so pervasive that Théophile Gautier in 1858 could describe the smile of Mona Lisa as "vague, infinite, inexpressible, like a musical thought."[46] This direction culminated in the late nineteenth century, with symbolist artists from Redon to Gauguin proclaiming the virtues of the enigmatic. Redon spoke for his generation when he wrote, "[m]y drawings inspire and cannot be defined. They determine nothing. They place us, like music, in an ambiguous indeterminate world."[47] The efforts of Liszt and Berlioz to endow music with articulate speech and powers of description seem to have gone unheard.

Clearly, painters listened to music with ears attuned to their own pictorial needs. Given their orientation, it is surprising that they were drawn to music irrespective of the composer's ideological affiliation (program or absolute music). This occurred despite considerable technical knowledge about music by artists. Painters who upheld a belief in music as abstract could find it embodied in the work of Berlioz and Wagner (Van Gogh's two favorites). Fantin-Latour's tastes encompassed the very divergent styles of Schumann, Brahms, Berlioz, and Wagner, while Delacroix admired Mozart, Chopin, and Rossini (and detested Berlioz). Gauguin surprisingly preferred the precision of Handel. Artists with more consistent tastes like Max Klinger, who admired Beethoven, Schumann, and Brahms, were the exception. Musicians, for their part, however, displayed little interest in or knowledge about the visual arts. Liszt, Mendelssohn, Chausson, Chabrier, and Debussy were unusual in their close contacts with painters.

The quest after "musical" painting yielded no single style, as a glance at the similarly titled canvases *Symphony in White, No.1 (The White Girl)* (1862) by James McNeill Whistler and *A Symphony* (1849–1852) by Moritz von Schwind, quickly confirms. Nonetheless, music represented an enduring inspirational model for artists seeking an alternative to painting which was narrative and descriptive. This did not necessarily lead to the diffuse forms of Delacroix, Turner, Fantin-Latour, or the late style of Corot. German art indebted to musical ideals, found in works by Arnold Böcklin, Klinger, and others, remained solidly three-dimensional and illusionistic. Most painters, however, admired music because it exemplified to them an art that was independent (of other art forms and the material world), self-referential and, as Hanslick maintained, comprised of an indivisible form and content. The desire to make painting be more like music thus motivated painters, paradoxically, to discover and use what was unique about their own medium. For this reason, the term "musical" became frequently synonymous with "painterly" and the opposite of "literary."[48] Painters sought to convey meaning through color and form, space and light; they used images symbolically to evoke mood, essence, and subjective states, in pointed contrast to the storytelling of narrative art.

Beginning with the German Romantics, landscapes were favored because their forms were interpreted as ciphers of meaning rather than material objects. To contemporaries, landscapes (especially those devoid of figures) dispensed with the conventional subject matter of religious and history paintings—nothing "happened" in them. Runge, who described landscape painting as an abstract art, achieved similar effects with the arabesque, while Friedrich came close to painting musical "nothingness" in his *Monk by the Sea* (1810).[49] This tradition continued in German art through the landscapes of the musically inspired painters Anselm Feuerbach, Klinger, and Böcklin, the last of whom said he wanted to evoke a "felt impression" like music without having to "render anything explicit."[50] The fusion between landscape, emotion, and musicality in German Romantic philosophy is explored more fully by Elizabeth Prelinger in Chapter 9 where she considers its legacy (and "negative" inversion) in Munch's *The Scream*. In France nature was also considered to be the subject most capable of endowing painting with an auditory "voice." Kermit Champa, in Chapter 5, discusses musical reception in French and British criticism, and landscape/music associations within the context of paintings by Corot and Monet.

After mid-century in both France and Germany opposition between narrative and nonnarrative art took on new implications as battle lines were drawn between academic painting (which was content oriented) and a realist style whose formal elements were equally important to conveying meaning. The influence of music contributed greatly to this development wherein paintings were "seen" rather than "read." The project of making art musical frequently involved a reduction of the concrete physical presence of the images depicted. Whether through the dissolution or flattening of forms, most painters turned away from mimetic description in order to enhance the communicative power of color, line, and shape. Of all the tools at the painter's disposal, color was universally regarded as the most evocative and musical (and also, like music, the most "feminine"). For John Ruskin, "the arrangement of colors and lines is an art analogous to the composition of music, and entirely independent of the representation of facts," while for Delacroix, colors and forms "seen from a distance reach the most intimate regions of the soul and convey what one may call the music of a picture. . . ."[51] Painters from Runge to Van Gogh emphasized the abstract nature of color relationships by referring to them as pictorial "symphonies." As Peter Schmunk elucidates in Chapter 8, Van Gogh's musical conception of color was an important factor in the development of his mature style as he moved from Nuenen to Paris to Arles. Gauguin summarized nineteenth-century attitudes in his response to a query about his painting *Tahitian Pastorals* (1892):

> I obtain symphonies, harmonies that represent nothing absolutely real in the vulgar sense of the word, with arrangements of lines and colors given as a pretext by any subject whatsoever from life or nature. These do not express any idea directly, but should make one think the way music makes one think, without the help of ideas or images, simply by the mysterious affinities between our brains and such arrangements of color and line.[52]

The concept of color as musical—providing the technical basis for linking the arts of sight and sound—stemmed from a belief in synesthesia prevalent throughout most of the nineteenth century. While Gauguin spoke of correspondences between harmonies of color and sound, comparing those in Beethoven's *Pathetique Sonata* with the "somber

harmonies of brown and dull violet in Delacroix," Liszt "tested" startled
orchestra members in Weimar by requesting them to "play" blue, violet,
and pink.[53] For many composers and painters, these affinities were an integral part of the creative process. Böcklin, for instance, played the flute
and bells while working in his studio. Karl Maria von Weber wrote in his
autobiography that he sought "certain combinations of timbre that
should correspond to the colour effects used by painters to convey the
light transitions between dawn, morning, afternoon and evening," and
Debussy described a composition as "an experiment . . . in finding the
different combinations possible inside a single colour, as a painter might
make a study in grey. . . ."[54]

Nineteenth-century enthusiasm for synesthesia began with E.T.A.
Hoffmann, whose ideas gained additional recognition through the pub-
licity of Baudelaire's writings. Hoffmann (who identified the hero of his
story *Kreisleriana* as "the little man in a coat the colour of C sharp minor
with an E major coloured collar") inspired Baudelaire's poem *Correspondances* and was frequently cited by him. Synesthetic experiences
described by Hoffmann in *Kreisleriana* haunted Baudelaire's aesthetic
vision. Hoffmann wrote: "It is not so much in the dream state as in the
preceding delirious stage, particularly when one has been immersed in
music, that a relationship is established between colours, sounds and per-
fumes."[55] For Baudelaire, similar associations occurred while listening
to Wagner (and while smoking opium), prompting him to theorize rhap-
sodically that "what would be truly surprising would be to find that
sound *could not* suggest colour, that colours *could not* evoke the idea of a
melody. . . ."[56]

Artists remained eager to enhance these moments of audio-visual
epiphany by combining image and sound in *Gesamtkunstwerk* productions. Runge, who had written an essay titled "Thoughts on the Analogy
of Color and Tone," hoped to see his drawings, *The Times of Day*, realized as paintings displayed in a cathedral-like setting with musical
accompaniment. A similar project was envisioned by his colleague
Friedrich. Increasingly, multimedia partnerships were forged by friends.
Moritz von Schwind planned a cycle of wall paintings for a room in
which Schubert's compositions would be played. Each wall was to represent poetry that had been set to music by Schubert. Later in the century a
concert of Debussy's music was performed in a Brussels gallery hung
with paintings by Gauguin and Renoir. Redon and Chausson played
Beethoven and Schumann in the more private setting of Chausson's
home, filled with his collection of contemporary French art.

These collaborations reflected a musical literacy on the part of painters which was typical of nineteenth-century middle-class society. While relatively few musicians could draw or had been raised in an artistic milieu (Mendelssohn and Debussy being exceptions), most painters possessed at least a rudimentary musical education. These included, among others, Ingres (who socialized with Gounod and Cherubini), Delacroix (a close friend of Chopin and member of a musical club with Gautier, Baudelaire, Balzac, and Boissard de Boisdenier), Von Schwind, Feuerbach, and Böcklin (founding members of a vocal quartet in Rome), Klinger (a talented musician who kept a piano in his studio and corresponded with Brahms), Redon (who played the violin with Chausson in a chamber group and described himself as having been "born on a sound wave"), Fantin-Latour and Bazille (who performed four-hand piano transcriptions with Edmond Maître), and Munch (a friend of Frederick Delius). Van Gogh was unusual in having been exposed to music only as an adult; Gauguin played a little piano but preferred the guitar, which was certainly more suited to his peripatetic lifestyle.

The centrality of music in nineteenth-century European culture occurred for a variety of social and economic reasons that have been investigated by William Weber, Leon Botstein, and Richard Leppert. The growth of public concerts, whose tickets after mid-century were offered at very reasonable prices, served to democratize the musical experience, just as exhibitions and the emergence of galleries made the viewing of art available to a wider audience. Technological innovations in printmaking (the invention of lithography and mechanized typesetting) made the production of sheet music commercially profitable and inexpensive for consumers. Periodicals devoted to the arts flourished, featuring articles aimed at both the general public and the professional; concerts and exhibitions were regularly reviewed. Amateur music groups, ranging from choral societies to string quartets and orchestras, were also a frequent part of bourgeois life. During the second half of the century more and more households owned pianos. These facts of everyday life establish a context for the essays in this book. The theoretical issues discussed were ultimately a product of the increased integration of music, art, and life during the nineteenth century, one that afforded growing opportunities for painters and musicians to experience art from Zelter's "other side."

NOTES

[1]Carl Friedrich Zelter, *Carl Friedrich Zelters Darstellungen seines Lebens,* ed. Johann-Wolfgang Schottländer (Weimar: Verlag der Goethe-Gesellschaft, 1931), 151. The translation is by Stephanie Campbell.

[2]Charles Baudelaire, "The Life and Work of Eugène Delacroix" (1863), quoted in Edward Lockspeiser, *Music and Painting: A Study in Comparative Ideas from Turner to Schoenberg*, (New York: Harper and Row, 1973), 47. The full text is reprinted in *The Mirror of Art: Critical Studies by Charles Baudelaire*, ed. and trans. Jonathan Mayne (Garden City, N.J.: Doubleday, 1956), 306–338.

[3]An extensive bibliography is provided by Philippe Junod in Chapter 2, "The New *Paragone:* Paradoxes and Contradictions of Pictorial Musicalism." Publications in English devoted to music and the visual arts in the nineteenth century include Edward Lockspeiser's book (see above); Andrew Kagan, "Ut Pictura Musica, I: to 1860," *Arts Magazine*, 60, no. 9 (May 1986), 86–91; Peter Vergo, "Music and the Visual Arts," *The Romantic Spirit in German Art 1790–1990*, ed. Keith Hartley (London: Thames and Hudson, 1994), 131–137; Matthias Kühn, "The Romantic Concept of a 'Union of the Arts,'" *The Romantic Spirit*, exh. cat. (New York: Pierpont Morgan Library, 1988); and the brief but thought-provoking recent article by the Liszt scholar Wolfgang Dömling, "Reuniting the Arts: Notes on the History of an Idea," in *19th-Century Music*, 18, no. 1 (Summer 1994): 3–9.

This book is an outgrowth of the session "Music and the Visual Arts: Cross-Currents in 19th-Century European Culture" held at the 1997 annual conference of the College Art Association in New York City. The panel was chaired by Peter Schmunk and myself with Kermit Champa and Jeffrey Kallberg as respondents. Special thanks go to Professor Kallberg and Dr. Stanley Boorman for their help with this project in its early stages. I would also like to thank series editor Martha Feldman for her comments and suggestions on the manuscript for this book.

[4]Dömling, 4. Karl Schawelka, *Quasi una Musica: Untersuchungen zum Ideal des 'Musikalischen' in der Malerei ab 1800* (Munich: Mäander, 1993). The same point is also made by Jean-Yves Bosseur in *Music: Passion for an Art* (N.Y.: Rizzoli, 1991), 93, and derives from opinions formulated in the eighteenth century by Diderot, D'Alembert, and others.

[5]Jean-Jacques Rousseau, *Dictionaire de Musique*, Paris, 1768, quoted in Carl Dahlhaus, *The Idea of Absolute Music*, trans. Roger Lustig (Chicago: University of Chicago Press, 1989), 49.

[6]Immanuel Kant, *Kritik der Urteilskraft*, 1790, Part I, Book 2, Section 53, in *Music and Aesthetics in the Eighteenth and Early-Nineteenth Centuries*, eds. Peter le Huray and James Day (Cambridge: Cambridge University Press, 1981), 221–222. Kant's response to music was generally one of testy irritation. He complained that its impressions "vanish altogether, or, if they are involuntarily recalled by the imagination, are more tiresome than pleasurable" (223).

[7]For a discussion of the emerging prestige of instrumental music within a context of German Romantic idealism see Mark Evan Bonds, "Idealism and the

Aesthetics of Instrumental Music at the Turn of the Nineteenth Century," *Journal of the American Musicological Society,* 50:2–3, Summer-Fall 1997.

[8]Ludwig Tieck, "Symphonien," cited and translated in John Neubauer, *The Emancipation of Music from Language: Departure of Mimesis in Eighteenth-Century Aesthetics* (New Haven: Yale University Press, 1986), 199–200. The notion of music's nonrepresentational nature, so essential to an understanding of music by visual artists, appeared in several documents at the turn of the century. Charles Rosen has emphasized the significance of Friedrich Schiller's remarks in his 1794 review of Friedrich Matthisson's poems. Schiller stated that music represents feelings by their form, rather than content (Charles Rosen, *The Romantic Generation* [Cambridge, Mass.: Harvard University Press, 1995], 127). A decade earlier Adam Smith had been even more explicit about the absence of external content in instrumental music: "Its meaning, therefore, may be said to be complete in itself. . . . What is called the subject of such Music is merely . . . a certain leading combinations of Notes. . . . The subject of a composition of instrumental music is part of that composition: the subject of a poem or picture is no part of either." ("The Imitative Arts," cited in Kagan, 89).

[9]E.T.A. Hoffmann, cited in Dahlhaus, 42.

[10]Rosen, 39–40.

[11]On changes in concert hall etiquette see William Weber, "Wagner, Wagernism, and Musical Idealism," in *Wagnerism in European Culture and Politics,* ed. David C. Large and William Weber (Ithaca and London: Cornell University Press, 1984), 30–31; Martha Feldman, "Magic Mirrors and the *Seria* Stage: Thoughts toward a Ritual View," *Journal of the American Musicological Society,* 48:3, Fall 1995, 423–483; and James H. Johnson, *Listening in Paris: A Cultural History* (Berkeley: University of California Press, 1995).

[12]Schawelka, 12, 53. This theory allows the author to present a definition of "musical" which applies to all paintings inspired by music. The customary meaning of the term as synonymous with "abstracting" is obviously inaccurate for most German art from Runge to Böcklin and Klinger.

[13]Wilhelm Wackenroder to Tieck, May 5, 1792, quoted in Schawelka, 53.

[14] Thomas Carlyle, "On Heroes and Hero Worship," 1852, cited in Kagan, 91.

[15]Anne-Louise-Germaine de Staël, *De l'Allegmagne,* 1810, in Le Huray and Day, 301. Her book was largely responsible for introducing German Romantic philosophy and culture to France.

[16]Johann Georg Sulzer, *Allgemeine Theorie der schönen Künste,*1793, quoted in Dahlhaus, 4. Sulzer's book was the first "dictionary" on aesthetics to give extensive coverage to music. In some passages (unlike the statement quoted above) he anticipates Romantic ideas about music and provides early

comparisons between painting and music, observing that "the visual and aural senses . . . affect the spirit and the heart." Translated in Le Huray and Day, 133.

[17]Arthur Schopenhauer, *The World as Will and Representation,* vol. I, section 52 (1819; reprint, trans. E.F.J. Payne, N.Y.: Dover Publications, 1969), 262.

[18]Ibid, 257.

[19]Schopenhauer, *The World as Will and Representation,* vol. I, 263 and II, 450. He described symphonic music as incorporeal: "[M]ere form without the material, like a mere spirit world without matter. We certainly have an inclination to realize it while we listen, to clothe it in the imagination with flesh and bone, and to see in it all the different scenes of life and nature. On the whole, however, this does not promote an understanding or enjoyment of it, but rather gives it a strange and arbitrary addition." His comments can certainly be taken as an indictment of program music, since the second volume was published in 1844.

[20]Schopenhauer, vol. I, 260.

[21]De Staël, 301. Delacroix paraphrased her in his journal entry from January 26, 1824: "This art [painting], like music, *is higher than thought;* [sic] hence it has the advantage over literature, through its vagueness." (*The Journal of Eugène Delacroix,* ed. Hubert Wellington [Oxford: Phaidon, 1980], 24.)

[22] Ludwig von Beethoven, cited in Lockspeiser, 13.

[23]The term "absolute music" was coined by Wagner in 1847; Liszt was the first to use the word "Programmusik." See Thomas S. Grey, *Wagner's Musical Prose: Texts and Contexts* (Cambridge: Cambridge University Press, 1995), 1; and Monike Fink, *Musik nach Bildern: Programbezogenes Komponieren im 19. und 20. Jahrhundert* (Innsbruck, Austria: Edition Helbling, 1987), 13.

[24]G.W.F. Hegel, *Aesthetics: Lectures on Fine Arts* (1835–1838; reprint, trans. T. M. Knox, Oxford: Clarendon Press, 1975), 901–902. The lectures were originally delivered in Berlin between 1820 and 1829.

[25]Dahlhaus, *The Idea of Absolute Music,* 14.

[26]Franz Liszt, *Lohengrin und Tannhäuser,* quoted in Baudelaire, "Richard Wagner and Tannhäuser in Paris" (1861; reprint in *The Painter of Modern Life and Other Essays,* ed. and trans. Jonathan Mayne, N.Y.: DaCapo Press, 1964), 133.

[27]Leon Botstein, "Listening through Reading: Musical Literacy and the Concert Audience," *19th-Century Music* XVI, no. 2, (Fall 1992): 144, and Grey, 9–12. Grey presents an especially convincing argument for the existence of program music as a presence equal to that of absolute music. He notes that "the dominating cultural role of opera, drama, poetry, and novels by the early nineteenth century increasingly led consumers of absolute music to listen against the grain of its autonomous appearance, so to speak, to listen for cultural, literary, or otherwise fictive meanings."

[28]Hegel, 953.

[29]Schawelka, 53.

[30]Hector Berlioz, "L'Imitation en musique," *Gazette musicale de Paris,* 1837, in Le Huray and Day, 483.

[31]Liszt, quoted in Franzsepp Würtenberger, *Malerei und Musik: Die Geschichte des Verhaltens zweier Künste zueinander* (Frankfurt: Peter Lang, 1979), 77. This book presents the most comprehensive survey of pictorial and musical interchange from the Renaissance through the twentieth century.

[32]Berlioz's landscape references were decidedly more exotic than Beethoven's Viennese woods. In *Grand Traité d'Instrumentation* (Paris 1843) he wrote: "In the thousand instrumental combinations offered by the orchestra may be found a richness and a variety of harmony and colour together with a wealth of contrasts unequalled in any form of artistic expression. . . . In repose the orchestra suggests the slumber of the ocean; in a state of agitation it recalls a tropical tempest. The orchestra sometimes explodes and it is then a volcano. Buried in the depths of the orchestra are the murmurs and the mysterious sounds of the primeval forest." Cited in Lockspeiser, 25.

[33]Passages from Wagner's 1870 essay "Beethoven" are translated in Lockspeiser, 15, and in *Music in European Thought, 1851–1912,* ed. Bojan Bujic (Cambridge: Cambridge University Press, 1988), 65–75.

[34]These works, and the circumstances surrounding their inspiration, are discussed by Monike Fink (15–16, 30). She also provides a lengthy bibliography on program music. *La Sposalizio* and *Il Pensieroso* were both published as part of the second volume of Liszt's *Années de Pèlerinage.* The other piano pieces in this series were derived from poetry. For further discussions regarding Liszt and painting see Würtenberger, 208–209, and Wolfram Steinbeck, "Musik nach Bildern: Zu Franz Liszts *Hunnenschlacht,*" in *Töne, Farben, Formen: Über Musik und die bildenden Künste,* (Laaber: Laaber Verlag, 1995), especially 17–19.

[35]Fink, 17–30. Her research has uncovered 711 musical compositions based on visual arts sources written during the nineteenth and twentieth centuries. Nearly two-thirds of these, however, were completed within the last fifty years. Throughout the nineteenth and early twentieth centuries all of the works were composed for orchestra or piano. Perennial favorites for musical inspiration included Dürer and Michelangelo, followed by Goya and, in the twentieth century, Picasso.

[36]For a more detailed discussion of Debussy within the context of the visual arts see Helga de la Motte-Haber, *Musik und Bildende Kunst: von der Tonmalerei zur Klangskulptur* (Laaber: Laaber Verlag, 1990), 109–117. This book is also valuable for illustrations of paintings (today frequently obscure) used as sources by composers.

[37]Julius Becker, "Ideen über Malerei und Musik," *Neue Zeitschrift für Musik* 33 and 34 (October 21 and 24, 1840): 129–131 and 133–134; Brendel, "Einige Worte über Malerei in der Tonkunst," *Neue Zeitschrift für Musik* 47 (1850): 242; and Louis Viardot, "Ut Pictura Musica," *Gazette des Beaux-Arts* I (January-March 1859): 19–29.

[38]Johann Jakob Engel, "Ueber die musikalische Malerei" (1780; reprint in *Johann Jakob Engels' Schriften,* vol. IV, Berlin: in der Myliussischen Buchhandlung, 1844), 136–156.

[39]Becker also suggested associations between instruments and specific colors, and between contours and the melodic line. Ultimately, though, he considered music to be a Romantic art form and stated that paintings could only be "musical" if they evoked states of mind and emotions similar to the musical compostions.

[40]Eduard Hanslick, *Vom Musikalisch-Schönen,* 1854, in *Music in European Thought, 1851–1912,* 12.

[41]Ibid., 19.

[42]Ibid., 36.

[43]Ibid., 19.

[44]Ibid., 18, 20.

[45]Baudelaire, "Richard Wagner and Tannhäuser in Paris," 137.

[46]Théophile Gautier, cited in Schawelka, 121. Gautier's comments appeared in an 1858 article on the Mona Lisa.

[47]Odilon Redon, quoted in Lockspeiser, 90.

[48]The reverse is true in music, where literary and visual influences are often difficult to distinguish. Schawelka discusses these issues with regard to painting in his chapter titled "Inhalte: Gegen die 'Anekdote,'" 140–152.

[49]Runge is cited in Schawelka, 132. Landscape painting was associated with music by Schiller and A. W. Schlegel (see Rosen, 130, and Schawelka, 120). Ludwig Tieck described history painting as the "bête noire" of "musical ideals" in his novel *Franz Sternbalds Wanderungen.* See Schawelka, 121. For considerations of the arabesque as a strategy of communication different from narration see Frances S. Connelly, *The Sleep of Reason: Primitivism in Modern European Art and Aesthetics, 1725–1907* (University Park, Penn.: Pennsylvania State University Press, 1995), 37–54. Elizabeth Prelinger discusses arabesques in her essay on Edvard Munch in this volume.

[50]Arnold Böcklin, quoted in Ludwig Hevesi, *Alt-Kunst, Neu-Kunst* (Vienna, 1909), 500, cited in Botstein, "Brahms and Nineteenth-Century Painting," *19th-Century Music* (Fall 1990): 163.

[51]For Ruskin's statement see Kagan, 91. Delacroix is translated in Lockspeiser, 41.

[52]Gauguin provided these comments in an interview for *L'Echo de Paris* (June 13, 1895). The statement is quoted in *The Art of Paul Gauguin,* exh. cat., Richard Brettel et al. (Washington, D.C. and Chicago: The National Gallery of Art and The Art Institute of Chicago, 1988), 284.

[53]Gauguin to Fontainas, March 1899, translated by John Rewald and reprinted in Herschel B. Chipp, ed., *Theories of Modern Art: A Source Book by Artists and Critics* (Berkeley: University of California Press, 1968), 75. The Liszt incident supposedly occurred in 1842 and is recounted via Friedrich Mahling in Würtenberger, 76.

[54]Weber's comments are reprinted in Lockspeiser, 15; Debussy's are included in an 1894 letter to Eugene Ysaye quoted in Dömling, 4.

[55]This passage from Hoffmann is quoted by Baudelaire in his review of the 1846 Salon and in his essay on Wagner and Tannhäuser. The translation is by Lockspeiser, 68.

[56]Baudelaire, "Richard Wagner and Tannhäuser in Paris," 116. Baudelaire also praised Wagner's ability to excel "in *painting* space and depth, both material and spiritual."

CHAPTER 2

The New *Paragone*
Paradoxes and Contradictions of Pictorial Musicalism

PHILIPPE JUNOD

> *. . . et si vis similem pingere, pinge sonum.*
> *(. . . and if you wouldst make a likeness of me,*
> *paint sound.)*
>
> AUSONIUS, *EPIGRAMMATA* XI

In 1859, the inaugural issue of the *Gazette des Beaux-Arts* presented as its lead article an essay with a provocative title: "Ut pictura musica," or "As with music, so with painting."[1] Its author, the writer Louis Viardot, husband of the singer Pauline Viardot and friend of Eugène Delacroix, claimed to address "a very new question for the first time." "Someday," he predicted, "a book will be written on the parallels between painting and music."[2] Yet Viardot had not done his homework, for comparisons between the arts—particularly between painting and music—had been common since the Renaissance. Beginning with Leonardo's seminal *Il paragone delle arti,*[3] the theme had received numerous treatments from diverse perspectives, extending from Venice (Marco Boschini) and Rome (Gianpietro Bellori) to Paris (Roger de Piles), from Classicism (Félibien) to Romanticism (Delacroix), and from music (Marc-Antoine Charpentier) and music theory (Vincenzo Galilei, Martin Mersenne) to philosophy (Athanasius Kircher, Nicolas de Malebranche). A significant turning point in this evolution occurred in the eighteenth century, when Father Bertrand Castel and Johann Leonhard Hoffmann ventured a literal interpretation of what was until then only a metaphor: the "color of sounds."[4]

The nineteenth century saw renewed interest in the *paragone* debate. Delacroix's defense of painting (conceived as an art of simultaneity) as superior to music (an art of succession in time) can be seen as a variation on Leonardo's thesis.[5] Indeed, from Runge to Wagner, Madame de Staël to Gauguin, Apollinaire to Kandinsky, many of the same questions were debated. In such discussions painting was most often defined in a dual opposition: to the material art of sculpture, on the one hand, and to the conceptual art of literature, on the other.

It is this historical continuity that allows me to speak of a new *paragone* emerging in the nineteenth century in the same manner that Irving Babbitt more recently referred to a "new Laocoon."[6] The new *paragone* for painting was music, which, over the course of the nineteenth century, became the touchstone for the value and authenticity of the painter's art. In the following essay, I provide a schematic overview of the development of this mode of thinking and identify some of the paradoxes implicit in such an endeavor.

THE OLD *PARAGONE*

The importance of the *paragone* dispute during the Renaissance is well known.[7] Though arguments over the relative status of the arts may seem somewhat futile today, at the time the stakes in the debate were high: to rescue painting from its inferiority as a merely "mechanical" art by redefining it as a dignified "liberal" activity. To do so, it was argued that painting was akin to music and literature, as well as to other cognitive disciplines whose "nobility" had been consecrated by tradition, at the same time as it was opposed to sculpture which remained bound to the material world. Leonardo used this logic in his attempt to prove, with a self-conscious sense of sophistry, that painting, "a thing of the mind," is both related (as "sorella" or "sister") and superior to music.

During the eighteenth century, the aesthetics of the *arti sorelle* became a veritable commonplace.[8] "Poetry, music, and painting are three sisters who should be inseparable," wrote Saint-Martin.[9] Jean-Etienne Liotard preferred another image: "All the arts have clasped hands together."[10] In a parallel fashion, the ancient authority of Horace and Simonides was employed to establish the complicity of painting and poetry, which was captured in the formula "*ut pictura poesis*" ("As with painting, so with poetry").

Lessing's *Laocoon* of 1766 seemed at first to deal a fatal blow to the dogma of *ut pictura poesis*.[11] Insisting upon the uniqueness of the different arts, Lessing distinguished between the natural signs and simultaneous perception of painting in contrast to the arbitrary signs and successive perception of poetry. Subsequently Heinse, Goethe, Herder, Fernow, and Quatremère de Quincy each in turn questioned the orthodoxy of the *arti sorelle* by distinguishing between spatial and temporal arts.[12] But this division of the arts with its insistence on the internal limits of each medium soon provoked a reaction from the Romantics.[13] Novalis, as well as Schelling and A. W. Schlegel, reaffirmed a belief in the unity of art.[14] And the Symbolists, heirs to the Romantics, sought also to combine rather than to distinguish. They brought together Baudelaire's "correspondences" with the synesthesias of Rimbaud's *Sonnet des voyelles* and Wagner's *Gesamtkunstwerk.*[15] In this tradition the "union," "coincidence," "fusion," or "synthesis" of the arts was believed to take place under the aegis of music, and music became the prototype of a universal language.[16]

Even before Lessing's *Laocoon,* Rousseau had sought to mark out the boundaries between the arts, insisting that "each sense has its own domain. The domain of music is time, while that of painting is space."[17] Baudelaire implicitly refuted this opposition when he wrote that Wagner excels "in painting space and depth."[18] Debussy went so far as to declare, paradoxically, that "music and poetry are the only two arts which move in space. . . ." He added, with prescience, "I may be wrong, but it seems to me that this idea will stir the dreams of future generations."[19]

In the nineteenth century we find more and more artists with double vocations.[20] What is more, encounters between painters, writers, and musicians in artists' ateliers fostered dialogue between the arts. In this regard one thinks of the exchanges that occurred in Dresden between such diverse figures as Runge, Friedrich, Carus, Tieck, Schlegel, Jean-Paul, Hoffmann, Novalis, and Weber. Similarly, the studios of Ary Scheffer and Delacroix were centers of interaction between painters, writers, and musicians in Paris. Comparatism in both the natural and human sciences was on the rise, and this mode of thought is evident in aesthetics as well. Thus, for example, Viardot refers to "comparative anatomy and physiology" in order to affirm that "at bottom, all arts . . . are but one and the same art—beauty revealed."[21]

With Romanticism, then, music replaced poetry as the ideal model of painting, and the notion of *ut pictura musica* supplanted that of *ut pictura poesis.*[22] The apparent redundancy of the numerous comparisons between music and painting in the nineteenth century, however, should not blind us to the diversity of theoretical viewpoints underlying the arguments. I would like to suggest a schematic classification of these viewpoints according to four interrelated rubrics: *parallelism, convergence, divergence,* and *succession.*

PARALLELISM

Parallelism establishes the functional equivalence of the arts by situating their kinship at the level of expression. "Are not all arts expressions of human thought or feeling?" wondered Lamartine, and cannot "one art translate another"?[23] Rodin in turn declared that "painting, sculpture, literature, and music are closer to each other than is generally believed. They all express the soul's feeling in view of nature. The means of expression are all that varies."[24] The underlying assumption is that each art is like a language whose meaning can be adequately translated into any other language. This view presupposes a divisibility of form and meaning, such that a single idea may find expression alternately in painting, music, or poetry.[25] Robert Schumann illustrated this point when he wrote that "for the painter, the poem becomes an image; the musician transposes the painting into sound. The aesthetic of one art is the same as that of another; only the materials differ."[26] But it is Liszt, creator of the symphonic poem, who perhaps best embodies this ideal of transposition. Liszt's project of setting to music a cycle of Kaulbach's paintings was intended to provide a description at once "poetic, musical, and pictorial."[27] While this "history of the world in painting and in sound" was only partially realized (in *The Battle of the Huns*[28]), Liszt also composed "transpositions" of Raphael's *Sposalizio* and Michelangelo's *Pensieroso* which have already attracted critical attention.[29]

CONVERGENCE

The second rubric, *convergence,* suggests an actual collaboration with other arts which has its roots in the theater. Schelling had viewed drama as the meeting place of all the arts—including poetry, music, painting, and dance—and attitudes and experiences of this kind only increased in number over the course of the nineteenth century.[30] Stendhal recommended the display of successive "decorations" during performances of Mozart and Haydn.[31] While in Rome in 1885, Liszt actually "illustrated" his *Dante-Symphony,* with pictures by Bonaventura Genelli depicting scenes from the *Divine Comedy.*[32] Inversely, Caspar David Friedrich created a series of four paintings (now lost) for the court of Saint Petersburg which were meant to be accompanied by music, "so that music and painting may be be brought into agreement, the one supporting the other."[33] Moritz von Schwind planned a cycle of paintings for his "Schubert room."[34] Reciprocally, Novalis proclaimed that "plastic works should never be viewed without music. . . ."[35] Tieck and Wackenroder also formulated a principle of the interaction of sight and hearing,[36] and this idea may have inspired Runge's painting *The Hours of the Day,* which he conceived as an interaction between visual and acoustical sensations, "an abstract, pictorial and musical poem, with choir, a composition for all three arts together, for which architecture should provide an appropriate setting."[37] The apogee of the notion of convergence is found in Wagner's *Gesamtkunstwerk,* an idea that has been systematically developed in the twentieth century, from the Viennese Secession to the Bauhaus, from Schoenberg's *Glückliche Hand* to Kandinsky's *Gelber Klang,* Scriabin's *Prométhée,* and Schlemmer's *Ballet triadique.*[38]

DIVERGENCE

Divergence, my third rubric for conceiving the concord of the arts, is the opposite of convergence. Proponents of the concept of divergence assume a primal unity of all the arts and thus regard their division into distinct media as a sign of decline.[39]

"All art flows from the same source," wrote Liszt in 1855.[40] The notion of divergence stems from the Platonic and Rousseauist myth of a universal, originary language prior to the fall of man. It thus seeks to recapture this lost unity, what Runge proclaimed as the "future meeting of music and painting."[41] At the end of the century, Edouard Schuré observed that "divine Art has been cut into pieces"[42] and should be returned to its "original unity": "The arts constitute a united whole. They are truly fertile only when they act together in harmony and support each other."[43]

SUCCESSION

Finally, I invoke the notion of *succession* to characterize a concept of chronological development which was introduced into the terms of comparison. From the successionist viewpoint, music is the logical and necessary outcome of the evolution of the arts. Schiller maintained this view when he wrote that "the plastic arts, in their highest form, must become music."[44] Schopenhauer, too, declared that "the goal of all art is to resemble music,"[45] an opinion echoed in Walter Pater's affirmation that "all art constantly aspires towards the condition of music."[46] The reason for music's superior status is that it was seen as the consummate artistic expression of human spirituality. Schlegel, Schelling, Tieck, and Hoffmann saw in music the culmination of a process of dematerialization and the advent of modernity, as did Hegel, for whom music, opposed to the materiality of sculpture, represented the final stage of Spirit expressed in art.[47] Carl Gustav Carus suggested that music is superior to sculpture in the same way that our sense of hearing is superior to our sense of touch.[48] And at the end of the century Van Gogh would write, "As it is now, painting promises to become more subtle—more music and less sculpture."[49] In similar fashion, Théodore de Wyzewa traced an evolution from sculpture to music and from sensation to emotion, by way of the notion.[50]

It was from this perspective that some writers attributed to each period a dominant art. Thus, for Heinrich Heine, ancient Egypt was the age of architecture, ancient Greece the age of sculpture, the Middle Ages that of painting, and the present day (i.e., 1841) the age of music, "art's final word."[51]

INITIAL PROBLEMS

The four viewpoints described above are compatible in that they each express a notion of the kinship between painting and music. Yet they do so by drawing on very different orders of meaning. At times the relationship is conceived within a metaphysical or cosmic order. A. W. Schlegel, Schelling, Novalis, Tieck, and Schopenhauer all referred to the ancient doctrine of the Harmony of the Spheres. Tieck spoke of the "soul's mystery" and saw in art sounds "of a divinity for the human heart,"[52] while for Runge, the term *musikalisch* was synonymous with *mystisch*.[53] At other times, however, music's kinship with painting is explained through physics (by the phenomenon of vibrations, the common denominator of sounds and colors) or through psychology (by synesthesia or by the analogy of effects on spectator and auditor).[54]

Likewise, the objects of comparison are also subject to fluctuation. Sometimes the languages of music and painting are at issue; at other times it is a particular composer and painter, or even two particular works.[55] In a famous open letter to Berlioz, Liszt wrote, "Raphael and Michelangelo helped me to better understand Mozart and Beethoven. . . . The Colosseum and the Campo Santo are not as foreign to the Heroic Symphony and the Requiem as one might imagine."[56] Viardot preferred comparing Beethoven to Rembrandt and Mozart to Albert Cuyp.

Similar ambiguities persist when it is a matter of comparing specific formal or stylistic elements. Structural homologies between works seen and works heard are not easy to establish. Charles Avison, one of the first writers to try to go beyond a metaphorical level of comparison, was aware of this difficulty in 1752.[57] If some equivalences seemed obvious, like that between timbre and visual texture, between the tonal system and visual perspective, or between pitch and luminosity (high = light, low = dark), others were less so.[58] There was general consensus with regard to "the analogy between the gradation of tones and the gradation of colors" which Rodolphe Töpffer, anticipating gestalt theory, qualified as a form of relation.[59] Moreover, the very terminology specific to music and the visual arts associates rhythm and plastic composition, melodic arabesque and line, and sonority and color. Rousseau held that "melody does for music exactly what drawing does for painting."[60] And Viardot makes "the quite natural comparison between melody and drawing, harmony and color."[61] Yet for Berlioz it is "instrumentation" that "is in music exactly what choice of color is in painting."[62] And in a conversation with Chopin recounted by George Sand, Delacroix declared that "harmony in music not only consists of the constitution of chords but also of the relations between them, of their logical succession, of what I would call, for want of a better term, their auditory reflections."[63] Baudelaire saw things in yet another light: "In color one discovers harmony, melody, and counterpoint."[64]

TWO IMAGES OF MUSIC

When one considers the body of these writings as a whole, what is most striking is the simultaneous presence, sometimes in the same authors, of arguments that depend on irreconcilable views of the nature of music. A. W. Schlegel, for example, perceived this apparent contradiction as one between music's appeal to feeling, on the one hand, and its basis in numerical structures, on the other.[65]

In the first case there is the subjective viewpoint, which sees music in terms of its emotional effect. Eighteenth-century British theorists such as Addison and Reynolds first introduced this aesthetics of receptivity, which calls upon the listener's participation; it later found adepts in Germany (e.g., Schopenhauer) as well as in France (e.g., Baudelaire). For Samuel Morse, music was the art of imagination par excellence from whence stems its tie to dream and suggestion.[66] And, as early as 1751, Diderot saw music as the language "whose expressions are the most arbitrary and least precise" and that "leaves more free-play to our imagination."[67] For Quatremère de Quincy, "The magic power of the musical art is to force us to give form to the most indefinite conceptions, to complete the contours of its vague sketches."[68] Liszt considered instrumental music "a poetic language" able to express "all that defies analysis."[69]

Citing Mme. de Staël, Delacroix maintained that painting and music were "above thought," and that "their advantage over literature lies in their vagueness."[70] And Paul Deschanel observed in 1854: "Music says more than speech, because it speaks with less precision; herein lies its superiority."[71] Music is thus opposed to the conceptual nature of spoken language.[72] Gauguin, too, affirmed that "in regard to colors, a poem should be more musical than literary" and "that, on the whole, painting seeks suggestion more than description, as in fact does music."[73] Odilon Redon, writing in the wake of Verlaine and Mallarmé, observed: "My drawings are suggestive, not definite. They do not determine anything. Like music, they place us in the ambiguous world of the indeterminate."[74]

At the same time, many of these same authors, making a traditional reference to mathematics, identified music with pythagorean proportion.[75] Here, mathematical structure was opposed to subjective feeling, to mood, to *Stimmung*. Thus, figures like Schelling, Goethe, Ruskin, and Schopenhauer referred to architecture as "music frozen in time," and music was considered to be the archetypal art of strict forms, such as the symphony and the fugue.[76] In this manner, each generation pursued Goethe's wish to find a rational anchor for painting akin to Rameau's notion of a "fundamental bass" which signals the roots of chords and anchors music in a tonal system.[77] In 1904, Adolf Hölzel still looked to theories of harmony and counterpoint to instruct in painting,[78] and, in April 1911, Kandinsky wrote to Schoenberg, "Now we, too, are entitled to dream of a Treatise on Harmony."[79]

ONE OR MANY?

Having examined some of the problems internal to the new *paragone,* we can now identify a major tension underlying the entire debate. It is a rivalry between *centripetal* and *centrifugal* tendencies in Western aesthetics, two distinct and opposed perspectives between which the pendulum of aesthetic understanding has swung back and forth.

On the one hand, there are those, such as the Romantics, Symbolists, and Surrealists, who sought to abolish boundaries between the arts. On the other hand, there are those, such as the Neoclassicists, Impressionists, and the diverse "purists" leading up to formalism and abstract painting, who sought to distinguish each art in its pure form. The centripetal tendency is well-illustrated in the twentieth century by the Fluxus movement, expressed in 1964 by John Cage's declaration on "the dialogue between the arts," which stresses their interdependence.[80] The centrifugal tendency is apparent in Adorno[81] as well as in Clement Greenberg who, significantly, invokes Lessing to support his plea for the specificity of each art; the substitution of music for poetry as the new model for painting is denounced by Greenberg as a "new confusion of the arts."[82] Yet paradoxically, Greenberg still finds some use for music: "But only when the avant-garde's interest in music led it to consider music as a *method* of art rather than a kind of effect did the avant-garde find what it was looking for." Greenberg's "but" captures the problematic tension between centripetal and centrifugal tendencies. To understand this apparent contradiction we need once again to return to the origins of the debate.

I noted above the social motives for the Renaissance rivalry between the arts. It will help now to examine the aesthetic dimension of the same debate, for the *paragone* dispute inaugurated by Leonardo and Benedetto Varchi played a key role in the construction of the "modern system of fine arts" that has been so well described by Paul Kristeller.[83] Two things were at stake: to define aesthetics as an autonomous field, yet at the same time to specify the identity of each of its family members. In other words, the task was to establish the unity of the concept of art (as distinct from nonart) while articulating the aims of each particular art. At one level, the goal was to organize what today are called the "plastic arts" or "visual arts"—what Vasari named the "arts of design [*disegno*]"—by proceeding *per genus et differentiam*. In this context, the association of sound and color makes sense, as it allows painting to retain its specificity in relation to sculpture and drawing.[84]

Attempts to classify the arts in a hierarchy multiplied in the eighteenth century. In their respective treatises, Dubos, Crouzaz, André, Batteux, Mendelssohn, and Sulzer, among others, pursued a unifying principle for art. Nonetheless, Diderot maintained that each art has its "particular hieroglyphs,"[85] and Rousseau, in Chapter XVI of his *Essay on the Origins of Language,* entitled "False Analogy between Color and Sound," denounces their mutual encroachment.[86] In 1786, following Lessing's example, Joshua Reynolds declared that "no art can be engrafted with success on another art. For though they all profess the same origin, and to proceed [*sic*] from the same stock, yet each has its peculiar modes."[87] In his *Essay on Imitation,* Quatremère de Quincy pointed out the dangers of borrowings between the arts.[88] And Schiller identified the same problem: "Each art accomplishes its own style to the extent that it is able to push back its limits while maintaining its specific features."[89]

The centrifugal tendency was heightened over the course of the nineteenth century as modernity became aware of the importance of the hand, the implement, and the materials of art.[90] This emphasis on pictorial workmanship had in fact, since Boschini, often been related to the craft of musical composition and performance. Constable, for example, in praising Titian's touch, calls him a "great musician."[91]

On several occasions Delacroix insisted on the importance of the painter's technique, "which adds to thought, without which thought is incomplete."[92] We see how this demand may come into conflict with the principle of unity. Liszt, himself a solid partisan of *ars una,* stresses musical technique in his acclaim of virtuosity, which he associates with the use of color in painting. Yet in recognizing that a painting must be seen in the original, he implicitly calls into question the legitimacy of printmaking and of literary translations.[93] Odilon Redon is even more explicit: "I think that suggestive art depends a great deal on how the material calls out to the artist. A truly sensitive artist will not find the same fiction in different materials."[94] Redon goes so far as to reproach Fantin-Latour for having forgotten that "color is incapable of translating the musical world."[95]

More than ever, then, the goal in the late nineteenth century was to preserve the specificity of each mode of expression. As Viardot writes, the task was to preserve "the variety of the arts within the unity of art."[96] However, reconciling centripetal and centrifugal tendencies often appeared as hopeless as the task of squaring the circle. Three examples will illustrate the difficulty.

In 1863, Baudelaire remarked, with regard to Delacroix: "Moreover, a diagnostic sign of our century's spiritual state is that the arts seek, if not to supply the place of one another, then at least reciprocally to lend each other new forces."[97] Elsewhere he denounced the threat of confusion: "Is it not a sign of decline that today each art wants to encroach upon its neighbor, and that painters introduce musical scales into painting. . . ?"[98]

Walter Pater, too, wavers between the famous claim that "all art constantly aspires towards the condition of music" and the competing insight that "each art . . . [has] its own peculiar and untranslatable sensuous charm."[99] To resolve the difficulty Pater is forced into some intellectual acrobatics: "But although each art has thus its own specific order of impressions, and an untranslatable charm, while a just apprehension of the ultimate differences of the arts is the beginning of aesthetic criticism; yet it is noticeable that, in its special mode of handling its given material, each art may be observed to pass into the condition of some other art, by what German critics term an *Andersstreben*—a partial alienation from its own limitations, through which the arts are able, not indeed to supply the place of each other, but reciprocally to lend each other new forces."[100] Here we recognize the very terms used by Baudelaire.

Wagner, the father of the *Gesamtkunstwerk,* also cautioned against the danger of hybrid forms: "The purity of a genre of art is thus the precondition of its being understood; on the other hand, the blending of arts can only mislead the understanding. . . . When the musician tries to paint, he makes neither music nor painting."[101]

THE ORIGINS OF ABSTRACTION

Music was able to serve for several centuries as a model for painting in part because it represented an ideal of immateriality. Goethe had declared that "the dignity of art appears most manifestly in music because it has no matter," while Herder located music's superiority in the fact that "it is spirit."[102] Similarly, Schopenhauer characterized music as "form without matter" and "soul without body."[103] Now this disembodiment appears to conflict with the modern appreciation of technique, material, and bodily engagement in specifying the arts. The issue is further complicated by another contradiction, between an ideal of expressivity and an ideal of purity, each derived from a distinct tradition.[104] Expressivity stresses the content of an artwork's message and, as we have seen, underlies the notion of translation between different arts. In contrast, purity emphasizes the form of the work and is the basis of its autonomy from other arts.

In music, a new awareness of the means of expression resulted in the development of orchestration and an emphasis on timbre itself. The debate, begun by Galileo Galilei two centuries earlier[105] over the respective merits of vocal versus instrumental music was rekindled in the nineteenth century.[106] Tieck and Wackenroder, followed by Schopenhauer, made a case for the superiority of instrumental music.[107] Viardot saw the new emphasis on intrumentation as a sign of modernity, which he associated with the development of landscape painting, while he associated vocal music with history painting.[108] And Signac compared the painter's "keyboard of colors" to the "orchestration of a symphony."[109]

All the same, instrumental music served theorists of the nineteenth century mainly as a model of a completely nonimitative art. Still wedded to a Baroque, Aristotelian tradition, Rousseau and other writers of the mid-eighteenth century had seen imitation as the common denominator between painting and music, that which, alone, "raises them" to the level of fine arts.[110] In contrast, Rodolphe Töpffer maintained that "imitation plays almost no role—expression is everything."[111] For Schopenhauer, whose hostility to words set to music was extreme, the autonomy of music was a metaphysical fact: music, he claims, would exist "even in the absence of the world."[112] The link between music and feeling was soon joined by an association of music and "decoration," consecrated by theorists of applied art such as Owen Jones and Walter Crane. [113] Here we should recall August Endell's well-known phrase announcing the start of a new art, an art made of "forms that mean nothing and represent nothing," which impress our soul "as only music can do with sounds."[114]

The roots of the aesthetics of nonfigurative painting are, thus, much older than its practice.[115] Citations could easily be multiplied. A few examples will suffice to illustrate the surprising continuity of the idea. For Novalis, "the musician draws the essence of his art out of himself—and he is above all suspicion of imitation."[116] For Stendhal, "subject matter is of little value to the painter; it is a bit like the words to a musical *libretto*."[117] Coleridge, a great defender of the unity of art, held that "[m]usic is the most entirely human of the fine arts, and has the fewest analoga in nature. . . ."[118] Hegel spoke of "that magic of colors" which threatens "to predominate to the point that the content is repressed . . . in which case painting . . . begins to resemble music."[119] Delacroix, once again citing Mme. de Staël ("Music, the first among the arts—what does it imitate?"[120]), coined the expression "music of the painting" to designate "those mysterious effects of line and color" which, in a letter to Baudelaire of October 8, 1861, he qualifies as a "musical game" [*partie musicale*].[121] Critics take up the expression, as does Gauguin, one of the first to make use of the notion of "abstraction."[122] Citing Delacroix in *Racontars de rapin,* where he announces that "colorful painting is entering into a musical phase," Gauguin speaks of the "musical role to be played from now on by color in modern painting."[123] Ruskin calls abstract relations between colors "musical," pleasant to the human senses . . . though they represent nothing."[124] But assuredly it is Whistler who proposed the most radical formulation of the idea when, to justify the musical titles he chose for his canvasses, he proclaimed: "The subject-matter has nothing to do with harmony of sound or of color."[125]

The ideal of "pure music" as the model of pictorial form is taken up by several modernist currents. It is reformulated in the twentieth century, notably, by Boccioni, Kupka, Delaunay, Macdonald-Wright, Schwitters, Picabia, Van Doesburg, Macke, Klee, Matisse, Moholy-Nagy, and Nicolas de Staël. Yet Appollinaire provides the most ingenuous formulation of its paradoxical nature: "Thus we are heading towards an entirely new form of art, which will be to painting (such as it has been conceived until now) what music is to literature. It will be a pure painting, in the same manner that music is pure literature."[126]

THE PARADOXES OF MUSICALISM

Musicalism, the predominant ideology of the new *paragone,* is thus marked with contradiction from its beginnings. Impregnated by the grand nineteenth-century currents of evolutionism and comparativism, wavering between rationalism and subjectivism, spirit and matter, it is divided between a nostalgia for lost unity and an insistence on the specificity of each art. It issues in, finally, a double paradox: painting defined as pure music, and modernism understood as a return to primitive origins.

These theoretical difficulties have certainly not stood in the way of a series of valuable artistic accomplishments. Perhaps they have even helped to provoke them, like the grain of sand that provokes a pearl. Still, one must inquire into the deep causes of these ambiguities. Can the contemporary confusion of spatiotemporal and audiovisual categories be explained simply in terms of the aging [*l'usure*] of the system of fine arts? What is the ideological scope of this phenomenon? A quest for original unity, which seems to accompany the will to transgress, is a common denominator of most twentieth-century avant-garde movements and this makes them heirs to the Romantic project. In this light, the new *paragone* may appear to be an attempt at compensation, a defensive reaction of a society faced with the challenges of modernity which feels threatened at its roots.

NOTES

This essay was translated from the French by Stephen Michelman.

[1]Louis Viardot, "Ut pictura musica," *Gazette des Beaux-Arts* I (1859), 19–29. Andrew Kagan has brought to light the importance of this text; see "*Ut Pictura Musica* to 1860,*" in *Absolute Art* (St. Louis: Grenart, 1995), 73–99.

[2]Dozens of works have in fact been devoted to the theme in the twentieth century, many since the great Stuttgart exhibit of 1985; see Karin von Maur, ed., *Vom Klang der Bilder,* (Stuttgart: Staatsgalerie, 1985). Among the most recent are Carlo Majer, Hubert Damisch, and Omar Calabrese, *Musica e pittura* (Milano: Mondadori, 1988); Philippe Junod, *La musique vue par les peintres* (Lausanne: Edita, 1988); Helga de la Motte-Haber, *Musik und bildende Kunst* (Laaber: Laaber Verlag, 1990); Jean-Yves Bosseur, *Musique, passion d'artistes*

(Geneva: Skira, 1991); Jacques Parrat, *Les relations entre la peinture et la musique dans l'art contemporain* (Nice: Z'Editions, 1993); Karl Schawelka, *Quasi una musica. Untersuchungen zum Ideal des "Musikalischen" in der Malerei ab 1800* (Munich: Mäander, 1993); Karl-Heinz Weidner, *Bild und Musik. Vier Untersuchungen über semantische Beziehungen zwischen darstellender Kunst und Musik* (Bern: Lang, 1994); Klaus Kropfinger, *Über Musik im Bild. Schriften zu Analyse, Ästhetik und Rezeption in Musik und bildender Kunst* (Köln: Dohr, 1995); Günter Metken, *Laut-Malereien, Grenzgänge zwischen Kunst und Musik* (Frankfurt: Campus, 1995); Elisabeth Schmierer et al., *Töne, Farben, Formen. Über Musik und die bildenden Künste* (Laaber: Laaber Verlag, 1995); François Sabatier, *Les miroirs de la musique. La musique et ses correspondances avec la littérature et les beaux-arts* (Paris: Fayard, 1995); Philippe Junod and Sylvie Wuhrmann, ed., *De l'archet au pinceau. Rencontres entre musique et arts visuels en Suisse romande* (Lausanne: Payot, 1996); Gottfried Böhm et al., *Canto d'amore. Klassizistische Moderne in Musik und bildender Kunst* (Basel: Kunstmuseum und Paul Sacher Stiftung, 1996).

Prior to 1985, the most important titles are Edward Lockspeiser, *Music and Painting: A Study of Comparative Ideas from Turner to Schoenberg* (New York: Harper, 1973); Franzsepp Würtenberger, *Malerei und Musik. Die Geschichte des Verhaltens zweier Künste* (Bern: Lang, 1979); and Reinhold Hammerstein, "Musik und bildende Kunst. Zur Theorie und Geschichte ihrer Beziehungen," *Imago Musicae* I (1984), 1–28.

[3]Leonardo da Vinci, *Il paragone delle arti,* ed. Claudio Scarpati (Milano: Vita e pensiero, 1993), chap. 29: "Come la musica si dee chiamare sorella et minore della pittura." The term *paragone* does not appear until 1817, in the Guglielmo Manzi edition.

[4]On Father Castel, see the proceedings of the 1995 Clermont-Ferrand colloquium (in preparation). On Hoffmann, who is less well-known, see Rainer Cadenbach, "Tonmalerei als Farbenkunst. J. H. Hoffmanns Versuch einer wechselseitigen Erläuterung von malerischer Harmonie und Tonkunst" in *Töne, Farben, Formen,* cit. n. 2, 93–112.

[5]George P. Mras, "*Ut pictura musica:* a Study of Delacroix's *Paragone,*" *Art Bulletin* 45, no. 3 (Sept. 1963), 266–271; "The Paragone," in *Eugène Delacroix's Theory of Art* (Princeton: Princeton University Press, 1966), 33–45; Günter Busch, "Synästhesie und Imagination. Zu Delacroix's kunsttheoretischen Äußerungen," in H. Koopmann, *Beiträge zur Theorie der Künste im 19. Jh.,* 2 vols. (Frankfurt: Klostermann, 1971), I, 240–255; Olivier Revault d'Allonnes, "La correspondance des arts selon Eugène Delacroix," in *Harmoniques* 5 (Paris: IRCAM, June 1989), 72–87.

[6]Irving Babbitt, *The New Laokoon: An Essay in the Confusion of the Arts* (London: Constable, 1910).

[7]See Leatrice Mendelsohn, *Paragoni: Benedetto Varchi's Due Lezioni and Cinquecento Art Theory* (Ann Arbor: UMI, 1982); Claire J. Farago, *Leonardo da Vinci's Paragone: A Critical Interpretation with a New Edition of the Text in the Codex Urbina* (Leiden: Brill, 1992); Lauriane Fallay d'Este, *Le paragone. Le parallèle des arts* (Paris: Klincksieck, 1992).

[8]Herbert Schueller, "Correspondences between Music and the Sister Arts According to 18th Century Aesthetic Theory," *Journal of Aesthetics and Art Criticism* XI (June 1953), 334–359; Jean H. Hagstrum, *The Sister Arts: The Tradition of Literary Pictorialism and English Poetry from Dryden to Gray* (Chicago: University of Chicago Press, 1958). Leonardo's terminology survived for many decades. Cf., for example, Samuel F. B. Morse, *Lectures on the Affinities of Painting with the other Arts* [1826](Columbia: University of Missouri Press, 1983). In 1865, Liszt defined poetry, painting, and music as the three "arti sorelle," which he hoped to unite within a single academy. Gauguin, in his *Cahier pour Aline,* once again described painting as "sister to music," and Wagner spoke of the "three originary sisters" ("*drei urgeborene Schwestern*") in "Tanzkunst, Tonkunst und Dichtkunst," *Gesammelte Schriften und Dichtungen,* 10 vols. (Moers: Steiger, 1976), III, 67.

[9]Louis-Claude de Saint-Martin, *L'homme de désir* [1790], in *Oeuvres majeures,* 6 vols. (Hildesheim: G. Olms, 1980), III, 79.

[10]See Jean-Etienne Liotard, *Traité des principes et des règles de la peinture* (1781; reprint, Genève: Minkoff, 1973), 24.

[11]Gotthold Ephraim Lessing, *Laokoon* (1766; reprint, Stuttgart: Reclam, 1964).

[12]"Die Poesie ist fürs Gehör und die Malerei fürs Auge." Wilhelm Heinse, *Ardinghello und die glücklichen Inseln* [1787](Stuttgart: Reclam, 1975), 698. On the *paragone,* see also pp. 12 and 171–180. "Eines der vorzüglichsten Kennzeichen des Verfalles der Kunst ist die Vermischung der verschiedenen Arten derselben." Johann Wolfgang von Goethe, "Einleitung in die Propyläen" [1798], *Werke,* Hamburger Ausgabe XII: *Schriften zur Kunst* (Hamburg: Wegner, 1967), 49. "Raum kann nicht Zeit, Zeit nicht Raum, das Sichtbare nicht hörbar, dies nicht sichtbar gemacht werden. . . ." Johann Gottfried Herder, *Kalligone. II. Von Kunst und Kunstrichterei* [1800] in *Sämtliche Werke,* 33 vol., ed. B. Suphan (Berlin: Weidmann, 1880), XXII, 187–188. While Lessing gives scant attention to music, Herder explicitly refuses any analogy between sound and color. Ludwig Fernow, "Über das Kunstschöne," in *Römische Studien,* 3 vols. (Zürich: Gessner, 1806), I, 308–309. Antoine-Chrysostome Quatremère de Quincy, *Essai sur la*

nature, le but et les moyens de l'imitation dans les Beaux-Arts [1823](Bruxelles: Archives de l'architecture moderne, 1980), 38, 72–76, and 341.

[13]Paul Böckmann, "Das Laokoonproblem und seine Auflösung in der Romantik," in Wolfdietrich Rasch, ed., *Bildende Kunst und Literatur. Beiträge zum Problem ihrer Wechselbeziehungen im 19. Jh.* (Frankfurt: Klostermann, 1971), 59–78. On the influence of German Romantism, see also Hugh Honour, "Frozen Music," in *Romanticism* (Harmondsworth: Penguin, 1979), 119ff.; and Peter Vergo, "Musik und bildende Kunst," in *Ernste Spiele. Der Geist der Romantik in der deutschen Kunst 1790–1990* (München: Haus der Kunst, 1995), 581–586.

[14]"Lessing sah zu scharf und verlor darüber das Gefühl des undeutlichen Ganzen, die magische Anschauung der Gegenstände zusammen in mannichfacher Erleuchtung und Verdunklung." See Novalis, *Schriften,* 4 vols., ed. Paul Kluckhohn and Richard Samuel (Darmstadt: Wissenschaftliche Buchgesellschaft, 1977), II, 557. Friedrich Willhelm Joseph Schelling, *Philosophie der Kunst* [1802–1803](Darmstadt: Wissenschaftliche Buchgesellschaft, 1990), 379–380. August Wilhelm Schlegel, "Übersicht und Einteilung der schönen Künste," in *Die Kunstlehre* [1801–1802](Stuttgart: Kohlhammer, 1961), 100ff.

[15]Wagner in fact makes explicit reference to Lessing's *Laokoon:* "Whenever Lessing sets boundaries and assigns limits to poetry, he misunderstands the *dramatic work of art* . . . which brings together all aspects of the plastic arts." Wagner, *Opéra et drame,* 2 vols. [1851](Paris: Plan-de-la-tour, 1982), I, 199.

[16]Such is the program of the *Revue wagnérienne,* published 1885–1888, in which Edouard Dujardin demands "the necessary union of the arts" (August 15, 1887; reprint Genève: Slatkine, 1968), III, 160. "Union," "fusion," and "totality" are a leimotiv of Théodore de Wyzewa's writings; see *Nos maîtres* (Paris: Perrin, 1895), 11, 20, 29, 50, and passim. See also Debussy's critique of Wagner and his "fusion of the arts," *Monsieur Croche et autres écrits* (Paris: Gallimard, 1971), 193.

[17]Jean-Jacques Rousseau, *Essai sur l'origine des langues* [1755](Paris: Aubier, 1974), 160.

[18]Charles Baudelaire, "Richard Wagner et Tannhäuser," [1861] in *Oeuvres complètes* (Paris: Gallimard, 1954), 1052.

[19]Claude Debussy, *Monsieur Croche et autres écrits, cit.* n. 16, 46.

[20]Cf., "Les écrivains-dessinateurs," *Revue de l'art* 44 (1979); and Würtenberger, *Malerei und Musik* (cit. n. 2), 50ff.

[21]Viardot, "Ut pictura musica," cit. n. 1, 26.

[22]This formula soon became a commonplace observation. See Kagan, "*Ut Pictura Musica* to 1860," cit. n. 1.

[23]Alphonse de Lamartine, *Cours familier de littérature,* 22 vols. (Paris: l'auteur, 1856–1866), VI, 398, 400.

[24]Auguste Rodin, *L'Art,* Entretiens réunis par Paul Gsell [1911](Paris: Gallimard, 1967), 126.

[25]Johann August Apel, "Musik und Poesie," *Allgemeine musikalische Zeitung* 9 (1806), 451ff.

[26]Robert Schumann, "Aus Meister Raros, Florestans und Eusebius Denk- und Dicht-Büchlein," *Gesammelte Schriften über Musik und Musiker* (Leipzig: Breitkopf und Härtel, 1891), I, 34.

[27]"[I]n poetischer, musikalischer und malerischer Form." Liszt, cited in Walter Salmen, "Liszt und Wagner in ihren Beziehungen zur bildenden Kunst," *Liszt-Studien* 3 (1986), 157.

[28]Wolfram Steinbeck, "Musik nach Bildern. Zu Franz Liszts *Hunnenschlacht,*" in Elisabeth Schmierer et al., *Töne, Farben, Formen. Über Musik und die bildenden Künste,* cit. n. 2, 17–38.

[29]Cf., W. Salmen, op.cit. n. 27; Jacqueline Bellas, "Franz Liszt, le grand transpositeur," in *Transpositions,* Actes du colloque de l'Université de Toulouse-Le Mirail, 15-16 mai 1986 (Toulouse: Université de Toulouse-Le Mirail, 1986), 223–233; and Jean-Jacques Eigeldinger, "Anch'io son pittore ou Liszt compositeur de *Sposalizio* et *Penseroso,*" in Philippe Junod et Sylvie Wuhrmann, ed., *De l'archet au pinceau,* cit. n. 2, 49–74. On these questions, see also Helga De la Motte-Haber, "Gemälde als Programm neuer musikalischer Formen," in *Musik und bildende Kunst,* cit. n. 2, 80ff.

[30]Friedrich Wilhelm Joseph Schelling, *Philosophie der Kunst* [1802– 1803](Darmstadt: Wissenschaftliche Buchgesellschaft, 1990), 380.

[31]Stendhal, *Vies de Haydn, de Mozart et de Métastase* (Paris: Champion, 1914), 8.

[32]Dezsö Legany, "Liszt in Rom—nach der Presse," *Studia Musicologica* 19 (1977), 39. *L'Osservatore Romano* of December 2, 1865, commented: "Cosi la galleria dantesca sarà inaugurata col concorso delle tre arti sorelle, la Poesia, la Pittura e la Musica." The pictures are no longer extant, and thus it is impossible to know precisely how the images and music were related in their presentation.

[33]C. D. Friedrich, letters of October 14 and January 12, 1835, to Joukowski, in Sigrid Hinz, ed., *C. D. Friedrich in Briefen und Bekenntnissen* (Berlin: Henschel, 1968), 65–70.

[34]Moritz von Schwind, *Briefe,* ed. Otto Stoessl (Leipzig: Biographisches Institut, [1924]), 253–254, 268.

[35]Novalis, *Schriften,* cit. n. 14, II, 37.

[36]Ludwig Tieck und Wilhelm-Heinrich Wackenroder, "Die Farben," in *Phantasien über die Kunst* (Berlin-Stuttgart: Spemann, [1886]), 42–46. See also Julius Becker, "Ideen über Malerei und Musik," *Neue Zeitschrift für Musik* 21 (Oct. 1840), 129.

[37]Runge, letter to his brother of February 22, 1803. This project anticipates Alexander Scriabin's great "Mystery"; cf., *Notes et réflexions,* trans. Marina Scriabine (Paris: Klincksieck, 1979).

[38]Michael Lingner, "Der Ursprung des Gesamtkunstwerkes aus der Unmöglichkeit 'absoluter Kunst.' Zur rezeptionsästhetischen Typologisierung von Ph. O. Runges Universalkunstwerk und R. Wagners Totalkunstwerk," in *Der Hang zum Gesamtkunstwerk* (Zürich: Kunsthaus, 1983), 52–69; Wolfgang Dömling, "Wiedervereinigung der Künste, Skizzen zur Geschichte einer Idee," in E. Schmierer, *Töne, Farben, Formen,* cit. n. 2, p. 119–126. On the misunderstandings with regard to the use of this idea, see Peter Vergo, "The Origins of Expressionism and the Notion of Gesamtkunstwerk," in S. Behr, D. Fanning, and D. Jarman, ed., *Expressionism Reassessed* (Manchester: University Press, 1993), 11–19, and Klaus Kropfinger, "Wagner—Van de Velde—Kandinsky," in *Über Musik im Bild, Schriften zu Analyse, Ästhetik und Rezeption in Musik und bildender Kunst* (Köln: Dohr, 1995), 431–448.

[39]A. W. Schlegel writes, "Allein die Einheit ist überall im Menschen früher als die Trennung." *Die Kunstlehre* (Stuttgart: Kohlhammer, 1961), 106.

[40]See Franz Liszt, "Clara Schumann," *Gesammelte Schriften,* 6 vols. (Wiesbaden: Breitkopf, 1882), IV, 193. Goethe evoked the image of streams flowing from the same mountain, but to stress their divergence; see *Farbenlehre, Didaktischer Teil,* V, "Verhältnis zur Tonlehre," (München: Deutscher Taschenbuch Verlag, 1970), 164. Later, Kandinsky echoes this idea: "All the arts derive from one and the same root . . . from the same trunk." ("Alle Künste kommen aus der gleichen und aus einer einzigen Wurzel . . . aus demselben Stamm.") Wassili Kandinsky, "Konkrete Kunst" [1938] in *Essays über Kunst und Künstler* (Bern: Benteli, 1973), 217.

[41]Philipp Otto Runge, letter of September 27, 1809, *Hinterlassene Schriften,* 2 vols. (Göttingen: Vandenhoeck und Ruprecht, 1965), II, 388.

[42]Edouard Schuré, *Histoire du drame musical* (Paris: Perrin, 1876), 5.

[43]Idem, *R. Wagner: son oeuvre et son idée* (Paris: Perrin, 1904), 301, 305. The same idea is found in Henry Van de Velde, *Aperçus en vue d'une synthèse d'art* (Bruxelles, 1895).

[44]Friedrich von Schiller, *Über die ästhetische Erziehung des Menschen* [1795] (Stuttgart-Berlin: Cotta, 1904), 84.

[45]Arthur Schopenhauer, *Werke,* 10 vols. (Zürich: Diogenes, 1977), X, 329.

[46]Walter Pater, "The School of Giorgione," [1877] in *The Renaissance* (New York: Boni, 1919), 111.

[47]Georg Wilhelm Friedrich Hegel, *Esthétique,* 3 vols. (Paris: Aubier, 1944), III, 301.

[48]Gustav Carus, *Briefe über die Landschaftsmalerei* [1835](Heidelberg: Lambert Schneider, 1972), 81–83.

[49]Vincent van Gogh, letter 528, August 1888, *Correspondance générale,* 3 vols., trans. M. Beerblock and L. Roelandt (Paris: Gallimard, 1990), I, 270.

[50]Théodore de Wyzewa, *Nos maîtres,* cit. n. 16, 16–19.

[51]Heinrich Heine, review of April 24, 1841, *Pariser Berichte 1840–1848* in *Werke, Säkularausgabe,* 27 vols. (Berlin: Akademie, 1970-1986), X, 99. This theory, to which Viardot subscribed, survives beyond Spengler and W. Pinder to the 1932 manifesto of the musicalist movement. See Henry Valensi, Charles Blanc-Gatti, Gustave Bourgogne and Vito Stracquadaini, *Manifeste du groupe des peintres "Les artistes musicalistes,"* in *Comoedia* 17, no. 4 (1932). See also H. Valensi, "L'allègement progressif de la matière à travers l'évolution de l'art," *Journal de psychologie normale et pathologique* (15 janv.–15 fév. 1934), 160–170, and idem, *Le musicalisme* (Paris: l'auteur, 1936).

[52]*Phantasien über die Kunst,* cit. n. 36, 74.

[53]Philipp Otto Runge, *Hinterlassene Schriften,* 2 vols. (Hamburg: F. Perthes, 1840–1841), I, 44. On Runge's occultist origins, see Heinz Matile, *Die Farbenlehre Ph.O. Runges, Ein Beitrag zur Geschichte der Künstlerfarbenlehre* (München: Mäander, 1979), 183.

[54]Philippe Junod, "De l'audition colorée ou du bon usage d'un mythe," in *La couleur. Regards croisés sur la couleur du Moyen Age au XXe siècle* (Paris: Léopard d'or, 1994), 63–81.

[55]This type of comparison seems to have first been employed by Giuseppe Carpani in *Le Haydine* of 1812, then plagiarized by Stendhal in 1815 in his *Vies* (cit. n. 31, 224: "I'm seized by the need to make comparisons") Cf., Helmut C. Jacobs, "Musik, Bild, Text—Stendhals literarische Visualisierung von Musik," in *Stendhal: image et texte* (Tübingen: Narr, 1994), 145–157.

[56]Franz Liszt, letter of October 2, 1839, *Artiste et société,* ed. Rémy Stricker (Paris: Flammarion, 1995), 187. Compare this with the following declaration by Schumann: "Der gebildete Musiker wird an einer Raphaelschen Madonna mit gleichem Nutzen studieren können wie der Maler an einer Mozartschen Symphonie." (op. cit. n. 26, 34) On this topos, see Martin Staehelin, "Mozart und Raphael. Zum Mozart-Bild des 19. Jh," *Schweizerische Musikzeitung* 117 (1977), 322–330; Walter Salmen, "Raphael und die Musik," in *Der Aquädukt* (München: Beck, 1988), 364–371.

[57]Charles Avison, "On the Analogies between Music and Painting," in *An Essay on Musical Expression,* cited by Kagan, op.cit. n. 1, 80–84. An earlier attempt at a term-by-term association of painting and music was made by Claude François Ménestrier, *Des représentations en musique ancienne et moderne* (1681; reprint, Genève: Minkoff , 1972), 73–75.

[58]The homology between luminosity and pitch is a constant from Arcimboldo to Bertrand Castel to Philipp Otto Runge. See A. B. Ceswell, "The Pythagorism of Arcimboldo," *Journal of Aesthetics and Art Criticism* 39, no. 2

(1980–1981), 155–161; Pavel Preiss, "Farbe und Klang in der Theorie und Praxis des Manierismus," in R. Pecman, ed., *Mannerism and Music of the XVIth and XVIIth Centuries, Colloquium Musica Bohemica et Europaea* (Brno, 1970), 163–170; and Tonino Tornitore, "Giuseppe Arcimboldi e il suo clavicembalo oculare," *Revue des études italiennes* 31 (1985), 58–77. It is curious to note that, contrary to his successors, Arcimboldo associates dark colors with high pitches. See also Bertrand Castel, *L'optique des couleurs* (Paris: Briasson, 1740), 300; and Philipp Otto Runge, "Gespräch über Analogie der Farben und Töne," in *Hinterlassene Schriften,* I, 168–170.

[59]Rodolphe Töpffer, *Réflexions et menus propos d'un peintre genevois* [1848] (Paris: Payot, 1928),172. See also Christian von Ehrenfels, "Über Gestaltqualitäten," *Vierteljahrsschrift für wissenschaftliche Philosophie* XIV (1890), 249–292.

[60]Jean-Jacques Rousseau, *Essai sur l'origine des langues* (Paris: Aubier-Montaigne, 1974), 149.

[61]Viardot, "Ut pictura musica," cit. n. 1, 25.

[62]Hector Berlioz, *A travers chants. Etudes musicales, adorations, boutades et critiques* (Paris: Calman Lévy, 1862), 8.

[63]George Sand, *Impressions et souvenirs* (Paris: Lévy, 1873), 81.

[64]Charles Baudelaire, *Salon de 1845,* in op. cit. n. 18, 613. In the twentieth century, Paul Klee would associate color and texture with polyphony. See Andrew Kagan, *P. Klee: Art and Music* (Ithaca and London: Cornell University Press, 1983), 77ff.

[65]August Wilhelm Schlegel, *Die Kunstlehre,* cit. n. 14, 205.

[66]Samuel F. B. Morse, *Lectures,* cit. n. 8, 50.

[67]Denis Diderot, *Lettre à Mademoiselle De la Chaux* in *Correspondance,* 16 vols., ed. Georges Roth (Paris: Minuit, 1955), I, 128.

[68]Quatremère de Quincy, op. cit. n. 12, 100.

[69]Liszt, foreword to *L'Album d'un voyageur* (Vienne: Haslinger, 1842).

[70]Eugène Delacroix, January 26, 1824, *Journal,* 3 vols., ed. André Joubin (Paris: Plon, 1932), I, 50.

[71]Paul Deschanel, *Physiologie des écrivains et des artistes ou essai de critique naturelle* (Paris: Hachette, 1864), 204.

[72]On the meaning of the opposition between music and literature, see James Kearns, *Symbolist Landscapes: The Place of Painting in the Poetry and Criticism of Mallarmé and His Circle* (London: Modern Humanities Research Association, 1989), 56 and 79ff.

[73]Paul Gauguin, *Racontars de rapin* (Paris: Falaize, 1951), 49; and idem, *Lettres à Daniel de Monfreid* (Paris: Falaize, 1950), 182.

[74]Odilon Redon, *A soi-même* (Paris: Corti, 1961), 26–27. On the connotations of music during the symbolist period, see A. G. Lehmann, *The Symbolist*

Aesthetic in France 1885-1895 (Oxford: Blackwell, 1968), 149–175; and Hendrik R. Rookmaaker, *Synthetist Art Theories* (Amsterdam: Zeitlinger, 1959), 210–220.

[75]See the contradictions analyzed by Laurence Ferrara, "Schopenhauer on Music as the Embodiment of Will," in Dale Jacquette, ed., *Schopenhauer, Philosophy, and the Arts* (Cambridge: Cambridge University Press, 1996), 183–199. Baudelaire, in the *Salon de 1859,* writes: "In certain respects, the colorist's art is obviously related to mathematics and to music." (op. cit. n. 18, 778.) Wassily Kandinsky, for example, *Point-ligne-plan* in *Ecrits complets,* ed. Philippe Sers, (Paris: Denoël-Gonthier, 1970), 54, 130.

[76]Cf., for example, Runge, *Hinterlassene Schriften,* cit. n. 53, I, 33, 36, 223.

[77]Wassily Kandinsky and Franz Marc, *Der Blaue Reiter* (1912; reprint, München: Piper, 1965). This analogy in fact goes back to Diderot's *Essais sur la peinture,* Chapter II: "The rainbow in painting is equivalent to the fundamental bass in music." See *Oeuvres esthétiques* (Paris: Garnier, 1959), 678.

[78]Adolf Hölzel in Walter Hess, *Das Problem der Farbe in den Selbstzeugnissen der Maler* (Mittenwald: Mäander, 1981), 98: "Ich meine, es müsse, wie es in der Musik einen Kontrapunkt und eine Harmonielehre gibt, auch in der Malerei eine bestimmte Lehre über künstlerische Kontraste jeder Art und deren notwendigen harmonischen Ausgleich angestrebt werden. . . ."

[79]Schoenberg-Kandinsky, *Correspondance,* in *Contrechamps* 2 (April 1984), 17.

[80]Richard Kostelanetz, *John Cage* (Köln: DuMont, 1973), 107.

[81]Theodor W. Adorno, "Die Kunst und die Künste," in *Ohne Leitbild. Parva Aesthetica* (Frankfurt: Suhrkamp, 1967), 168–192.

[82]Clement Greenberg, "Towards a Newer Laocoon," [1940] in *The Collected Essays and Criticism,* 4 vols., ed. John O'Brian (Chicago: University of Chicago Press, 1986–1993), I, 23–38. See also "Modernist Painting" [1960], ibid., IV, 85–93. In 1981, Greenberg attempted once again to denounce the multimedia "invasion" of the art scene and to restore the purity of the plastic arts; see "Intermedia," *Arts Magazine,* 56, no. 2 (Oct. 1981), 92–93.

[83]Paul O. Kristeller, "The Modern System of the Arts: a Study in the History of Aesthetics," *Journal of the History of Ideas* XII (1951), 496–527; and XIII (1952),17–46.

[84]Roger De Piles, *L'idée du peintre parfait* [1699](Paris: Gallimard, 1993), 62; and idem, *Cours de peinture par principes* [1709], ed. Thomas Puttfarken (Nîmes: Chambon, 1990), 154.

[85]Denis Diderot, *Lettre sur les sourds et muets* [1751], ed. P. H. Meyer (Genève: Droz, 1965), 81.

[86]Moreover, this chapter contradicts Rousseau's earlier claim that "sounds are never more energetic than when they resemble colors." Op. cit. n. 17, 91.

[87]Joshua Reynolds, *Discourses on Art,* ed. Robert R. Wark (New Haven: Yale University Press, 1975), 240.

[88]Quatremère de Quincy, *Essai sur la nature, cit. n. 12,19, 68, 96, 332, and passim.*

[89]Friedrich von Schiller, *Über die ästhetische Erziehung des Menschen* [1795] (Stuttgart-Berlin: Cotta, [1904]), 85.

[90]I have developed this point in *Transparence et opacité. Essai sur les fondements théoriques de l'art moderne* (Lausanne: L'Age d'homme, 1976), chap. V and VI.

[91]"It is striking to observe with what consummate skill the painter, like a great musician, has varied his touch and execution. . . ." John Constable, *Discourses,* ed. R. Beckett (Suffolk Records Society, 1970), 48.

[92]Eugène Delacroix, *Dictionnaire des Beaux-Arts,* ed. Anne Larue (Paris: Hermann, 1996), 86–89, and idem, *Oeuvres littéraires,* 2 vols. (Paris: Crès, 1923), II, 62.

[93]Franz Liszt, "R. Wagner," *Gesammelte Schriften,* 6 vols. (1880–1883; reprint, Hildesheim and New York: Olms, 1978), III, 235.

[94]Odilon Redon, *Lettres d'Odilon Redon 1878–1916* (Paris-Bruxelles: van Oest, 1923), 33.

[95]Odilon Redon, *A soi-même, cit. n. 74, 156–157.

[96]Louis Viardot, "Ut pictura musica," cit. n. 1, 26.

[97]Charles Baudelaire, "La vie et l'oeuvre de Delacroix," in *Oeuvres complètes, cit. n. 18, 856.

[98]Charles Baudelaire, "L'art philosophique," in ibid., 926.

[99]Walter Pater, "The School of Giorgione," cit. n. 46, 111, 107.

[100]Ibid., 110.

[101]Richard Wagner, *Opéra et drame, cit. n. 15, I, 201. Cf., Walter Salmen, "Liszt und Wagner in ihren Beziehungen zur bildenden Kunst," cit. n. 27, 153.

[102]Goethe, *Maximen und Reflexionen,* no. 769, in *Werke, cit. n. 12, XII, 473. Herder, *Kalligone, cit. n.12, II, 187.

[103]Arthur Schopenhauer, *Die Welt als Wille und Vorstellung* [1818](Leipzig: Kröner, 1911), 160.

[104]The tradition of expressivity derives from Aristotle's concept of the mimetic nature of *ethos,* further developed in the baroque doctrine of affects and in Poussin's theory of "modes." The tradition of purity has roots in Pythagoras and Vitruvius.

[105]Erwin Panofsky, *Galileo as a Critic of the Arts* (Den Haag: Nijhoff, 1954).

[106]Wolfram Steinbeck, "Musik über Musik. Vom romantischen Sprach-problem der Instrumentalmusik zu Liszts symphonischer Dichtung *Orpheus,*" *Schweizer Jahrbuch für Musikwissenschaft,* Neue Folge, no. 15 (1995), 163–181.

[107]Ludwig Tieck und Wilhelm Heinrich Wackenroder, "Das eigentliche innere Wesen der Tonkunst und die Seelenlehre der heutigen Instrumentalmusik," in *Phantasien über die Kunst,* cit. n. 36, 67–75.

[108]Louis Viardot, "Ut pictura musica," cit. n. 1, 25.

[109]Paul Signac, *D'Eugène Delacroix au Néo-impressionnisme,* ed. Françoise Cachin (Paris: Hermann, 1964), 108.

[110]Rousseau, *Essai sur l'origine des langues,* cit. n. 17, 151.

[111]Rodolphe Töpffer, *Réflexions et menus,* cit. n. 59, 231.

[112]"[S]o ist die Musik . . . auch von der erscheinenden Welt ganz unabhängig . . . könnte gewissermassen, auch wenn die Welt gar nicht wäre, doch bestehen . . ." Arthur Schopenhauer, *Die Welt als Wille und Vorstellung,* cit. n. 103, 52, 156.

[113]In a letter to Frizeau of July 27, 1909, Odilon Redon speaks of "decorative painting, what your friend calls 'musical painting,' which could more aptly be described as: suggestive painted surface." Cited in *Gazette des Beaux-Arts* 111 (mai-juin 1988), 328. See also Ernst H. Gombrich, "Some Musical Analogies," in *The Sense of Order: A Study in the Psychology of Decorative Art* (London: Phaidon, 1979), 285–305.

[114]August Endell, "Formen, Schönheit und dekorative Kunst," *Dekorative Kunst* 1, no. 1 (1898), 75.

[115]Peter Vergo, "Music and Abstract Painting: Kandinsky, Goethe and Schönberg," in *Towards a New Art: Essays on the Background to Abstract Art* (London: Tate Gallery, 1980), 41–63. Kagan, "*Ut Pictura Musica* to 1860," cit. n. 1, 84–85, has demonstrated Adam Smith's importance in this regard. See also Otto Stelzer, *Vorgeschichte der abstrakten Kunst* (München: Piper, 1964).

[116]Novalis, *Schriften,* cit. n. 14, II, 574; see also III, 559: "Die eigentliche sichtbare Musik sind die Arabesken, Muster, Ornamente."

[117]Stendhal, "Promenades dans Rome," in *Voyages en Italie* [1829] (Paris: Gallimard, 1973), 634.

[118]Samuel T. Coleridge, "On Poesy or Art," *Biographia Literaria* (Oxford: Clarendon, 1907), 261.

[119]Hegel, *Esthétique,* cit. n. 47, III, 258.

[120]Germaine de Staël, *De l'Allemagne,* (Paris: Charpentier, 1869), 480.

[121]Eugène Delacroix, *Oeuvres littéraires,* cit. n. 92, I, 66.

[122]Paul Gauguin, letters to Schuffenecker of August 14 and October 8, 1888 in *Oviri, écrits d'un sauvage* (Paris: Gallimard, 1974), 40, 42.

[123]Letter to Fontainas of March 1899. Gauguin used musical metaphors on several occasions, notably in an interview with Tardieu (*Echo de Paris,* May 13, 1895), in *Avant et après, Notes synthétiques,* as well as in his commentary on his painting *Manao Tupapau;* cf., *Gauguin* (Paris: Grand Palais, 1989), 280.

[124]"These abstract relations . . . whether of colours or sounds, form what we may properly term the musical or harmonic element in every art . . . are pleasant to the human senses or instincts, though they represent nothing and serve for nothing." John Ruskin, *Aratra Pentelici: Six Lectures on the Elements of Sculpture,* chap. I: "Of the Division of Arts," in *Works* (London: Allen, 1905), XX, 207.

[125]James McNeil Whistler, *The Gentle Art of Making Enemies* [1890](New York: Dover, 1967), 127.

[126]"On s'achemine ainsi vers un art entièrement nouveau, qui sera à la peinture, telle qu'on l'avait envisagée jusqu'ici, ce que la musique est à la littérature. Ce sera de la peinture pure, de même que la musique est de la littérature pure." Guillaume Apollinaire, "Du sujet dans la peinture moderne," *Soirées de Paris* 1 (février 1912), reprinted in *Les peintres cubistes* (Genève: Cailler 1950), 14.

CHAPTER 3

Seeing Music
Visuality in the Friendship
of Johann Wolfgang von Goethe
and Carl Friedrich Zelter

STEPHANIE CAMPBELL

> *Die Nachahmung ist uns angeboren, das*
> *Nachzuahmende wird nicht leicht erkannt.*
>> —GOETHE, *WILHELM MEISTERS LEHRJAHRE*

Carl Friedrich Zelter (1758–1832), remembered today chiefly as Goethe's friend and Mendelssohn's teacher, played an important part in the developing musical scene in early nineteenth-century Berlin. Under his leadership the Singakademie became the premiere choral institution in Germany and the orchestra he organized to accompany the choir helped pave the way for the founding of the Berlin Philharmonic. He also founded the music department at Humboldt University and established the first Liedertafel, a social organization devoted to the singing and composing of part-songs for male chorus. His diverse and often innovative body of solo lieder consists of approximately two hundred songs. In addition, Zelter was important as a collector of scores, an early authority on J. S. Bach, and a teacher of voice and composition. Despite his impressive musical accomplishments, Zelter did not become a professional musician until the age of fifty. For more than half of his adult life, Zelter earned his living as a master mason.

Trained in the visual medium of architectural drawing, Zelter approached music from a strongly visual orientation. As a child, he felt no particular interest in music until his father took him, at the age of eleven or twelve, to see an opera for the first time. In his autobiography, Zelter described the experience using a visual metaphor:

> I saw the sound of the singers coming, as it were, but the orchestra as a
> whole was a tremendous, engrossing puzzle to me. . . . From the time
> of these perceptions forward, my gaze was drawn toward the theater
> and I swam in a sea of joy.[1]

At the age of seventeen, Zelter was forced to wear a blindfold during a
long convalescence from scarlet fever. During this period of sightless-
ness he felt the first stirrings of a serious musical calling and spent his
time practicing the violin and keyboard. Zelter's description, again, includes a strong visual component:

> In this long night of awakening new strength, I sought out the keyboard
> and groped around on the keys. My fingers found notes, thoughts were
> formed for the notes, and pictures formed themselves from the
> thoughts. I improvised in my own way and for the first time became
> truly familiar with the keyboard without the use of my eyes.[2]

Zelter presents these events as a turning point and source of conflict in
his life; not until the summer when he was supposed to begin his work as
a mason did he realize that "all of [his] senses were directed toward
music."[3] Significantly, this musical awakening occurred in a visual
void—the "images" aroused (however indirectly) by the music seem to
substitute for the missing sense. Throughout his life, Zelter continued to
describe his musical experiences in visual terms.

    Johann Wolfgang von Goethe, Zelter's friend and correspondent for
more than thirty years, also approached his life and art from a visual
standpoint. In his autobiography *Dichtung und Wahrheit,* after describing an early attraction to drawing and painting, Goethe explains: "The
eye was the primary organ with which I grasped the world."[4] A visual
way of thinking inevitably affected the musical life of both Zelter and
Goethe—Goethe, in his theorizing about music, and Zelter, not only in
what he said about music, but also in his compositional process. While
the shared visual orientation of the two friends may have contributed to
their close relationship, it did not lead to complete unanimity. Goethe
and Zelter took different positions with respect to tone painting, a visual
analogy for the musical reflection of a wide variety of phenomena.
Curiously, though, Goethe took no notice of this difference of opinion
when he cited his friend Zelter's songs to support his own views on tone
painting.

    In his theoretical writings Goethe explored the relationship between sound and color. His scientific study of color, *Farbenlehre,* includes several observations about musical sound. He acknowledged that tone and color were separate phenomena, operating on different senses, but were united in that "both may be derived from a higher formula."[5] According to Goethe, tone and color conform to "universal law (separation and tendency to union, rising and falling, weight and counterweight)" like rivers that flow in different directions from a single mountain.[6] Goethe's theory comprises a system of opposing pairs which he called "plus" and "minus." After recommending that the methodology of his theory of color be applied to music, he suggested that the fundamental polarity of music was major and minor, thus equating it with light and darkness in his theory of color. Later in the *Farbenlehre* Goethe again cited major and minor as the principal difference between keys and went on, despite his caution that color and tone may not be directly compared, to make an analogy between the visual and musical arts:

> We would be justified in drawing a comparison between a picture with a powerful effect and a musical work in a major key, or a painting with a gentle effect and a work in a minor key.[7]

Goethe's outline for a *Tonlehre,* undertaken two years after the completion of the *Farbenlehre,* represents his attempt to apply his methodology to music. While refraining from a direct comparison to painting or color, he cited the contrast between major and minor as "the polarity in the theory of tone" and "the basis for all music," again implying that it parallelled the opposition between light and darkness in his theory of color.[8] The sketch remained undeveloped despite his efforts to enlist the aid of Zelter, who disagreed with Goethe's basic premise.

Although Zelter rarely expressed open disagreement with Goethe, the two debated the nature of the minor scale intermittently from 1808 to 1830, during which time it became something of a sore subject. In 1808 Goethe asked his friend why the minor mode was so often encountered. Drawing, perhaps indirectly, on Rameau's influential harmonic treatise, Zelter replied that the minor third is a variant of the major third, which is more natural since it occurs when a string, or monochord, is divided into five parts, while the minor third does not occur in the harmonic series at all, although as the monochord is divided into smaller and smaller proportions the interval comes closer to the minor third. Goethe contended that the frequent occurrence of minor keys in folk music proved that both were gifts of nature; since humankind was the highest manifestation of nature, the human ear was a far more reliable indicator than any string.[9] Zelter answered with a fuller explanation, giving ground where he could, but defending his original position. For a time the subject was dropped.

In 1826 Goethe asked for Zelter's comments on his outline for the *Tonlehre*, which they had discussed during Zelter's visit in the summer of 1810, and Goethe had then put aside. A cautionary remark in Goethe's letter accompanying the sketch suggests that Zelter still disagreed with his basic premise: "If something can be contributed to its completeness, I would be happy. You will accept the methodology."[10] Zelter avoided commenting directly on the issue, although in 1828 he answered Goethe's request for information on seventeenth-century music with the rather pointed suggestion that music's source of descriptive power was the operation of consonance and dissonance:

> What light and shadow is in modern painting can be thought of as chromatic (dissonant) in modern music, since at this point music acquires a descriptive, dramatic character it did not have before. Thus the seventeenth century divides the serving art from the ruling, which stands on its own.[11]

Short of challenging Goethe's premise, against which he had been cautioned, Zelter came as close as he dared to saying that consonance and dissonance, rather than major and minor, is the fundamental polarity of music theory. In the course of proposing a slight change in wording for the *Tonlehre* the following year, Zelter again mentioned "the theory of dissonance, through which music becomes an art," and in the next paragraph "the theory of consonance and dissonance in relation to a key tone, by which music becomes an art of artists."[12] This undercurrent of disagreement in an exchange usually characterized by a genuinely sympathetic outlook (supplemented by occasional bursts of obsequiousness on Zelter's side) reveals the strength of Zelter's commitment to his own theories about the source of music's descriptive power.[13]

Like Goethe, Zelter connected seeing and hearing, music and painting, at the level of universal law. In his autobiography, Zelter recounts a dispute that arose in 1783 when, while discussing Goethe's *Werther* with his friend Jeanette Ephraim, he introduced a comparison with painting. To Jeanette's protest that painting was just as irrelevant to the novel as music would be, Zelter replied:

> There is only one Art; painting and music are only different fields, part of this general Art; one must know the boundaries, but also how it

looks from the other side; yes, the painter who is musical, just as the composer who paints, these are the true, genuine artists; conversely, the dry historical copier, like the notesetter, could never be called an artist in spirit and in truth.[14]

At this point, Jeanette's painting instructor and her family, which had been drawn into the argument, asked Zelter whether he disagreed with the general condemnation of musical "painting," citing the portrayal of such things as "roaring lions, hissing snakes, and crowing roosters" in music. The musical reflection of these kinds of specific details, a practice commonly called "word painting," met with strong critical disapproval at the time.[15] Convinced that he had been misunderstood, Zelter remained silent. The main point of his comparison, that both painters and composers must begin with an act of imagination in order to be artists rather than copyists, had been brushed aside.

In a speech for an art festival in 1820, Zelter explicitly located the connection between seeing and hearing in the "inner imagination." He compared one of the paintings on display, Raphael's *St. Cecilia* (patron saint of church music), with a musical work performed by the *Singakademie,* a *Crucifixus* setting by Lotti:

> The words "Crucifixus" and so on, which are familiar throughout Christendom, are stretched by our master into a baseline, a painterly foundation, in order to build the picture of the cross upon it. As the seeing eye changes into the ear in Raphael's "Cecilia" standing before us, so in this piece the ear changes to the spiritual eye through the inner imagination, where the eternal cross, on which the sins and shame of all the world are atoned, miraculously raises itself. Towards the end the piece gradually raises itself into a colossal harmonic mass, in which reason and meaning sink and dissolve into humility and worship.[16]

The image that Zelter finds in Lotti's music does not depend on any sort of overt musical representation but on the familiar text, the harmony (i.e., the operation of consonance and dissonance), and the inner imagination. While it is certainly possible to listen to a *Crucifixus* setting without visualizing a cross, much as one may view the *St. Cecilia* painting without imagining music, the association is a natural one for a listener inclined to visualization, as Zelter seems to have been.[17]

Zelter's strong visual imagination affected his compositional process. As a young man, he prepared counterpoint exercises for his teacher Carl Friedrich Christian Fasch without the aid of pencil and paper, turning the music over in his mind as he walked from his home in Berlin to Potsdam where Fasch was employed. He typically began the process of song composition by looking at the poem on the page, committing it to memory as he read it aloud repeatedly. On occasion Zelter credited the inspiration of the song to the poem's appearance on the page: He attributed the funereal rhythm of his setting of Goethe's *Klaggesang* to the mournful look of the poet's handwriting.[18] In 1810 he explained to Goethe: "Whenever I have your verses before my eyes, it always seems to me as though they adopted a melodic form by themselves and did not want to speak at all, only to sing."[19] Autograph notebooks of Zelter's songs tend to support the idea that the melody, at least, was complete before anything was committed to paper. Sketches showing the evolution of a melody are infrequent and, in laying out the text, Zelter often had a well-developed idea of how much room would be necessary for the music.

The process that began by taking the poem off of the page, as it were, and out of the composer's actual sight, culminated in returning the finished work to the page, where it literally became visible to the composer again. At this point Zelter perceived the song differently than during the phase when the song had belonged only to the "inner eye," and often became dissatisfied:

> Only when it is printed and stands plainly before me do the right notes announce themselves, and what is there pains me.
>
> In making this observation only now, when the song stands fixed and finished before me, I share it with you for this reason: one does not know what one is making and would be lost if God did not know it.
>
> Good work also wants to have hands, and not until the thing stands in front of my eyes do I see where the climax belongs. Now I will actually have to begin studying architecture; oh, to be thirty years younger![20]

After the song (composed in a matter of hours or, at most, days) was on the page, Zelter would set it aside for a time and then return to revise it, usually not radically, over the course of months or even years.

Although in one of the complaints quoted above, Zelter finds his work lacking in architecture, he was certainly not a novice in this respect, being a successful builder of houses. He had thought about the connection between musical structure and architecture for a long time. According to August Wilhelm Schlegel, who in 1798 advised Goethe to make

Zelter's acquaintance, Zelter claimed a relationship between building and composing and insisted that, while building might not be musical, composition was indeed architectural.[21] Zelter never stated explicitly in what sense composing resembled building, but his analogy can be extended to his process of notating songs. He tended to notate the music in layers, writing out the melody first, then the bass line, and finally filling in details of the accompaniment. Very often pencil sketches remain in place underneath the ink, so that, much as a building covers a wooden framework, the finished song consumes or covers its initial outline. Some of Zelter's unfinished songs resemble cutaway diagrams of a building, revealing the layers of work underneath by their varying degrees of completion.

Zelter sometimes employed spatial analogies to describe his compositional process. Twice he compared composing to sculpting from the living material that aids in its own creation.[22] About his compositional process Zelter remarked: "I would never have known how to set anything to music without first imagining a plastic model."[23] In Zelter's imagination, stamped with a visual orientation, an idea that was spatial in origin could be translated into sound. While both Zelter and Goethe admitted a fundamental connection between visual and aural phenomena, Goethe's cautious comparisons of music and painting, sound and color, contrast with Zelter's broader connection of music with images and shapes.

Goethe disliked musical reflections of specific details of a text. He disapproved of through-composition on the grounds that it paid "a false attention to detail."[24] In a letter to Zelter, Goethe praised Zelter's choral setting of his ballad *Johanna Sebus* for a higher kind of tone painting that he found only imperfectly in the music of other composers:

> It is a kind of symbolism for the ear, through which the object, in so far as it is in motion or not in motion, is neither imitated nor depicted, but created in the imagination in an entirely unique, incomprehensible way, because the signified seems to have almost no relationship with the signifier.[25]

With his statement that the movement of objects is not imitated or depicted, Goethe takes issue specifically with the musical representation of motion. Goethe goes on to make a concession that seems to contradict his opposition to tone painting: "Obviously, the thunder can rumble and the waves rage in a completely natural way in the music."[26] Since the subject of the ballad is a storm and flood, however, Goethe's admission of the representation of thunder and waves applies not so much to a specific text painting as to an overall stormy affect.

Ten years later, in 1820, Goethe made the following frequently quoted statement in another letter to Zelter: "To paint notes with notes, to thunder, to crash, to babble and splash is detestable. A minimum of it can be used as a final touch in exceptional cases, just as you do."[27] The phrase "to paint notes with notes" refers to the musical representation of sound, a somewhat different variety of tone painting than that singled out ten years before. Each of his examples (thunder, crash, babble, and splash) has an aural component. In this letter, Goethe proceeds to explain his idea of desirable tone painting:

> The purest and highest painting in music is that which you practice: the important thing is to put the listener in the mood that the poem sets; then the shapes form themselves in the imagination according to the situation in the text, without knowing how they came about.[28]

Goethe's "pure and high" tone painting excludes all musical representation except that of a general affect. If it matches that of the poem, then mental images based on the text can be formed. For Goethe, music and images are already related at the fundamental level of universal law; therefore, music need not depict specific details of a text in order to stimulate the visual imagination.

In a comment reported by the actor Eduard Genast about Schubert's setting of *Erlkönig,* Goethe seems to find appropriate tone painting: "I have heard this composition once before and it did not say anything to me, but performed like this, the whole forms itself into a visible picture."[29] Although Goethe spoke disparagingly about the song elsewhere, and in this instance was more or less constrained to say something positive about the song since Genast had kindly arranged for Wilhelmine Devrient-Schröder to sing it for the poet, here he singles out musical depiction for praise. In a later remark Goethe admired "the clatter of the horse," which he might be expected to find offensive as a representation of sound.[30] However, the repeated eighth notes run through the whole song and represent not only the horse but also a general character of urgency. Rather than a "false attention to detail," Schubert's representation of the horse grows out of the overall affect.

Given his broader view of the connection between the music and images, perhaps it is not surprising that Zelter embraced a more detailed variety of tone painting than Goethe did. He responded to Goethe's 1820

criticism of tone painting with praise of Beethoven's character symphonies, particularly *Wellington's Victory,* and Haydn's oratorios, *The
Creation* and *The Seasons,* all well-known for lavish tone painting. He
reminded Goethe that genius cannot be quarreled with and suggested
that one could feel entirely at ease about a programmatic piece if, upon
removing the extramusical element, the music functioned on its own.

In 1802 Zelter had passionately defended Haydn's *Creation* against
accusations of superficial depiction in the Leipzig *Allgemeine musikalische Zeitung.* In his review, Zelter broaches the controversial topic by
observing that the individual movements of Haydn's symphonies and
quartets each have a unique character or "elemental spirit" and concluding that all of Haydn's instrumental works are the composer's own variety of "paintings for the ear."[31] The poem itself, Zelter explains, is a
succession of pictures, like a row of paintings. He compares the representation in the work to a shadow play for the inner eye, brought to life
by music and the imagination. Zelter's detailed interpretation of the
overture, or *Representation of Chaos,* elicited words of approval in a letter from Haydn himself.[32]

If Haydn is always painting, as Zelter suggests, then his response to
an overtly descriptive text with musical depiction is only to be expected.
After hearing a performance of the *Creation* many years later, Zelter remembered his earlier review and wrote to Goethe:

> For me it was as if I really enjoyed it today for the first time since I
> publicly defended it thirty years ago against reproaches of the inadmis-
> sible depiction of exotic subject matter. What my predecessors had
> overlooked was the simple circumstance that the text is concerned pre-
> cisely with the superficialities of the creation story, and now it is a mat-
> ter of how the task is carried out. . . . Now since the chaos functions
> clearly, beneficially, powerfully, and delightfully as art without sung
> words, I envision removing the words from the entire work and observ-
> ing what ignorant opinion takes for [mere] brushwork, from the rum-
> bling and growling of the behemoth and lion to the notes of the
> nightingale, as a series of charming events that the sensitive ear enthu-
> siastically wants to unravel. And it was good![33]

Because the music is more than superficial tone painting, depiction only
adds to the musical experience. In his 1802 review, Zelter had singled out
the representation of the nightingale as "praiseworthy behind our powers
of expression," observing: "One sees with the highest admiration how

the composer seizes every opportunity of using his art to express all that it can and will."[34]

Clearly Zelter was far more tolerant of specific musical depiction than Goethe. Given his conservative outlook in other matters, Zelter's acceptance of tone painting despite a climate of critical disapproval demonstrates his capacity for independent judgement and is perhaps related to his visual orientation. Curiously, admiration for the tone painting in *Wellington's Victory,* generally considered a low point in Beethoven's body of work, was one of the deciding factors in conquering Zelter's initial resistance to Beethoven. Zelter respected Beethoven not in spite of, but at least in part because of his tone painting.

In praising Zelter's "pure and high" tone painting, Goethe mentioned three works by name: *Johanna Sebus* and two solo lieder, *Um Mitternacht* and *Ruhe*. Each of these works contains examples of localized, specific word painting. In much the same way that Schubert's *Erlkönig* combines a general affect of urgency with the sound of the horse, Zelter includes storm music throughout much of the work, especially in the piano introduction. Aside from the generalized storm music, however, the music contains detailed representation of the sort Goethe claimed to dislike. In the choral refrain at the words *die Fläche saust,* quick-moving melismas rush against slower-moving voices and a dominant pedal point to suggest the water spreading over the land. In one of the solo verses, the piano seems to react to the motion of the word *schwoll,* or "swelled," with a little rise and fall (Figure 3–1). The ascending arpeggio on the words *zum Himmel hinauf,* that is, "up to heaven," is the sort of spatial analogy one might encounter in a sixteenth-century madrigal (Figure 3–2). Near the end of the ballad, Zelter extends the word *überall,* or "everywhere," through repetition, indicating the extent of the flood. Thus, the literal depiction in *Johanna Sebus* includes the representation of motion, position, and quantity.

Figure 3–1. Carl Friedrich Zelter, *Johanna Sebus,* mm. 70–72.

Figure 3–2. Zelter, *Johanna Sebus,* mm. 148–149.

As an example of Zelter's most attentive and careful text-setting, *Um Mitternacht* is perhaps an especially significant indicator of his practical approach to the relationship between words and music. In varied strophic form, the three strophes present speechlike yet expressive declamation and an interesting variety of rhythmic and melodic detail. Nevertheless, the relationship between words and music is not totally abstract. Among the many musical reflections of individual words and phrases are two descriptive gestures on the words *Stern* and *Gestirn,* both meaning "star(s)": a bit of coloratura, perhaps suggestive of shimmering, on *Stern* (Figure 3–3), and an ascending leap of a ninth on *Gestirn,* representing height (Figure 3–4).

In the profoundly peaceful and beautiful *Ruhe,* a setting of Goethe's well-known "Über allen Gipfeln ist Ruh," Zelter treats the text with more restraint than in the other two examples, but with a great attention to detail. The stops and starts in the piano, the fermatas, and a unison between

Figure 3–3. Zelter, *Um Mitternacht,* mm. 14–15, first strophe.

Figure 3–4. Zelter, *Um Mitternacht,* mm. 12, second strophe.

spü - rest du kaum ei - hen Hauch

Figure 3–5. Zelter, *Ruhe*, mm. 8–9.

melody and bass line in the ninth measure contribute to a general sense of rest and stillness. The most specific instance of text-painting occurs on the limiting word *kaum*, or "scarcely," which is isolated and cut short by eighth rests on either side (Figure 3–5).

One writer on the subject of Goethe and music has remarked disparagingly that Zelter's music for *Ruhe*'s line *"Die Vögelein schweigen im Walde"* ("The birds fall silent in the woods") sounds more as if the line were *"Die Vögelein singen im Walde."* ("The birds sing in the woods.")[35] The setting contains two more examples of this kind of ironic, reverse symbolism: the rather conspicuous multiplicity of notes on the word *einen* in the phrase "you sense scarcely a single breath" (Figure 3–5) and the gradual slowing during the repetitions of the word *balde,* ("soon") (Figure 3–6). One calls to mind Goethe's statement that the signifier seems to bear no relationship to the signified. In *Ruhe* much of the tone painting is accomplished by signifiers, not *without* a relationship, but with a negative one. Stillness, silence, and swiftness are evoked partly through their opposites.

Even in the works that Goethe singled out as exemplifying the "purest and highest" in tone painting, Zelter went far beyond the representation of a general affect and connected music and text in a wide variety of ways. In fact, Zelter's song output is generously sprinkled with tone painting, from early songs such as "Die Braut am Gestade," which presents a descending octave leap on the word "sinkend," not to mention the oscillation on the words "strüdelt das Schiff" (Figure 3–7), until his last dated song, "Abschied," where the piano interpolates lark imitations. If Goethe had considered Zelter's setting of "Gleich und Gleich," which consists largely of coloratura in imitation of a bee in flight, he might have

war - te nur, bal - de, bal - de, bal - de ruhst

Figure 3–6. Zelter, *Ruhe*, mm. 11–12.

nun   stru - delt   das   Schiff   sin - kend!

Figure 3–7. Zelter, *Die Braut am Gestade*, mm. 72–76.

acknowledged that Zelter's tone painting was sometimes more than a "final touch."[36]

Although both Zelter and Goethe admitted a connection between music and the visual imagination, they took different positions with respect to tone painting, a practice that assumes a relationship between aural and other phenomena. Goethe's apparent failure to acknowledge the divergence may be interpreted in two ways: either Goethe was more tolerant of detailed word painting than his statements on the subject have generally led his readers to believe, or his brotherly devotion to Zelter caused him to develop a blind spot concerning his friend's activities. Zelter's songs may have succeeded with Goethe because they transcended specific text painting by portraying general affect as well. Perhaps the arguments that Zelter had presented on behalf of Haydn may be brought to his own defense: (1) for Zelter, as for Goethe, all music is connected to the visual imagination, so specific details are not out of place should the text suggest them; and (2) the music functions on its own, even if the tone painting is not recognized.

Particularly in his later years, Zelter was seen as a conservative force in music; Beethoven once sent greetings "to Zelter, the faithful guardian of the true art."[37] Goethe's counsel to Zelter that they hold firmly to the views with which they started and so become the last representatives of a great age suggests that the two friends saw themselves as belonging more to the past than the future.[38] Nevertheless, in their discussion of a connection between the senses, rooted in the inner imagination, Zelter and Goethe laid hold of a thread that was to become increasingly important in the nineteenth century.

NOTES

[1]Carl Friedrich Zelter, *Carl Friedrich Zelters Darstellungen seines Lebens,* ed. Johann-Wolfgang Schottländer, vol.4 of *Schriften der Goethe-Gesellschaft* (Weimar: Verlag der Goethe- Gesellschaft, 1931), 16.

[2]Ibid., 34–35.

[3]Ibid.

[4]Johann Wolfgang von Goethe, *Dichtung und Wahrheit,* vol. 5 of *Johann Wolfgang Goethe Werke* (1812; reprint, Frankfurt am Main: Insel, 1993), 203.

[5]Goethe, *Zur Farbenlehre,* ed. Gerhard Ott and Heinrich Proskauer (1810; reprint, Stuttgart: Freies Geistesleben, 1979). Translated by Douglas Miller in *Scientific Studies,* vol. 12 of *Goethe's Collected Works* (Princeton: Princeton University Press, 1988), 276. All other translations are my own.

[6]Goethe, in Miller, 276.

[7]Ibid., 293.

[8]Goethe, "Theory of Tone," in Miller, 302.

[9]Only three years earlier Zelter had read Goethe's translation of and commentary on Diderot's satirical *Le Neveu de Rameau.* One wonders whether his introduction of ideas stemming from a theorist on the opposite side of the French *querelles* from that of Diderot, towards whom Goethe was sympathetic, was the result of courage or naiveté.

[10]Goethe to Zelter, September 6, 1826, *Briefwechsel zwischen Zelter und Goethe,* ed. Max Hecker (1833; reprint, Frankfurt am Main: Insel Verlag, 1987), 2:506.

[11]Zelter to Goethe, [August 1828], *Briefwechsel,* 3:73.

[12]Ibid. [May 1829], *Briefwechsel,* 3:173.

[13]Eventually Zelter withdrew from his original position that the minor third was derived from the major, greatly relieving Goethe's mind on the subject. He never capitulated, however, on the issue of consonance and dissonance standing in the place of light and shadow. See Zelter to Goethe, April 14, 1831, *Briefwechsel,* 3:459–460.

[14]Zelter, *Darstellungen,* 151.

[15]For a summary of eighteenth-century attitudes towards "word painting" or "tone painting," see Richard Will, "Programmatic Symphonies of the Classical Period" (Ph.D. diss., Cornell University, 1994), 98–120.

[16]Enclosure in a letter from Zelter to Goethe, April 19, 1820, *Briefwechsel,* 2:66.

[17]According to Ettore Camesasca, Raphael's *St. Cecilia* was returned to Bologna in 1815 after having been confiscated during the Napoleonic invasion. Presumably the work displayed at the art festival was a copy. See Camesasca, *All the Paintings of Raphael,* trans. Luigi Grosso (New York: Hawthorn Books, 1963), 2:79–80.

[18]Zelter to Goethe, June 16, 1828, *Briefwechsel,* 3:589.

[19]Zelter to Goethe, March 19, 1810, *Briefwechsel,* 1:279.

[20]Zelter to Goethe, January 29, 1818, *Briefwechsel,* 1:627; December 2, 1816, 1:576; and June 14, 1809, 1:256.

[21]August Wilhelm Schlegel to Goethe, June 10, 1798, quoted in Walther Victor, *Carl Friedrich Zelter und seine Freundschaft mit Goethe* (Berlin: Das neue Berlin, 1960), 15–16.

[22]Zelter to Goethe, March 24, 1818, *Briefwechsel,* 1:642, and February 3, 1823, 2:220–221.

[23]Ibid., 221.

[24]Goethe, *Johann Wolfgang Goethe Tag—und Jahreshefte,* ed. Irmtraut Schmid, in *Johann Wolfgang Goethe Sämtliche Werke,* series I, vol. 17 (Frankfurt am Main: Deutscher Klassiker Verlag, 1994), 72.

[25]Goethe to Zelter, March 6, 1810, *Briefwechsel,* 1:277.

[26]Ibid.

[27]Goethe to Zelter, May 2, 1820, *Briefwechsel,* 2:68.

[28]Ibid.

[29]Eduard Genast, *Aus dem Tagebuche eines alten Schauspielers* (Leipzig: Voigt und Günther, 1862), 2:280–281.

[30]J. G. von Quandt, quoted in *Goethes Gedanken über Musik* (Frankfurt am Main: Insel, 1985), 50.

[31]Zelter, "Recension," *Allgemeine Musikalische Zeitung* 4 (March 10, 1802): 385–396.

[32]Haydn to Zelter, February 25, 1804, *Joseph Haydn: Gesammelte Briefe und Aufzeichnungen,* ed. Dénes Bartha (Kassel: Bärenreiter, 1965), 436–437.

[33]Zelter to Goethe, April 28, 1830, *Briefwechsel,* 3:332–333.

[34]Zelter, "Recension," 394.

[35]K. Mitchells, " 'Nicht nur lesen! Immer singen!' Goethe's 'Lieder' into Schubert Lieder," *Publications of the English Goethe Society* 44 (1974): 78.

[36]On the other hand, since Zelter had sent the song to Goethe less than a year before Goethe's 1820 letter quoted above, the praise may have been tinged with admonition.

[37]Ludwig von Beethoven to Ludwig Rellstab, [May 3, 1825], *Briefwechsel Gesamtausgabe,* ed. Sieghard Brandenburg (Munich: Henle, 1996), 6:58.

[38]Goethe to Zelter, [June 7, 1825], *Briefwechsel,* 2:375.

CHAPTER 4

Fingal's Cave and Ossian's Dream
Music, Image, and Phantasmagoric Audition

THOMAS S. GREY

> *As when a shepherd of the Hebrid Isles,*
> *Placed far amid the melancholy main,*
> *(Whether it be lone fancy him beguiles,*
> *Or that aerial beings sometimes deign*
> *To stand embodied to our senses plain),*
> *Sees on the naked hill, or valley low,*
> *The whilst in ocean Phoebus dips his wain,*
> *A vast assembly moving to and fro,*
> *Then all at once in air dissolves the wondrous show.*
>
> —JAMES THOMSON,
> "THE CASTLE OF INDOLENCE"(1742).

FINGAL'S CAVE

"Staffa, with its crazy basalt pillars and caverns, is in all the picture-books," writes Karl Klingemann, travelling companion of the young Felix Mendelssohn, reporting on their excursion to the Scottish Highlands during the summer of 1829 in a joint letter to the Mendelssohn family back in Berlin.

> We were put into skiffs [from the steam-ship], and bounced over the seething waters ... towards the all-too famous Fingal's Cave. A greener roar of waves has certainly never washed into a stranger cavern—its many columns resemble the insides of some monstrous organ,

black, resounding, sitting there alone and quite, quite without purpose—the broad gray expanse of the sea before it and within it.[1]

Klingemann goes on to poke fun at his fellow travellers (himself and
Felix included) for all the physical discomforts they have undergone in
order to edify themselves with the sight of this natural wonder:

> The crew of the steamship breakfasted nearly alone, for few others
> could keep hold of a teacup, and altogether the *Ladies* were falling like
> flies, followed by an occasional *Gentleman;* I wish that my travelling
> brother-in-misfortune had not been among these, but he is on better
> terms with the sea as an artist than as a man or as a stomach.[2]

Indeed, what Klingemann sketched in satirical prose his friend Felix
Mendelssohn famously sketched in music, as well as in a pen-and-ink
drawing. Or almost. The sketch of what became the opening twenty-one
bars of the *Hebrides* Overture and a drawing of "The Hebrides and Morven" were both executed on August 7, 1829, actually the day *before* the
excursion by steamer and skiff to Fingal's Cave, as R. Larry Todd has
noted.[3] The pen-and-ink drawing is not actually of Fingal's Cave at all,
but a tranquil view of the Firth of Lorn near Oban on the western coast of
Scotland, with a glimpse of the ruins of Dunollie Castle through the
branches of an oak tree. The musical sketch was sent to his family as a
kind of sounding postcard, along with a short note explaining that it
should convey "how strangely he was affected by the Hebrides" ("wie
seltsam mir auf den Hebriden zu Muthe geworden ist").[4] Though the musical sketch seems to have preceded the actual excursion to Staffa, its relative proximity has encouraged some fancifully embroidered tales from
the writers of program notes. One Charles O'Connell, for example, recounts that Mendelssohn notated these twenty-one measures "while he
sat in a tossing skiff within the cave itself" (scarcely likely, given
Mendelssohn's indisposition on the occasion, and the fairly elaborate detail of this *particell* sketch).[5] The normally sensible D. F. Tovey even
claims that the composer wrote the sketch "while actually standing in
Fingal's Cave."[6] This might have been a mischievous joke on Tovey's
part. He spent much of his life in Scotland as a professor of music at Edinburgh University, and must have been aware that the cave is filled with
water—as much as twenty-three feet, even at low tide, according to one
source. A contemporary drawing of the site by J. M. W. Turner demonstrates the point; a highly stylized contemporary view, from a German illustrated travelogue, corresponds much more closely to Klingemann's
description of the site (see Figures 4–1 and 4–2).

Figure 4–1. J.M.W. Turner, *Fingal's Cave, Staffa,* steel engraving by E. Goodall for Walter Scott, *Poetical Works,* vol. 10, 1833–1834.

Figure 4–2. Engraving of Fingal's Cave from Barthélemy Faujas de Saint–Fond,
Reise durch England, Schottland und die Hebriden, vol. 2 (Göttingen, 1799), 32.

At any event, critics are understandably at pains to stress Mendelssohn's visual receptivity to nature in the genesis of the *Hebrides* Overture. It is an attractively Romantic notion, Mendelssohn as *plein air*
composer (following the lead of Beethoven, who was known to wander
about the Vienna Woods, sketchbook in hand, breathing inspiration from
the picturesque surroundings). In Beethoven's case, there is a certain
poignancy to the thought of the deaf composer translating the silent landscape into musical themes. With Mendelssohn, his genteel accomplishment in drawing and painting makes the idea of his also sketching a
landscape "in tones" an irresistible one. Klingemann's musical, even synaesthetic, account of the cavern—the "green roar" of the waves and his
evocation of the site as a kind of uncanny musical instrument ("resembling
the insides of some monstrous organ, black, resounding, and . . . quite
without purpose")—provides further encouragement along these lines.

Even if Mendelssohn actually did jot down his sketch the day *before*
the uncomfortable boat ride, he had at least spent several days on the
coast and would have had a sense of the general ambiance and topogra-
phy. But Klingemann's initial remark about the site of Fingal's Cave is
suggestive: "[I]t's in all the picture books." Felix and Karl, after all, were

making this excursion for the same reason as the rest of their fellow tourists: to see firsthand a famous sight, an inspiring natural phenomenon. As much as anything, Mendelssohn was inspired by the anticipation of the sight—that is, by a mental image of what he *expected* to see.

Their trip through Scotland represented a relatively recent albeit well-established type of visual *Bildungsreise:* the "picturesque" Scottish Highlands tour. This was a Romantic alternative to the continental "grand tour" with its emphasis on a classical literary heritage, though art (classical and Renaissance) was also part of that program, which Mendelssohn would carry out the following year. Among the various "picturesque" itineraries in the British Isles, including Wales and the English Lake District, the Scottish tour emphasized the grander, more rugged and "sublime" end of the picturesque spectrum, inevitably colored by several decades of enthusiasm for Ossianic poetry with its "melancholy grandeur" and its abundance of darkly brooding, windy and mist-enshrouded Highland landscapes.[7] More recently, the novels and poetry of Walter Scott had contributed much to the popular mystique of the Highlands landscape, and his estate of Abbotsford was another stop on Mendelssohn's itinerary. The picturesque tour was thus specifically geared towards two related activities: landscape sketching and the viewing of natural landscapes as potential pictures (either as a source of material for the artist, or simply as a repository of visual experiences for the reader of Ossian, Scott, and related Romantic literature). It is certainly no accident, then, that a musician trained in the techniques of drawing and painting, and well-acquainted with a culture of "literary" landscape appreciation, would bring away from Scotland compositional projects grounded in visual stimuli: the *Hebrides* Overture and the "Scottish" Symphony.

For over a hundred years, at least, the *Hebrides* has been regarded as the quintessential "musical landscape." And while it is not my principal goal here to reiterate and embellish this century of critical tradition attached to the piece, it is still necessary to begin with landscape. Ironically, it seems to have been Richard Wagner, Mendelssohn's most notorious critical nemesis, who is principally responsible for the tradition of appreciating the *Hebrides* as a "masterpiece of musical landscape painting." This phrase originates in an interview between Wagner and the English critic Edward Dannreuther which found its way into the first edition of *Grove's Dictionary.*[8] The passage can be further traced to a variety of pronouncements recorded in Cosima Wagner's diaries, though these were later cleansed, either by Wagner or Dannreuther, of various venomous qualifications. In an entry from 1869 Wagner calls the work "clear, smooth, melodious, as definite in form as a crystal, but also just as cold; such an enormous talent as Mendelssohn's is frightening, it has no place in the development of our music. A landscape painter, incapable of depicting a *human being.*"[9]

This two-part theme is restated and varied in a number of later entries: Mendelssohn's consummate technical and formal skill, his affinity with visual *surfaces,* as the counterpart to his cultural and racial "inadequacy" as Jew, his fundamental alienation from "the purely human." (It scarcely needs to be pointed out that the phrase "our music" places Mendelssohn beyond the pale of the "German" musical tradition as such.) In one of these later entries, for example, we read:

> He [Mendelssohn] listened well and received impressions of a landscape—for instance, at the beginning of the [*Hebrides*] Overture the building up of the triad is full of atmosphere, but it is not the human heart and its sighing which he has reproduced, or Nature itself, but a landscape. And I can never think of a character like his as being capable of rapture.[10]

How Wagner claims to distinguish between the musical evocation of a natural landscape and a merely painted one is a puzzling point. But it is clear enough that his *hommage* to Mendelssohn's skill as a musical landscape artist is a backhanded compliment, at best, designed to marginalize the composer as a man of genuine though limited talent, with an affinity for the appearances of things (whether natural imagery or musical styles), but no feeling for their true, inner essence. And for Wagner, landscape clearly signified a lesser pictorial genre; inattentive as he was to painting in general, he surely remained blind to any revolution in the status of landscape effected by the likes of Friedrich, Constable, or Corot earlier in the century.

We might also question how closely Wagner attended to Mendelssohn's *musical* "landscape" in the *Hebrides* Overture. Perhaps it is *his* response one might accuse of superficiality, of failing to hear beneath the surface. The "surface," in this case, constitutes the opening group of the composition, the first forty-six measures. This opening remains a remarkable feat for a twenty-year-old composer writing in the age of Hummel and Spohr. Wagner's appreciation of it tallies with most subsequent responses. The sophisticated layering of rhythmic patterns that repeat but also continually transform themselves, the dark-hued harmonic expansion of the opening gesture under the sustained F# of the violins, the variety of wave- and windlike "swells" at different rhythmic levels, in different registers, and against different triadic and diminished harmonies—all of these seem to be executed with an artless simplicity that sounds utterly "natural" and that never fails to conjure up an appropriate repertoire of seascape images in receptive audiences provided with even just the minimal cues (Hebrides, seaside, clouds, wind). This has been the burden of countless appreciative glosses on—or critical "sketches" of—the piece since Wagner's time, if not before. But Mendelssohn's famous "seascape" effects are not the whole picture (or story).

One reason the opening group is so readily associated with desolate, uninhabited land- or seascape images probably has to do with the striking absence of distinct *melodic* material. Foregrounding repetitive motivic patterns, shaded by dynamic, rhythmic, and timbral variation, Mendelssohn manages to convey a strong sense of vacant, natural space and natural rhythms. But with the emergence of the *cantabile* second theme in the baritonal register of cellos and bassoons we are suddenly encouraged to construct a subjective presence, a "viewer" to inhabit the hitherto desolate scene (Figure 4–3).

The philosopher Jerrold Levinson has offered a small but detailed musical-expressive analysis of this second theme as conveying the feeling of "hope," embedded within a larger, general philosophical aesthetic argument that music is indeed capable of expressing such relatively "complex" emotions without the aid of verbal prompting.[11] Michael P. Steinberg cites Levinson in a recent tribute to Mendelssohn in the *New York Times* (on the 150th anniversary of his death), taking the *Hebrides*

Figure 4–3. *Hebrides* Overture, second theme, mm. 47–57.

as a point of departure in reconsidering various biographical and critical themes (among them the role of visual stimuli in the composer's oeuvre and the related critical polarity of "surface" and "depth"). Following up Levinson's argument about the expressive "depths" of the second theme—both of them cite Tovey's opinion of the melody as the "greatest Mendelssohn ever wrote," incidentally—Steinberg asserts that with the emergence of this theme the musical discourse acquires the character of a "first-person narrative voice."[12] In his eagerness to defend the composer against Wagner's, and much of posterity's, verdict about a talent for conveying landscape impressions (i.e., superficial, cold, and disengaged), Steinberg unnecessarily perpetuates dichotomies that Mendelssohn's music itself brilliantly transcends: image versus narrative, surface versus depth, imitation versus expression, and programmatic or representational versus absolute music.

Nonetheless, his intuition about the "first-person" quality of the second theme, in its musical context, is nicely compatible with my own reading of the theme as signalling a subjective presence within the initially vacant landscape. In my reading the theme serves the same purpose as certain figure types in landscape painting, above all the Romantic *Rückenfigur* (the typically pensive solo figure viewed from behind), inviting us to imagine ourselves similarly inhabiting the depicted landscape and meditating on it from "within" the scene.[13] Here the arching lyrical phrase, with its expression of hope and intimate confidences, reaches out to us from the musical "picture" with a song, inviting us to sing along, as it were—to share its central situation or perspective within the composition. In the music, as in a painting, this subjective dimension sets the images (or sounds) of the "landscape" in relief and helps to release their expressive or symbolic potential.

OSSIAN'S DREAM

But just what does this subject see? Where does he fix his sights? For a fleeting moment the initial "seascape" motive returns, perched dramatically on a hushed *(pianissimo)* °vii7/V in B minor. This quickly resolves into a heroic, *marziale* transformation of the main motive in D major, by way of closing theme, accompanied by brass fanfares and timpani (mm. 70–95). Following Levinson's purely affective reading of the second group, we could hear in this closing section the affirmative realization of his "hopes." The effect, in both musical-expressive and musical-structural terms, anticipates the character transformations of the Lisztian symphonic poem (whose "stories" tend, in fact, to translate rather easily into a succession of such affective labels, matched up to more or less traditional formal functions).

The "story" becomes somewhat more complex, however, in the ensuing development, though without abandoning the pictorial impulse. The topical references of the closing group (the *marziale* fanfares) spill over into the opening section of the development, where they mingle with wisps of the original "seascape" motive in the lower strings, against a shimmering, "misty" backdrop of triadic tremolos in the violins. Most striking is the effect of spatial dislocation or differentiation achieved by means of dynamic and timbral contrasts: "trumpet calls," alternately sounded by mixed woodwinds, horns, and actual trumpets, echo from different quarters of the imaginary musical space. The tremolo "backdrop" contributes to the sense of depth, providing a kind of aural "surface" against which the perceived depth or distance of the trumpet calls can be measured (Figure 4–4). These heroic summons elicit a new marchlike motive—presumably intended to sound fierce, rough-hewn, and Caledonian (though for the latter one can only point to the single, slow-motion "Scotch-snap" toward the end of the passage, m. 121). Strangely, for a work of such obsessive motivic organicism, this wholly new idea flashes across the scene for a mere ten measures and then disappears, never to be heard again (Figure 4–5).

Before these intimations of battle can coalesce into some more extended action, they are broken off by a quiet reminiscence of the second theme in the strings, in D, with wistful minor-subdominant inflections (the B-flats of mm. 124–28). The "hopeful" upward-striving contour of the theme is reversed at the end of the phrase; the muted scoring and dynamics, the tonality (D, as in the exposition), and the rhythmic *ritardando* all conspire to mark the passage as a moment of reminiscence and reflection, an interruption in the formal process of development (see mm. 123–130).

Commentaries on the *Hebrides* are, on the whole, oddly reticent to address these distinctive features of the development, let alone explain them in any way. They do cite, routinely, a comment from a letter of Mendelssohn's expressing his dissatisfaction with the development section in its original version of 1830:

> But *The Hebrides* I can't have performed here [in Paris] yet, since, as I told you [Fanny], I don't consider it finished yet; the middle section in *forte* in D major is very stupid, and the whole so-called development

Figure 4–4. *Hebrides* Overture, "trumpet calls" in opening of development, mm. 96–111.

Figure 4–5. *Hebrides* Overture, new march–like theme in development, mm. 112–123.

[*sogenannte Durchführung*] tastes too much of counterpoint rather than of whale-oil [*Tran*] and sea-gulls and salt-cod [*Laberdan*], while it should be the other way around.[14]

But what do these trumpet calls have to do with seagulls? What does the tranquil "reminiscence" have to do with whale oil or fish? What does the fragmentary "march" music have to do with anything—even with the exposition?

Mendelssohn's letter suggests, at any rate, that he wanted a more "characteristic" development than what he had composed at first. He was notoriously cagey about disclosing the intentions behind his music to anyone, however, even to his sister. (A famous letter to a relative stranger, one Marc-André Souchay, regarding the thought content of the "Songs without Words" is consistently cited as Mendelssohn's brief for the Romantic "ineffability" of musical meaning— that there is finally nothing to "say" about it.)[15] Nevertheless, I don't believe that he expected listeners to approach his *Hebrides* Overture with no ideas at all, even if he was undecided as to just how they *should* approach it. This indecision is registered in the variety of titles Mendelssohn attached to the work, without ever deciding on any definitive one. The work began life with the atmospheric but indistinct title, *Overture to the Lonely Isle,* soon altered to *The Hebrides* (altered, that is, from a generic landscape to a topographical or "portrait" landscape).[16] It was first performed in London as the *Overture to the Isles of Fingal,* and at its Gewandhaus premiere, in Leipzig, it was billed more concretely (and suggestively) as *Ossian im Fingals-Höhle* ("Ossian in Fingal's Cave"). The published versions equivocate between *The Hebrides* and *Fingal's Cave*—an equivocation that was thus passed down to us.[17]

Fingal's Cave was, as we have seen, a geological curiosity: the large cavern with its weird columnar formations of basaltic rock cut into the coast of Staffa. The name was attached to the site in the wake of the Ossianic craze that swept Europe in the later eighteenth century, and which was by no means extinguished by Mendelssohn's time. The impulse for Romantic tourists like Mendelssohn and Klingemann to visit the site, and the Scottish Highlands in general, derived in large part from the fashionably wild, brooding, and "sublime" ambiance of the Ossianic poems and the fascination they continued to exert on European culture at large. Almost from the moment of its publication the poetry was suspected of being largely a product of its "editor and translator," James Macpherson, with some thin foundation in fragments of written and oral traditions, tailored to modern sensibility and cravings for an archaic-mythic national past. This "product" was especially strong on atmosphere and "image" (also in the modern, commercial sense), though weak on actual mythic or epic content.

It is almost impossible to read Macpherson's Ossian poems for the plot. They cultivate the epic gesture assiduously, but narrative content and structure scarcely at all. Heroes live exclusively to do battle on blasted heaths by roaring mountain streams, to die courageously, and to hover about their descendants as wailing nocturnal spirits, riding on clouds and meteors, and portending an endless cycle of future battles and deaths which generate in turn more spirits and more portents. Women exist to mourn the dead, raise tombs to them, console the living, and fill out the overall chiaroscuro of the setting by beckoning the occasional ray of sun through the storm clouds or moonbeam through the nocturnal mists and shadows. Above all it is the ghosts and shadows of fallen heroes who dominate the epic landscape of the Ossian poems.

This glorification of arms and battle through an archaic northern hero cult, set against the modishly "sublime" Highlands background, much endeared the Ossianic style to Napoleon at the time of his major military campaigns. Several visual artifacts of the Napoleonic Ossian fad offer evidence of this poetic tradition's influence on the pictorial arts in the nineteenth century in images that can bring us back to Mendelssohn's revised development section. In François Gérard's 1801 painting, *Ossian Invoking the Spirits* (Figure 4–6), the tones of the bardic harp are echoed by celestial harps in the upper left, while a heroic group clusters around the royal shade of Fingal, Ossian's father, to the right (the spearheads of Fingal's warriors ranged behind the king are only faintly visible). The atmospheric lunar backlighting of the ruined castle is a favorite Romantic

Figure 4–6. François Gerard, *Ossian on the Banks of the Lora, Invoking the Spirits through the Tones of his Harp,* 1801–1810, oil on canvas, 184.5 × 194.5 cm., © Elke Walford Fotowerkstatt Hamburger Kunsthalle/Altbau.

motif, of course, but in conjunction with the diaphanous spirit forms occupying the center of the picture this lighting effect might also recall, more specifically, the illuminated *spectacles d'optique* that had been a popular form of fashionable entertainment for some decades, from de Loutherbourg's "Eidophysikon" of the 1780s to Daguerre's "dioramas" of the 1820s and 1830s.[18]

As in Gérard's picture, the somewhat more solid phantoms of Ingres's *Dream of Ossian* (1813, originally designed as a ceiling decoration for Napoleon's bedroom at Monte Cavallo) are portayed as projections of the bard's inspired fancy (Figure 4–7). While in some of the numerous sketches for this painting the figures are illuminated variously by the moon or by starlight, the finished oil painting portrays the light as emanating (symbolically) from the head of the dreaming Ossian.[19] The busier, almost psychedelic composition of Anne-Louis Girodet-Trioson's *Ossian Receiving the Napoleonic Officers* (1802) transposes the bard himself to the spirit world, where he welcomes the fallen heroes of recent battles into the realm of eternal mythic glory. Here, any remnants of the sublime Highlands landscape tradition have been obliterated by the grandiose poses of modern history painting, translated into the spectral fantastic mode. The explicit portrayal of Ossian's blindness in Girodet's painting might draw our attention, in retrospect, to the downcast and concealed state of his eyes in the pictures of Gérard and Ingres: both images serve to stress the "inner vision" of the poetic imagination as the source of those phantom apparitions Ossian invokes.

Significantly, it is precisely an *image* of the Ossianic world that provides the common ground between these paintings and Mendelssohn's overture, as I shall argue, rather than any concrete mythic-epic content drawn from Macpherson's poetic collections. None of these pictures illustrates a specific episode from the poetry. Each of them, on the other hand, takes as its central image the apparition of spirit forms hovering above and around the figure of Ossian, who preserves their memory in his bardic lays. The image is indeed a constantly recurring one throughout the various poetic epics attributed to "Ossian." The following excerpts are merely a small sampling:

On Lena's dusky heath they stood, like mist that shades the hills of autumn: when broken and dark it settles high and lifts its head to heaven.

"Peace," said Cuchullin, to the souls of the heroes; "their deeds were great in danger. Let them ride around me on clouds, and shew their features of war . . ."

Figure 4–7. J.-A.-D. Ingres, *Dream of Ossian,* 1812–1813, later reworked, oil on canvas, 348 × 275 cm., Musée Ingres, Montauban.

The ghosts of the lately dead were near, and swam on gloomy clouds, and far distant, in the dark silence of Lena, the feeble voices [of death] were heard.[20]

It is Fingal, in the crowd of his ghosts.

Around her [Comala, at the moment of her death], from their clouds, bend the awful faces of her fathers. . . .[21]

Lovely is the mist that assumes the form of Oscar!

The ghosts of Ardven pass through the beam, and show their dim and distant forms . . . . The songs of Ossian have been heard, and thy ghost has brightened in the wind, when thou didst bend from thy cloud to hear the song of Morven's bard.

Oscar goes to the people of other times; to the shades of silent Ardven, where his fathers sit dim in their clouds, and behold the future war.[22]

These passages also convey something of the central significance of the Ossianic oeuvre itself: the memorialization of an archaic, mythic history in song and in dream; that is, in the poetic imagination. Construed in this way, it becomes less difficult to reconcile the appeal of the Ossian poems for the Romantic generation with the widespread knowledge of their inauthenticity. Ossian was a symbol not of any factual, historical past, but the past of the Romantic imagination, and of the generative, creative power of that imagination itself.[23] Explaining the popularity of the Ossianic poems to late-eighteenth-century audiences in terms of their infusion with a contemporary ethos of the "sentimental," John Dwyer also points to the role of these misty specters as emblems of memory; they are mental images that constitute the emotional bond between the living and the departed.[24]

The frontispiece to the earliest editions of Macpherson's poems already confirms the centrality of this image: the blind Ossian is portrayed seated beneath a lone tree, balancing his harp on his outstretched hand, while a group of youthful spirit-figures looks on from a bank of clouds in the upper-right-hand corner (Figure 4–8). *Malvina Mourning the Death of Oscar* (1790) by the Danish artist N. A. Abildgaard, one of the few pre-Napoleonic paintings inspired by Ossian poetry, does refer directly to an episode from the poem, but chooses to portray the fallen Oscar as a cloud-borne spirit. (Both the mourning Malvina and her ghostly hero

Figure 4–8. Frontispiece, *Fingal: An Ancient Poem in Six Books, together with several other Poems* (London: T. Becket and P. A. De Hondt, 1762.) Courtesy of Department of Special Collections, Stanford University Libraries.

make a point of echoing the curve of the crescent moon above them.)[25] In these images, as in the paintings from the Napoleonic-era, the Ossianic landscape becomes a landscape of the dreaming mind, populated by the spirit forms of deceased heroes and commemorating their heroic exploits. "The more uncertain and fugitive the figures and scenes that haunt Ossian," as Pierre van Tieghem says, with reference to the Napoleonic era representations of the subject, "the more we are disposed to dream with him."[26]

I don't necessarily mean to suggest that Mendelssohn was familiar with any of these specific paintings—although it may be worth noting that he was in Paris at the time he wrote to Fanny about his plans to revise the development section of his overture. (A copy of Gérard's painting, furthermore, hung at this time in the Neues Palais in Potsdam, where cultured Berliners like the Mendelssohn family would likely have been aware of it).[27] But the thematic kinship among these pictures underscores what must have been a generally familiar image of the Ossianic tradition: a symbolic montage of bardic fancy, spectral heroes, and darkly sublime, rugged landscapes. The images that Ossian "dreams" are also those that would have inhabited the imaginations of susceptible Romantic tourists gazing on the wild and desolate landscape of the Hebrides or the dim, ominously "resounding" interior of Fingal's Cave.

*   *   *

With this cultural background in mind, we can begin to appreciate how Mendelssohn's overture is more than just a proto-impressionistic "landscape" composition inspired by coastal scenery and atmosphere. Rather, the work records, as it were, the *act* of viewing this landscape (albeit a highly stylized act), in which the spectator not only contemplates the scene before him—with all its changing effects of wind and wave, light and shade, and so on—but also invests it with shades of an imagined mythic history. The act, as I imagine it, goes something like this. (Here I recapitulate briefly before picking up with the development.) The first theme evokes qualities of the natural landscape itself, as so often described. The second (which is significantly the first "real" theme, as a melodic entity) draws our attention to the subjective consciousness of the viewer. (To my mind, it matters not whether we construe this presence as first person or third person—*pace* Steinberg—either as "us" or as another, although the point that the theme invites subjective identification is an important one.) With the *marziale* transformations of the opening motive in the close of the exposition (mm. 77–95) this viewing subject, inspired by the conjunction of natural grandeur and its mythic past, projects onto the landscape the heroic aura of that imaginary, poetic "history."[28]

The development, then, acquires the character of a dream sequence: "Ossian's Dream" becomes that of the viewer, lost in poetic reverie. (To anticipate the moral of the story: it is, above all, the *listener's* dream. The imaginative process enacted in this overture and the poetic-visual allusions I am attributing to it create a metaphor, I maintain, for the process of imaginatively engaged listening and interpreting appropriate to a large body of Romantic music, aesthetically congruent with Mendelssohn's work.) At the outset of the development, the viewer/listener projects onto the misty background of the original scene (recall again both upper and lower strings in mm. 96–122) a brief, dreamlike Ossianic fantasy sequence. Heroic calls to arms echo from distant quarters. Figures appear, fleetingly (the march fragment, mm. 112–122). Next, the viewer/listener returns to the present for a moment of dreamy reflection, as these airy visions temporarily recede (see the subdued reminiscence of the second theme, mm. 123–130). This moment of reflection brings the original ("phenomenal") landscape back into view, briefly, as the development references figures from the opening group (mm. 132–148). The development of these opening-group motives leads via F minor to B-flat minor for the final episode of the development, a distinctively "ghostly" disembodied transformation of the main motive, *pianissimo, staccato e leggiero,* developed antiphonally between woodwinds and strings (Figure 4–9).

Figure 4–9. *Hebrides* Overture, "spectral" battle-music (development of main theme), mm. 149–158.

With the repertoire of early Romantic Ossianic imagery in mind, it is not hard to picture this episode—through the mind's eye of our constructed viewing/listening subject—as a resumption of the dream sequence, a return to the internalized poetic dream world in which the mists and clouds of the immediate landscape are seen as coalescing into the shapes of those phantasmic warrior shades of Gérard, Ingres, and Girodet. They engage in a brief antiphonal "battle" which quickly gains steam (so to speak) and reaches a stormy climax, at which point the whole scene suddenly evaporates like a wisp of fog (see the chromatic scales in the flutes at m. 178). The battling figures are exposed for the vaporous, imaginary substance they "really are," and we are returned to the desolate and melancholy landscape where we began. But not quite: as if to confirm this phantasmic reading of the developmental "dream sequence," Mendelssohn inserts a fragmentary fanfare transformation of the main motive into the recapitulation, like a stray phantom warrior whom winds or wakefulness have failed to rout from the scene (Figure 4–10). I could pursue this metaphorical scenario through the recapitulation and coda (where our phantom warriors reappear, in fact, suggesting that the fanfare fragment was also an anticipation of future developments, within a so-called "terminal development"). But this much should suffice to make the point.

Such a scenario naturally raises all kinds of questions about authorial "intentions" and the limits of musical representation—questions I do not intend to tackle here. I would simply add that they were questions for Mendelssohn, too, who (proper German Romantic that he was) never stooped to the writing of "coarse" verbal programs, and remained chary even of simple characteristic titles. This does not mean, however, that he did not or would not have encouraged "imaginative" listening in his audience. The scenario I have been sketching is not exactly a "program" (though it may approach one); it is meant rather to suggest a mode of interpretive listening, one that was—I think—accessible to and cultivated by audiences of Mendelssohn's time, or at least by some part of them. As important as the visual or imaginative details, to me, is the essential fluidity of the scenario and the kind of listening it represents. One need not,

Figure 4–10. *Hebrides* Overture, fanfare-interpolations in recapitulation, mm. 184–187.

and finally cannot, distinguish precisely between what is heard and what is "seen" (imagined), or even between the details of visual images (now clouds, now spectral figures), which does not prevent these from being also motives, themes, and transformational variants. In closing, though, I would like to offer one further contextual layer to these thoughts towards a "visual" audition of Mendelssohn's overture, by which I want also to reinforce the exemplary or broadly metaphorical value of this individual case.

PHANTASMAGORIA AND "VISUAL" AUDITION

Plot, as I have suggested, is not a strong point of the Ossianic epics. Nor is it a strong point of music, for the most part. (I am discounting, for the moment, the notion of musical form as metaphorical "plot.") Music's fundamental ineptitude at telling stories, in the way that language does, has been the basis for critical rejection of program music for as long as the concept has existed. This attitude usually overlooks, however, the possibility that music might tell stories in a *different* way, or a different kind of story—something more like a story told in pictures, for instance, or like a dream, a sequence of fugitive images, a "hieroglyphic" text that eludes the grasp of waking logic.[29]

As narrative, Macpherson's Ossian poems partake of just such a dreamlike quality. The bardic poet is obsessively haunted by phantoms of the past ("professionally" haunted, one might say, since it is his vocation to act as the voice of memory and collective nostalgia, clinging to names, deeds, and phantom images of the deceased). A large population of spectral ancestral beings is forever hovering about the margins of the story, often displacing the story altogether, so that nothing remains but fragmented recollections of past exploits, a vaporous atmosphere dense with reminiscences and forebodings, but devoid of strongly directed present action. Confusions of character identity, narrative line, and time frame are compounded, as Fiona Stafford notes, "by the fact that the entire poem [of *Fingal,* in this case] is being sung by Ossian, who seems to make little distinction between the living and the dead."[30]

During the epoch of Ossian's greatest influence, in the decades around 1800, there developed a popular genre of "magic lantern" projection devoted to the visual "realization" of ghosts and spirits, and known—in the colorfully pretentious style of early commerical jargonizing—as the *phantasmagoria.* (A loosely metaphorical application of the term remains in the modern critical vocabulary thanks to Adorno, who adapted it from Karl Marx, to signify "consumer"—or for Adorno, also aesthetic—products from which all signs of productive labor have been effectively expunged.) The whole technology of the magic lantern, as it was developed across the second part of the eighteenth century, was in fact closely associated with the notion of phantom apparitions: the practical achievements of modern science were deployed to "realize" the paranormal phenomena that Enlightenment reason had exposed as fiction and superstition. The very technology itself—the projection of light images by means of illuminated transparencies—suggests a rationalized, demystified version of the psychological phenomenon of "seeing ghosts."[31]

The *fantasmagorie* inaugurated by the Belgian polymath scientist and showman Étienne-Gaspard Robertson in Paris in 1798 refined the illusionistic potential of the traditional magic lantern technique by plunging spectators into complete darkness and thus concealing from view the screen (a gauze or muslin scrim) so that the projected images would appear to hover freely in midair. By attaching rollers to the projection apparatus the images could be made to increase or decrease in size, simulating spatial advance and retreat.[32] At first, the subject matter of the phantasmagoria tended towards the grossly sensational rather than the literary or poetic. In the manner of a psychic medium, Robertson would claim to raise from beyond the grave the specters of deceased persons, ranging from Revolutionary heroes, villains, and martyrs (Rousseau, Voltaire, Robespierre, Marat, etc.) to the former wives and lovers of "ordinary" spectators planted in the audience. When, after alleged royalist leanings led to a one-year exile in Bordeaux, Robertson reopened his phantasmagorical entertainment in Paris within the atmospheric precincts of an abandoned Capuchin convent near the Place Vendôme, he expanded his repertoire to include a broader range of literary and imaginative scenes.[33] These immensely popular exhibitions were resumed in Paris around 1800 and continued under Robertson's direction for another six years. The phantasmagoria travelled to London in 1802, where it created a similar sensation, and in one form or another it was familiar throughout the Continent within the first decade of the nineteenth century. Given this chronology of the phantasmagoria and its widely documented influence on the popular imagination, it seems plausible that it also served as a model of spectral visualization in contemporary artistic representations of the Ossian poems, with their thematic focus on the bard's phantasmic imagination, whether singing or dreaming.[34]

A suggestive link between phantasmagoria, music, and the imagery of the Ossianic paintings is offered by Jean-François Le Sueur's briefly famous opera *Ossian, ou les bardes* (1804)—a product of the same Napoleonic context that generated the paintings of Gérard, Ingres, and Girodet. In Act 4 of the opera (whose plot is freely invented, not directly based on Macpherson's poems) Ossian has been captured by the Scandinavian enemies of the Caledonian people. Together with a Pyladeslike companion, Hydala, he is being held prisoner (as the libretto indicates) in

> a vast cavern cut in the rock, called in the poems of Ossian the Circle of Brunco [where] the Scandinavians detain their captives destined to be sacrificed to Odin. This cavern displays a terrifying aspect: in the center one sees a statue of Odin, and—according to the poems of Ossian—one hears nothing but the groaning of phantoms; it is open to the sky at the top and to the back.[35]

Ossian invokes the "shades of our fathers," and, left alone by Hydala (who somehow escapes to seek help), he gradually succumbs to a Gluckian *Sommeil* ("Le Sommeil d'Ossian," a brief sleep aria), followed by an extended fantastic dream sequence ("Le rêve d'Ossian"). As Ossian falls asleep, the stage directions specify that

> the objects he has just described, and of which he has so often sung, begin to retrace themselves on his mind *(viennent se retracer sur son esprit)*. The decor presents approaching clouds. The aerial palace opens up and presents to view the heros and the lesser bards.[36]

At this point an elaborate spectral *divertissement* ensues, with the shades of fallen heroes, bards, and young maidens singing in chorus to the accompaniment of celestial harps.[37]

Not surprisingly, it has been suggested that Ingres's painting took its imagery directly from this scene in Le Sueur's opera. The connection becomes even more explicit with the stage direction, further on in the scene: "The heroes, seated on their vaporous thrones, are armed with spears and shields."[38] The cover illustration to a much later piano-vocal score, from the 1880s, clearly links this scene of Ossian's dream in prison to the content of the Ingres painting, though somewhat insipidly transformed and debased (Figure 4–11). At the same time, the underlying "phantasmagoric" inspiration of the scene is strongly suggested

Figure 4–11. François Le Sueur, *Ossian, ou les bardes.* Frontispiece to piano-vocal score (Paris: Théodore Michaelis, 1804).

towards the end, following a pantomimed chorus in which the assembled shades ask what has silenced Ossian's song: "The whole of this elevated portion of the theater," we read, "should be enveloped in a light and transparent gauze, giving the objects a soft and distant quality."[39] At the close of this *Tableau Aërien* the shades "gradually lose their form, and everything dissolves like a mist, as the poems of Ossian put it, dispersed by the midday sun." As Ossian awakens, he reaches out after these phantom shapes that retreat from his grasp.[40]

Interesting as these details from LeSueur's opera are as part of a possible visual/conceptual background to the *Hebrides,* the music of the opera is, almost without exception, distressingly feeble. A later work, however, and one that was surely composed with an intimate knowledge of Mendelssohn's overture, would seem to confirm the continuity of these background images through the strongly marked musical images it deploys. Niels Gade's 1840 concert overture, *Nachklänge an Ossian* ("Reminiscences of Ossian"), op. 1, manages to convey through musical character alone (or rather, in conjunction with its title) a relatively distinct impression of the "dreaming Ossian" scenario. In the extended slow introduction a stark, folklike "bardic" theme emerges softly, against the dreamy, vaporous background of oscillating string figures and quietly strummed chords on the harp (Figure 4–12).

Across the introduction we hear this "bardic" theme achieve greater substance, and, when it is eventually stated by the full orchestra in unison, *fortissimo,* it aquires a grimly heroic tone; the whole process suggests Ossian's heroic vision of the shades of his ancestors gradually taking shape in his mind (and before the aural/visual imagination of the listener). Following the slow introduction, the main Allegro adopts the agitated character of a battle scene, complete with fanfare gestures and trumpet calls. Contrasted with this "din of battle" is a characteristically lyrical, major mode second theme that presumably connotes the presence of those consoling female figures who, in the poems, provide an occasional ray of light as respite from the gloomy scenes of battle. Where Mendelssohn's second theme returns in the course of the development, as if to mark the surrounding "dream vision" as the projection of an implicit poetic subject (as I have argued), Gade touches back—to similar effect—on the introductory "bardic" theme at the point or recapitulation in the main Allegro. The coda to the overture functions as a frame, reprising the introduction in something like reverse order: the "bardic theme" gradually divests itself of its heroic stature, and the musical

Figure 4–12. Niels Gade, Overture *Nachklänge an Ossian,* op. 1, "bardic" theme from introduction.

substance diminishes to a quiet whisper as Ossian's "dream" fades away into silence.[41]

If this whole "phantasmic" visual background to the Ossianic tradition was as well-defined as I am suggesting, we might reasonably ask if Mendelssohn's audiences heard it conveyed by (or themselves "projected" it on) his overture. I cannot answer that question with any authority at present. On the whole, I suspect that audiences heard these things rather *less* clearly than Mendelssohn expected they would, or should. (The same applies, I think, to the cases of his "Italian" and "Scottish" Symphonies, whose visual-connotative backgrounds he seems to have wished for audiences to intuit without any verbal prompting on his own part.) Yet I do think that the basic outlines of such a reading (or hearing) of the overture's development as a kind of Ossianic dream sequence, peopled by the warrior shades of Macpherson's epic poems, was readily available to some portion of the audience. Julius Benedict, for instance, a musically educated English acquaintance of the composer, did register these basic outlines, which he expressed in terms of a free succession of Ossianic images or "pictures": "One might fancy that one heard, now the lament of Colma [*recte:* Comala?] on the solitary shore, now the passionate accents of Fingal, or again, the strife and din of the distant battle."[42]

Even Wagner, who is in some part responsible for the nearly exclusive focus on the "landscape" qualities of the work, confessed that in his view the piece "requires a program," and recalled how he had been puzzled when he first heard it performed under the title *The Hebrides*, "which meant nothing to him—he did not understand it at all" (as Cosima relates).[43] Later on, during one of the frequent performances of the piece in piano arrangement in the salon at Wahnfried, Wagner drew attention to the *staccato e leggiero* episode at the end of the development (the "phantasmic battle" section of my scenario), exclaiming: "That is tremendously beautiful, ghostly!" Cosima goes on to identify the passage as "a sustained progression of the oboes against the staccato of the other instruments pages 25–26 in the score of the Hebrides Overture."[44] Finally, one of the overture's first critics, not a wholly sympathetic one, anticipated Wagner's initial "confusion" in terms that are revealing. Reviewing the original published score of 1834, Ludwig Rellstab complained first of the "monotonous repetitions" of the principal motive throughout the work, but then further of what he perceived as disruptions of formal syntactic coherence—most likely (though he does not particularize) the dramatic intrusions and transformations across the development and its interruption by the pensive reverie of the second group. "As accompanying music to a painting, to a story set on these islands," he writes, "much of this might become more intelligible, clearer, and acquire a distinct significance."[45]

Like Wagner, perhaps, Rellstab sensed a fantastic "action" taking shape within the musical landscape, but an action whose forms and outline he was unable to grasp. The hesitation between "painting" (*Gemälde*) and "story" (*Handlung*) is especially telling: Rellstab responds to the score as a species of "film music without film," so to speak—as the musical accompaniment to an absent *pictorial* narrative. "The composer," Rellstab adds, "evidently had the idea of representing in this work the somber, thrilling nature *(schauerliche Natur)* of the setting in conjunction with its poetic-historical sublimity." He perceived, in other words, something of the interaction of visual or representational levels at work here: a sonic landscape that becomes the setting for "poetic-historical" reminiscences projected onto it (with the composer's assistance) by the viewer/listener's imagination. Yet he was disoriented by the result. His mistake was to listen for narrative coherence, a "story," instead of being content with "pictures." There *is* a story of sorts encoded here (as I have been suggesting); but, like most *musical* stories, it thwarts the discursive logic of narrative prose, resembling instead the phantasmagoric illogic of dreams—silent pictures illuminated by the subconscious mind. Despite the numinous presence of Ossianic heroes in the development, the story is not really about them, per se. As in the paintings, it is not the enactment of any one particular Ossianic tale, but more a generic "image" of the poetic corpus as a whole. Musically, it is above all a story about the experience of viewing landscape: a progression from the objective viewing of natural phenomena (Fingal's Cave, or the Hebrides) through the imaginary projection of fragments of mythic history onto these, and back again to "nature," at the end. (The interaction of exterior and interior "vision" continues in the recapitulation and coda.)

If, as Terry Castle has argued, the "spectral technology" of the phantasmagoria gradually came to serve as a way of figuring or imaging visual imagination itself in the nineteenth century (as the internal projection of images by the "mind's eye" on the screen of the imagination), then perhaps the resonance of this figure in the *Hebrides* Overture and its background in Ossianic imagery and painting can be taken as a model for understanding the elusive status of musical "representation" during this same period.[46] The pictures or stories one might hear in a wide range of Romantic musical compositions are necessarily projections of the listener's imagination. As such, it is generally difficult or even impossible to distinguish clearly between the ontological status of "picture" (or image) and "story" in this music. A storylike quality may be suggested by the succession of fleeting, phantasmic musical "images" in a composition, but an attempt to fix these impressions in narrative prose is quite as difficult (or impossible) as fixing in language the incoherent images and fragmented stories of dreams. Technical analysis of the music, like the analysis of dreams, may or may not be revealing in its own terms, but neither seems remotely capable of recapturing the original experience in any truly recognizable way.

Like Ossian's singing and harping, listening to music conjures phantasmic visions that speak to us in some ancient and forgotten tongue. Like the visions of Ossian's dream, they elude the grasp of interpretive logic when we reach out to them upon waking from the musical experience (as it were). As the critic William Hazlitt remarked of the Ossianic style and tone: "[T]he annihilation of the substance and the clinging to the shadow of all things as in a mock-embrace, is here perfect." For Hazlitt, the probability that Ossian himself is merely an imaginary figment only underscores his value as a symbol of melancholy reflection on the shadowy intangibility of things past:

> It if were indeed possible to show that this writer was nothing, it would only be another instance of mutability, another blank made, another void left in the heart, another confirmation of that feeling which makes him so often complain, 'Roll on, ye dark brown years, ye bring no joy on your wing to Ossian.'[47]

I find it hard to resist hearing in the concluding measures of the *Hebrides* (Figure 4–13) the image of Ossian "clinging to the shadow of all things," reaching out for the phantoms of his dream world (note the "grasping"

Figure 4–13. *Hebrides* Overture, thematic, and textural dissolve in closing measures.

effect of the accented downbeat chords, as compared to the fugitive rec-
ollection of the second theme in the flute): I would not want to imply that
all attempts to listen for "meaning," however construed, are doomed to
revert to the bleak, desolate void of the Ossianic landscape—to come up
empty-handed. Still, similar to whatever *images* we might hear in music,
meaning too remains essentially vaporous and volatile, shifting and
transforming like the musical material itself. But as with a dream, that
does not make the experience—or the memory of it—any less real.

NOTES

[1]Letter of August 10, 1829, in Sebastian Hensel, *Die Familie Mendlessohn
1729–1847* (Berlin: B. Behr's Verlag, 1882), 1:231. (Translations my own unless
otherwise identified.)

[2]Ibid., 230–231 ("Ladies" and "Gentleman" in English in original German
text). Fingal's Cave as an object of artistic and particularly musical attention in
the Romantic era is documented by Matthias Wessel, "Die Fingalshöhe," chap. 8,
Die Ossian-Dichtung in der musikalischen Komposition (Laaber: Laaber-Verlag,
1994), 193–208; see also 209ff. for a catalogue of Ossian-inspired musical compositions from the late eighteenth century onwards.

[3]R. Larry Todd, *Mendelssohn: "The Hebrides" and Other Overtures* (Cambridge: Cambridge University Press, 1993), 29.

[4]The pen-and-ink drawing, now part of the M. Deneke Mendelssohn collection in the Bodleian Library, Oxford, is reproduced in Todd, "Of Sea Gulls and
Counterpoint: the Early Versions of Mendelssohn's *Hebrides* Overture," *19th-
Century Music* 2:3 (March 1979), 205. A facsimile of the musical sketch of August 7, 1829, accompanying a note of August 11, 1829, is included in Hensel,
1:235; Todd ("Of Sea Gulls and Counterpoint") gives a transcription of the
sketch (199).

[5]Charles O'Connell, *The Victor Book of Overtures, Tone-Poems, and Other
Orchestral Works* (New York: Simon and Schuster, 1950), 277

[6]Donald Francis Tovey, "Illustrative Music," vol. 4 of *Essays in Musical
Analysis* (1937; reprint, London: Oxford University Press, 1972), 91.

[7]Malcolm Andrews, *The Search for the Picturesque: Landscape Aesthetics
and Tourism in Britain, 1760–1800* (Stanford: Stanford University Press, 1989)
Andrews summarizes the history of the picturesque movement in England and
details four of the major tours on the basis of the extensive picturesque travel literature of the period. See in particular Chapter 8, "The Highlands Tour and the
Ossianic Sublime," pp. 197–240. As Andrews points out, this itinerary was
prompted quite explicitly by the Ossian craze, and tourists regularly brought

along Macpherson's poetry to fuel their receptivity to the landscape. Chronologically, Mendelssohn's tour should be regarded as a later echo of the picturesque movement, which in its "strong" form had largely run its course by the beginning of the century. The popularity of Scott (as mentioned above) did help to revive the tradition. By Mendelssohn's time (as his letters with Klingemann demonstrate) the earlier touring practices were starting to merge with something resembling the practices of modern tourism, in which the legacy of the "picturesque" would later be perpetuated through the technology of photography.

[8]The remarks on Mendelssohn are frequently cited and can be found, for instance, in Friederich Niecks, *Programme Music of the Last Four Centuries* (1907; reprint, New York: Haskell House, 1969), 169.

[9]*Cosima Wagner's Diaries,* ed. M. Gregor-Dellin and D. Mack, trans. G. Skelton (New York and London: Harcourt Brace Jovanovich, 1978), 1:170 (entry of December 7, 1869; emphasis in original).

[10]Ibid., 608 (entry of March 14 , 1873). Cf., vol. 2, p. 319: "In the evening we go with Herr R. [Josef Rubinstein] through the three Mendelssohn overtures, of which the *Hebrides* impresses us as truly masterly, *Calm Sea and Prosperous Voyage* less so, because of certain weak sentimentalities, and *A Midsummer Night's Dream* perhaps least of all. R. says he is outstanding as a landscape painter—but oh, when his heart starts to stagger! . . . It is a pity he saw elves just like gnats, but musically it is very well done" (entry of June 6, 1879).

[11]Jerrold Levinson, "Hope in *The Hebrides,*" in *Music, Art, and Metaphysics: Essays in Philosophical Aesthetics* (Ithaca, N.Y.: Cornell University Press, 1990), 336–375.

[12]Michael P. Steinberg, "Beneath a Smooth Surface, Mendelssohnian Depths," *The New York Times,* November 2, 1997, 37–38. "This great melody carries another musical gesture [i.e. besides Levinson's "hope"], pioneered by Mozart and taken into the Romantic era by Beethoven: the effect through which a musical voice becomes a first-person narrative voice. . . . *The Hebrides* opens with a descriptive theme that seems to take a third-person voice, the voice of scene-painting. But the sweep of the second theme carries a double shift, from [M. H. Abrams's] mirror to the lamp, from third-person to first-person voice" (38).

[13]See, for example, Joseph Leo Koerner, *Caspar David Friedrich and the Subject of Landscape* (New Haven and London: Yale University Press, 1990), 211ff.

[14]Letter of January 21, 1832, in (Felix Mendelssohn-Bartholdy, *Reisebriefe aus den Jahren 1830 bis 1832,* ed. Paul Mendelssohn Bartholdy (Leipzig: Hermann Mendelssohn, 1865), 328–329.

[15]The letter to Souchay (October 15, 1842) does not deny the existence of an emotional or otherwise significant "content" to music, only the difficulty of

circumscribing this in language. The immediate point of the letter, in fact, is that music's ineffable meaning (expression) is *less* open to misconstrual than is language, which Mendelssohn (in presciently poststructural terms) sees as endlessly contingent and ambiguous. A translation of the relevant passage can be found, among other places, in Leon Botstein, "The Aesthetics of Assimilation and Affirmation: Reconstructing the Career of Felix Mendelssohn," in *Mendelssohn and his World,* ed. R. Larry Todd (Princeton: Princeton University Press, 1991), 31.

[16]On the significance of the site-specific "topographical" or "portrait" landscape in Romantic art see Charles Rosen, *The Romantic Generation* (Cambridge, Mass.: Harvard University Press, 1995), 131 and 151–153 He is speaking principally of literary landscape description. Rosen, citing Ramond de Carbonnières *(Observations faites dans les Pyrénées, 1789)* on the interaction of landscape observation with subjective memory and imagination, states: "A site has a sentimental as well as a geological history: the buried strata of the past are directly evoked by the sensations of the present." Ramond wrote: "I extended on to Nature the illusion that she had caused to be born, uniting with her—by an involuntary movement—the times and events of which she had stirred up the memory" (153).

[17]See Todd, *Mendelssohn: The "Hebrides" and other Overtures,* 26–27, 34–36, as well as "Of Sea Gulls and Counterpoint," 198. Todd sugggests, if only in fairly general terms, that revisions to the development reflect Mendelssohn's desire to strengthen "characteristic" or implicitly programmatic elements: "It was likely the attempt to combine musical, literary, and pictorial aspects of the work that led Mendelssohn to reconsider passages in the early versions that exhibit a certain [i.e., excessive] contrapuntal rigor" (198).

[18]On de Loutherbourg's spectacles and their position in early Romantic visual culture, see Christopher Hussey, *The Picturesque: Essays in a Point of View* (London: F. Cass, 1927), 239–240; Gösta Bergman, *Lighting in the Theatre* (Stockholm: Almqvist and Wiksell, 1977), 228–231; and Richard Altick, *The Shows of London* (Cambridge, Mass.: Harvard University Press, 1978), 117–127. On Daguerre and the diorama see especially Helmut and Alison Gernsheim, *J.-L.-M. Daguerre: The History of the Diorama and the Daguerreotype* (London, 1956), 20–45; and Altick, Chapter 12, "The Diorama," 163–172. I have discussed at greater length the possible relation of these visual technologies to aspects of musical "imagery" in Mendelssohn's music—in terms of specific visual repertoires as well as metaphors of visual (and musical) "animation"—in my essay *"Tableaux vivants:* Landscape, History Painting, and the Visual Imagination in Mendelssohn's Orchestral Music," *19th-Century Music* 21:1 (Summer 1997), 38–76.

[19]The shadow cast by Fingal's spear on the shields of the spectral warriors in the background seems calculated to draw attention to this imaginary light source

as literally the "light" of the internal imagination, projected outwards. A number of the nine drawings and watercolor sketches for the picture are reproduced in the exhibition catalogue, *In Pursuit of Perfection: The Art of J.-A.-D. Ingres,* ed. Patricia Condon (J. B. Speed Art Museum: Lousiville, Ky., 1983), 46–51 and 159. Compare these images of Ossian's "internal" light as described in *The War of Caros:* "Daughter of Toscar, bring the harp; the light of the song rises in Ossian's soul," and further on, "And bring me the harp, O maid, that I may touch it when the light of my soul shall arise" (in *Fingal: An Ancient Poem in Six Books, together with several other Poems* [London: T. Becket and P. A. DeHondt, 1762], 95, 103). In *Conlath and Cuthóna* Ossian addresses the ghost of Conlath, calling attention to the vaporous "substance" of the image and the illuminating role of memory and poetic imagination: "O that mine eyes could behold thee, as thou sittest, dim, on thy cloud! Art thou like the mist of Lano; or an half-extinguished meteor? Of what are the skirts of thy robe? Of what is thine airy bow? . . . Come from thy wall, my harp, and let me hear thy sound. *Let the light of memory rise on I-thona, that I may behold thy friends*" (ibid., 122; emphasis added).

[20]From *Fingal: An Ancient Epic Poem, in Six Books,* in *The Poems of Ossian, Son of Fingal,* trans. James Macpherson, Esq. (Edinburgh: J. Robertson, 1792; reprint, ed. Jonathan Wordsworth, Poole, England and New York: Woodstock Books, 1996), 20, 23 ("It was the opinion then," Macpherson adds in a footnote, "that the souls of the deceased hovered round their living friends; and sometimes appeared to them when they were about to enter on any great undertaking"), and 30 (the words "of death" are missing from the 1792 edition, though present in the 1762 original).

[21]From *Comala: A Dramatic Poem,* in *Fingal: An Ancient Poem in Six Books,* 91 and 94.

[22]From *The War of Caros,* in ibid., 95, 97, and 100.

[23]William Wordsworth alluded to this imagery of vaporous phantoms, in a satirical vein, as emblematic of "Ossian's" essentially imaginary, fictional status, largely the invention of a modern author and a modern sensibility: "All hail, Macpherson! Hail to thee, Sire of Ossian. The Phantom was begotten by the snug embrace of an impudent Highlander upon a cloud of tradition—it travelled southward, where it was greeted with acclamation, and the thin Consistence took its course through Europe, upon the breath of popular applause" (cited from introduction to *The Poems of Ossian, Son of Fingal,* ed. Jonathan Wordsworth [n.p.]).

[24]"Misty memory and ethereal spirits merge in the twilight world of the Ossianic poems," writes Dwyer: "In effect, the ghosts of the Ossianic poems are memories, and Macpherson often deliberately blurs the distinction between 'actual' spirits and mental images of the deceased or absent recalled either by the waking or dreaming consciousness of Ossian and other epic heroes. (Johan

Dwyer, "The Melancholy Savage: Text and Context in the Poems of Ossian," in *Ossian Revisited*, ed. Howard Gaskill [Edinburgh: Edinburgh University Press, 1991], 190–191). Dwyer goes on to compare here the role of "ghosts and shades" as signs of sentimental attachment in Macpherson, as well as other aspects of "decaying and autumnal" setting and atmosphere, to similar elements in the expressly sentimental writings of Henry Mackenzie *(The Man of Feeling* and *Julia de Roubigné)*.

[25]Several additional French paintings of Ossianic subjects from the early nineteenth century are mentioned by Pierre van Tieghem in his chapter on "La peinture ossianique (1801–1817), in *Ossian en France* (Paris: F. Rieder and Cie., 1917), 2:141–165. Gros, for example, painted Malvina singing to the harp in order to "open up to [the spirit of] Oscar the palace of clouds" (156). A painting by Forbin exhibited in 1806 portrays Ossian revisiting the ruins of his ancestral castle (Selma) and the deserted heath "that was the theater for the exploits of his forefathers. . . . He succumbs to a profound reverie, as he imagines passing before him—amidst the howling of storms about his head—the shade of his father Fingal, leaning upon his brother and upon Moïna. A young girl carries in triumph the fruits of their aerial chase, and their dogs follow them, barking" (158; the description is taken from a catalogue of the original 1806 exhibit). A female English painter by the name of Elizabeth Harvey also exhibited *Malvina and Oscar* at the same salon of 1806, depicting (again according to the catalogue) "the sea and Fingal's cave" in the background, and the sky "strewn with humid mists" (160).

[26]Van Tieghem, 157.

[27]See the letter of Alexander von Humboldt to François Gérard of November 15, 1832: "Votre *Ossian* est très avantageusement placé dans les grands appartements du Château de Potsdam, beaucoup plus habitué que le château de Berlin" *(Correspondance de François Gérard, peintre d'histoire* etc., ed. Henri Gérard [Paris: Typographie de A. Laine et J. Havard, 1867], 281).

[28]Compare this response to the landscape of the River Rhine in an early tribute to its "romantically" picturesque character: "here new slopes of mountains and, on the peaks of one another, old fortresses awakened by their position and structure a hundred ghosts of knightly romance" (Aurelio di Giorgio Bertòla, *Viaggio pittorico e sentimentale sul Reno,* 1795; cited from Rosen, 136.

[29]Theodor Adorno addressed this characteristic confounding of narrative and visual responses to the musical experience in a passage from his posthumous collection of critical reflections on Beethoven (though this particular passage was stimulated by the first-movement development of Schubert's "Great" C-major Symphony): "Images of the material world appear in music only in a desultory, eccentric fashion, flashing before us and then vanishing; yet they are

essential to it precisely in their decaying, consumed state . . . We are *in* music the same way we are in dreams" (trans. Stephen Hinton, "Adorno's Unfinished *Beethoven," Beethoven Forum* 5 [1996], 146). For a discussion of hieroglyphs used in "musical" paintings, see Elizabeth Prelinger's essay in this volume, "Music to Our Ears? Munch's *Scream* and Romantic Music Theory."

[30]Fiona Stafford, *The Sublime Savage: A Study of James Macpherson and the Poems of Ossian* (Edinburgh: Edinburgh University Press, 1988), 141: "On the whole, *Fingal* tends to leave the reader uncertain as to which characters have actually appeared in the main action and which survive only in the memories of the protagonists. . . . As in Sterne's contemporary novel, *Tristram Shandy,*" Stafford adds, "a baffling series of recollections is made coherent only through the development of the narrator as the focal point" (141).

[31]This is one of several paradoxes attending the status of spirit apparitions in the Age of Enlightenment as analyzed in several of Terry Castle's essays collected in *The Female Thermometer: 18th-Century Culture and the Invention of the Uncanny* (New York and London: Oxford University Press, 1996). See, for example, "Phantasmagoria and the Metaphorics of Modern Reverie," 140–167; "The Spectralization of the Other in *The Mysteries of Udolpho,*" 120–139; and "Spectral Politics: Apparition Belief and the Romantic Imagination," 168–189. A theme shared by all of these essays, pertinent to the case of Macpherson's Ossian, is the role of the spectral apparition as a figure for the "conjuring" powers of the Romantic imagination in general, in the positive, productive sense of poetic invention or fancy, as well as in contested cases of hallucination, delusion, or other forms of alleged psychological "imbalance." The "historic Enlightenment internalization of the spectral," Castle claims, "the gradual reinterpretation of ghosts and apparitions as *hallucinations,* or projections of the mind introduced a new uncanniness into human consciousness itself. The mind became a 'world of phantoms' and thinking itself an act of ghost-seeing" (17).

[32]Accounts of the origins and early history of the phantasmagoria can be found in Richard Altick, *The Shows of London* (Cambridge, Mass: Harvard University Press, 1978); Terry Castle, "Phantasmagoria" (cf., note 32); and Anthony Newcomb, "New Light(s) on Weber's Wolf's Glen Scene," in *Opera and the Enlightenment,* ed. Thomas Bauman and Marita Petzoldt McClymonds (Cambridge: Cambridge University Press, 1995), 61–88. All of these sources refer principally to the *Mémoires récréatifs scientifiques et anecdotiques d'un physicien aéronaute* by the inventor of the phantasmagoria, Etienne-Gaspard Robertson, ed. Philippe Blon, 2 vols. (Langres: Clima, 1830–1834).

[33]Cf., Castle, "Phantasmagoria," 144–151, and Newcomb, "New Light(s)," 61–68. These included such episodes as the ghost of Samuel conjured before Saul by the Witch of Endor, the ghost of Banquo appearing to Macbeth, a

sequence of *tableaux fantastiques* after Henry Fuseli's *The Nightmare,* a vision of a "bleeding nun" inspired by G. E. Lewis's *The Monk* (the inspiration, in turn of Scribe's libretto *La nonne sanglante,* considered by Berlioz and composed by Gounod), an image of Edward Young—of "Night Thoughts" fame—interring the remains of his deceased daughter, the "Agony of Ugolino" after Dante's *Inferno,* as well as assorted scenes from classical mythology.

[34]One of Robertson's predecessors, a certain Guyot, demonstrated the projection of magic-lantern images on smoke—a suggestive technique in view of the vaporous phantom imagery predominant in the Ossian poems and pictures (Castle, "Phantasmagoria," 146, and n. 5).

[35]Le Sueur, *Ossain, ou les bardes,* libretto by P. Dercy and Jean-Marie Deschamps, (1804; reprint of the full orchestral score, New York: Garland, 1979), 349.

[36]"Pendant le sommeil d'Ossian, les objets qu'il vient de décrire, et qu'il a souvent chantés, viennent se retracer sur son esprit. La décoration offre les nuages qui s'approchent. Le palais Aërien s'ouvre, et laisse voire d'abord les héros et les Bardes inférieurs" (ibid., 388).

[37]There are only two harp parts in the score, although somewhere between eight and twelve instruments were used when the piece was played at the Opéra.

[38]"Les héros, assis sur des Trônes de vapeurs, sont armés de leurs lances et leurs boucliers" (Le Sueur, *Ossian*).

[39]"Toute cette derniere partie élevée du Théâtre doit être voilée d'une gaze légère et transparent, qui adoucisse et éloigne les objects. Ce Tableau Aërien doit être dans le coté opposé à celui où l'on apperçoit de loin le palais du Tonnerre où courent mille météores" (ibid., 409).

[40]"Les ombres perdent leur forme et leurs traits, et tout s'évanouit comme un brouillard, disent les poësies d'Ossian, qui se fond au Soleil du midi Ossian, endormi, s'agite, tends les bras vers les objets qui disparoissent" (ibid., 431). Matthias Wessel draws attention to the metaphorical value of Le Sueur's scene in his chapter on Fingal's Cave (see "Die Höhle als Traumstätte" in *Die Ossian-Dichtung in der musikalischen Komposition,* 201–205).

[41]In reviewing a performance of Gade's "Ossian" overture in 1855, Eduard Hanslick drew attention to the impression of "Valkyries rushing about in the clouds" that he associated with this piece and Gade's subsequent "manner" deriving from it: "Das starke Anschlagen des Localtons, der im 'Ossian' volksthümlich ergreifend wirkt, wurde bei Gade alsbald Manier,—man wird es mit der Zeit endlich satt, immer die Walkyren im Nebel herumtraben zu sehen" (Eduard Hanlsick, *Sämtliche Schriften,* ed. Dietmar Strauss [Weimar, Vienna, Cologne: Böhlau Verlag, 1995] I, 3: 37). The main theme Hanslick identifies as "trotzig-kriegerisch" ("defiantly warlike").

[42]Julius Benedict, *Sketch of the Life and Work of the Late Felix Mendelssohn Bartholdy* (London, 1850), 20; cited from R. Larry Todd, *Mendelssohn: The "Hebrides" and Other Overtures,* 82. (While it is not absolutely clear whether the "lament of Colma on the solitary shore" is suggested by the opening group or the second theme, the "strife and din of distant battle" must surely allude to the opening of the development.)

[43]*Cosima Wagner's Diaries,* 2: 626–627 (February 18, 1881).

[44]Ibid., 325 (June 17, 1879). These remarks also found their way into the interview with Dannreuther, though with the "ghostly" predicate removed: "Note the extraordinary beauty of the passage where the oboes rise above the other instruments with a plaintive wail like sea winds over the sea" (as cited in Niecks, 169).

[45]Ludwig Rellstab, "Ouverture aux Hébrides (Fingals-Höhle), composé par J. Mendelssohn-Bartholdy," *Iris im Gebiet der Tonkunst* 5 (1834): 50. ("Als begleitende Musik zu einem Gemälde, zu einer Handlung auf jenen Inseln möchte vieles verständlicher, klarer werden, vieles sein ganz bestimmte Bedeutung erhalten.")

[46]Terry Castle, "Phantasmagoria and the Metaphorics of Modern Reverie," 140–167.

[47]William Hazlitt, quoted in Stafford, *The Sublime Savage,* 149.

CHAPTER 5

Painted Responses to Music
The Landscapes of Corot and Monet

KERMIT SWILER CHAMPA

> *Music is pre-eminently the art of the 19th century because it is in a supreme manner responsive to the emotional wants, the mixed aspirations and the passionate self consciousness of the Age.*
>
> —REV. H. R. HAWEIS, 1871

Speaking as the most renowned and popular preacher in England, Haweis stated succinctly the trope of music's preeminent status in the arts of Europe in the second half of the nineteenth century.[1] Hardly an original thinker, Haweis safely assumed that his words would be accepted as self-evident. They had been anticipated by John Ruskin[2] and they were to be elaborated upon by Walter Pater, James Whistler, Oscar Wilde, and R.A.M. Stevenson in England over the next twenty-five years to form a critical discourse the chief substance of which was to ascertain precisely the nature of music's supremacy and how it might guide the other arts. As the discourse developed, the notion that form and content were one in music was set ever more firmly in place. That notion was accompanied by the belief that form and technique were essentially similar as well. This "oneness" ultimately emerged as an aesthetic standard thought to be variously manageable by each individual art.

The relationship between English critical discourse (modeled on a loosely Schopenhauer-derived and Ruskinian definition of music's master aesthetic status) and actual artistic production is, however, a highly vexed one. With the exception of Whistler's work, comparatively little painting emerges to mirror what advanced criticism demanded. Edward Burne-Jones's version of pre-Raphaelite work, while immersed in a local variant of Wagner worship, was not, properly speaking, modeled on music. Instead it sought to retain a connection both to something like pure musical feeling and a dramatically flat form of narrative. Like Swinburne's poetry, it hesitates to surrender its literacy to the mounting call for an art that is only (and at once) meaning and appearance.[3] It is then the strange case in England that a musically modeled critical discourse becomes itself virtually free-standing and able ultimately to perpetuate itself only allegorically, using historical figures such as Giorgione, Watteau, and Velasquez rather than more modern English ones.[4] Why Gainsborough is overlooked as a historical English focus in favor of the always conceptually elusive Turner remains a historiographical puzzle and an interesting one, if one not pursued here.

In France, there is nothing like the cumulative critical-theoretical tradition dedicated to music's preeminence that one finds in England. Yet there is, paradoxically, a far higher degree of application of much looser notions of music as some sort of aesthetic talisman for all the contemporary arts. What seems to be at the root of the paradox is the historical situation, more or less unique to France, where music itself rather than an elaborately theoretical discourse defining it, initiated and controlled the formation of a broad-based cultural ideology. As the musicologist Leo Schrade was first to explore in the 1930s, a phenomenon he referred to as Beethovenism emerged in France, first as an aesthetic enthusiasm and second as a condition of musical experience cumulatively so powerful as to demand definitions both of itself and of the art form it so powerfully reasserted—namely, symphonic music.[5] Schrade was the first to document in detail the veritable competition for a definitive characterization of Beethoven's music by the cultural elite of the generation of 1830, including Balzac, Hugo, Stendhal, and, most of all, Berlioz.

Featured prominently in the newly founded concerts of the Paris Conservatory under François-Antoine Habeneck, Beethoven's music rapidly became the high cultural staple in the Parisian diet for half a century. It was ultimately Berlioz who would manage the most compelling descriptions of what was heard. What he described and the way he described it acted to inscribe the aesthetic preeminence of concert music more durably in France than anywhere else in Europe, and at an earlier date. Most importantly, Berlioz's descriptions accounted for experiences rather than aesthetic principles in the abstract, experiences regularly shared by an ever-increasing number of Parisian concertgoers and ama-

teurs of music accustomed to hearing piano and/or chamber transcriptions in domestic settings up and down the bourgeois social scale.[6] By
the early 1860s in France and particularly in Paris, concert music was
everywhere to be heard. Piano sales, sheet music sales, music lessons,
and concert tickets experienced an economic boom the magnitude of
which was historically unprecedented.

Already in 1835, Paris had been characterized as a perpetual concert; by 1865 that concert was incessant to the point of threatening to
drown out all other forms of high cultural production.[7] Music was literally being worshipped. In Berlioz's words (speaking of Beethoven, always the traditional focus of musical discourse by mid-century) one
could expect music to have "a mysterious likeness to all possible things,"
to be "everything," a place where "the dreamer will recognize his dream,
the sailor his storm, Elijah his whirlwind in which his vehicle carries him
off, Erwin von Steinbach his cathedral, the wolf his forests."[8] As Schrade
characterized the situation, not only had music—particularly Beethoven's—become a cultural obsession, but Berlioz managed to give a
powerful verbal account of its effect, an account stressing vagueness of
signification rather than offering formal explanations. Wrote Schrade: "A
new way of speaking of music arose and led into spheres that had hitherto been tightly closed."[9]

This new way of speaking about music, a manner drenched in hy-
perbole, had a pervasive effect on commentary about the other arts as
well. Charles Baudelaire's long essay on Delacroix, for example, is conceived and developed, at least in part, in a mode of discourse emulating
Berlioz's writings about music, and the same is true of the writings of
many of Baudelaire's fellow critics, in the 1850s in particular.[10] To be de-
scribable in musical terms became a signal of the highest aesthetic accomplishment for a painting or a work of writing. To stand in the line of
historical tradition (or to be responsive to academic norms) was an increasingly less honorable achievement than to participate in music's
essence in some remarkable way. Exactly how that participation might
be first managed and then recognized through interpretation was never a
standardized operation. But how could it have been since the whole notion of music's expressive richness, as romantically conceived, rested on
vague, portentous suggestion rather than closed linkages between signifiers and things signified?

For any art to be musical it had to be free of mediating signifiers and,
instead, to offer unfixed signs that left "meaning" to the particular psychological response of the spectator. Narrative was the archenemy of the

musical, but nature as a domain of complex sensuous and psychological experience was not. In fact, nature as a site of reverie had the potential to offer exactly what the nonmusical arts needed in order to partner music—namely, infinite variability and rules of order that could be perceived as so elaborate and open-ended as to be virtually sublime.[11] Nature as the domain of origin, evolution, and notation was an ideal source for the poetic or pictorial image that might speak as music was believed to. Even more than "history" (another "period" obsession), nature promised infinite reservoirs of associative but only loosely anchored feeling.

What nature provided, and music demanded, was readily found in modern French painting, particularly in landscape painting, which had moved increasingly toward center stage in the 1850s. Lacking links to the prestigious painting tradition established in representations of the human figure, landscape practice needed a critical discourse which could account for it seriously. A latent musical discourse seems to have required at the same time exactly the kind of imagings that landscape painting (particularly that of Camille Corot and Théodore Rousseau) provided—imagings that were storyless but pregnant with unspecified moods. This quality opened the door to "musical" interpretation, and that interpretation rose gradually to a point of such respectability that landscape's antinarrative "difference" from academically revered history painting eventually came to be perceived as its aesthetic strength.[12]

What later music-featuring discourse in England lacked—namely, ready applicability to actual contemporary aesthetic practice—France possessed in its artistic problem child of the generation of 1830: nonnarrative and generally antipicturesque landscape painting. This practice fused perfectly with the experiential character of French romantic musical descriptions, so perfectly that it would be difficult to imagine either the painting or the musically modeled discourse having flourished without the fusion. By the 1860s the fusion had produced around Corot's work a virtual identity between image and ideology. Corot himself took pains to reinforce this identity with numerous studio interiors (Figure 5–1) produced in the late 1850s and 1860s that feature a model seated in a chair in front of an easel that bears a Corot landscape painting. In each picture the model holds an instrument, a lute or mandolin, sometimes playing "to the picture," sometimes seeming to pause as if suspended between playing and looking.[13]

To judge from the reminiscences of his influential friends, Corot lived the life appropriate to a perfect romantic mélomane.[14] He sang

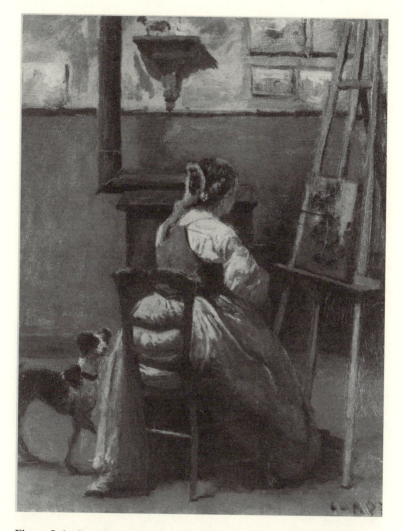

Figure 5–1. Camille Corot, *The Artist's Studio,* c. 1865–1870, oil on panel, 40.6 × 33 cm., The Baltimore Museum of Art, The Cone Collection, formed by Dr. Claribel Cone and Miss Etta Cone of Baltimore, Maryland. BMA 1950. 200.

among friends, played the violin, and maintained subscriptions to all the important concert and opera series in Paris. He had engravings of his favorite composers prominently displayed on the walls of his studio, and perhaps most importantly, he seemed never to read, staying thoroughly out of touch with the written word, whether literary or journalistic. The picture of Corot that emerges from his first biographer and his contemporary (and later) critics is clearly one that the artist facilitated simultaneously with his painting and his personal being. He was one who lived "beyond words" in an intelligent fantasy world where music reigned supreme, even as (and presumably particularly when) he painted.[15]

Corot's *The Concert* (Figure 5–2), a major effort for the Salon of 1855, was probably the first and most significant step the artist took in public to insist that a sense of musical feeling permeated his work. His insistence was broadly accepted and the critical appreciation which developed subsequent to 1855 is consistent in describing his paintings in musical terms. Corot's biographer Alfred Sensier seems responsible as well in the 1870s for collecting Theodore Rousseau and Rousseau's work under the same musical mantle, though earlier Rousseau criticism had not been totally lacking in literary-dramatic conjecture. Defenseless after his sudden death in 1868, Rousseau was increasingly joined discursively to Corot as melomane and maker of pictorial music.[16] But it was Corot rather than Rousseau who stood both during his lifetime and there-

Figure 5–2. Jean-Baptiste-Camille Corot, *The Concert,* 1844, oil on canvas, 98 × 103 cm., Musée Condé, Chantilly.

after as musical painter par excellence. Interpretations of his painting throughout the century following his death are remarkably consistent in elaborating, or simply repeating, how it was that he came to occupy this niche. So secure had Corot's position become in this regard that even during his lifetime his particular way of painting in its narrow tonalities and soft webs of brushwork and his half-real, half-idyllic motifs came literally to stand for what musical painting looked like.[17]

It is a fairly simple task to question the apparently perfect fit between Corot and musical painting. Certainly a great deal of self-construction and many historiographical reinforcements to that construction were contrived in one way or another to produce both commercial and ideological effect. Yet the fact remains that the musically constructed Corot was a successful and durable presence, so successful that it constituted something like a near closure to any wider pursuit of musically modeled painting in France. How to manage musical feeling pictorially without looking like Corot was a significant question for the younger painters emerging in the 1860s. One option was not to paint landscape; the other was to reconfigure it totally.

In different ways, the work of Henri Fantin-Latour and Paul Cézanne grappled with the first option, the former in an allegorical mode with certain ongoing echoes of Corot kept alive in lithographic images featuring musical subjects largely drawn from Wagner operas, and the latter attempting to produce something like a painting that "sounded" like music in the *Overture to Tannhäuser* from the late 1860s.[18] The second option was pursued by painters who based their work in landscape practice, but who drove that practice in directions that Corot would never have conceived. Preeminent among these painters was Claude Monet, whose reception as a landscape painter in the 1860s was to be a very frustrating one, largely, one suspects, because his work could not be seen to follow in any clear way from Corot's esteemed precedent. Monet's work did not look musical. This being the case, its aesthetic substance was for a time open to question.

Corot had made landscape painting an honorable category through its overt associations with music, but he does not seem to have managed beyond his own paintings to elevate the category in a wholesale fashion. And, given the fact that "genre" painting had become the most popular norm in academic painting in the 1860s and that variously confrontational forms of figure painting were the norm in the work of the academic opposition—Edouard Manet's and to a certain degree the late efforts of Gustave Courbet—Monet's landscape practice lacked any reliable nonmusic-based ideological support for itself. His work was neither overtly musical nor was it figural. It was remarkably resistant to classification, yet pictorially intense and self-certain. Not surprisingly, these qualities took some time to be understood and respected. It seems clear in retrospect that, as a dedicated landscape painter, Monet had done the only thing possible to loosen the hold exercised by Corot (or perhaps by the less personal phenomenon of Corotism). He turned Corot's practice inside out and in doing so made it difficult (almost intentionally, it seems) to have his work understood via music, or at least understood in the same way and in the same terms as Corot's.

All that was suggestively vague in Corot's practice, all that evoked memory and reverie and thus stood apart from particular moments in time, was jettisoned systematically by Monet over the course of the 1860s. Monet's opposing strategy, as seen in such works as *Cliffs of Etretat* (Figure 5–3), featured bold rhetorical effects of clear color evoking

Figure 5–3. Claude Monet, *The Porte d'Amont, Etretat,* c. 1868–1869, oil on canvas, 79.06 × 98.43 cm.sight. Courtesy of the Fogg Art Museum, Harvard University Art Museums, Gift of Mr. and Mrs. Joseph Pulitzer Jr.

bright light and seemingly particular moments delivered by remarkably vigorous passages of brushwork which were never allowed to resolve rhythmically as Corot's did. As has so often been noted, Monet seems to have taken his cue from the newly popular Japanese woodblock prints, where stark abbreviations of colored shapes produced momentary natural effects that were astonishingly clear and which acted along with abrupt contrasts of light and dark, characteristic of the 1860s photograph, to destabilize conventional notions of what best accounted for the way "seeing" actually felt.[19]

By 1869 and exemplified by work done at the weekend resort of La Grenouillère near the village of Bougival on the Seine not far from Paris, and at Etretat in Normandy, Monet had devised a practice of landscape painting that made his images seem to point forward at the spectator instead of drawing the specator into a picture space, "facing" the spectator confrontationally with a seemingly unprocessed incident of vision.[20] Monet's images began to feature a comprehensive sense of "being right there," replacing any Corot-type signs of musical-poetic processing with opposing signs that suggested the lack of aesthetic processing of any sort. These seemingly unmediated effects along with their graphic, coloristic forwardness made Monet's paintings' aggressive visual presences comparable to the most assertive of Manet's figural works. The sense of landscape as passive and receptive of gaze and figure painting demanding or dominating of gaze is brilliantly problematized by Monet at just the historical point when serious landscape painting, because of what had become the more or less musical commonplace issuing from Corot, seemed destined to collapse into utter predictability.

By manipulating eyesight rather than courting memory and reverie, Monet gave landscape a thoroughly new prospect. But would this prospect square with music? In order for any squaring to occur, music would have to be reconceived. It would need to be understood in a post-Romantic way as more purely generative than associative in effect. It would have to be viewed as a sensuous motor rather than a sensuous reflection or extension of the psychologically anticipated. Music would ultimately have to be granted its force *as sound,* in order for Monet's presentations of emphatic visibility to be comprehended as being aesthetically consonant with it.

There are suggestions in the criticism of the early 1870s that in the wake of the Franco-Prussian War serious music, which was traditionally coded German, was being ideologically recoded when associated with the arts of France. Most significant in this regard is the marginalizing of

Wagner who had, during the 1860s, dominated the discourse surrounding modern music, especially in Paris. A far simpler version of the musical model can be seen applied to the work of Monet and his associates Camille Pissarro and Alfred Sisley when they were first described together in 1872 by the critic (and friend of Monet) Armand Silvestre. This version of the model seems calculated by implication to stress musicality, but of a pure and anti-Wagnerist sort. Silvestre wrote:

> What immediately strikes one in looking at this painting is the immediate caress which the eye receives—it is harmonious above all. What finally distinguishes it is the simplicity of means in achieving this harmony. One quickly discovers in effect that the secret is based completely on a very fine and very exact observation of the relation of one tone to another. In reality it is a scale of tones, reconstructed after the works of the great colorist of the century, a sort of analytic procedure which does not change the palette into a banal percussion instrument as one might at first believe. . . . When one has cleared from the choir all those who sing out of tune, the discord will not be great, I suppose. There will be an even larger place for those with good voices, and the trio of which I speak seems to me to have the principal merit of making seem commonplace the use of the diapason.[21]

Silvestre's rhetoric is significant for the present discussion since he forges a new form of identity between landscape painting and music, one that does not allude to a particular composer, like Beethoven or Wagner, but which instead moves discursively between crossover terms like harmony, tone, scale, voice, etc. Romantic effusions are nowhere to be found, as Silvestre draws an aesthetic identity into being which he suggests is a natural one. He stresses refinement of effect in contrast to "banal percussion," "discord," and the "commonplace use of the diapason." This can be read, and likely would have been read by contemporaries, as a negative reference to Wagner and by implication to music as (just and always) German. In a remarkably inventive way, Silvestre uses the musical model itself to replace actual music as the new guiding force of the discourse. That force has gone over into what would be termed a few years later the "new painting."[22]

With Silvestre's description of post-Corot landscape in France—a description very likely reflecting Monet's agreement, at least in part—there appears a new dynamic in the partnering of music and landscape practice, one that is marked more by give and take than by one-sided em-

ulation. But the question remains whether—and if so, to what degree—
artists such as Monet were conceptually alert to this dynamic and active
in its production. We have Silvestre's words, *not* Monet's, to rely on. To
frame the question differently, one would have to ask how knowledgeable Monet was of the link in critical-aesthetic discourse between ambitious landscape painting and musicality in the latter 1850s and 1860s
and, further, how seriously he perceived the desirability or necessity of
maintaining that link in his own work.

On the basis of what has been introduced so far in this essay, I would
argue that Monet could not but have been alert to and concerned with the
utility, even the necessity, of retaining a musical quality in his work as he
set out to reconfigure serious landscape practice that had been so completely identified with Corot's manner of imaging. Some form of definable musicality was the one thing Monet literally needed to have carried
over in some form from Corot commentary to eventual Monet commentary. The means he discovered to assure this was to foreground chromatic
nuance and variety in his work, features that would eventually facilitate
the kind of description Silvestre was the first to provide. Without insisting on elaborately conscious preconceptions on Monet's part, it seems
highly plausible to imagine him realizing that to paint landscapes that
were not subject to a "musical" understanding would be an act of sheer
folly. In a certain sense, the necessity of all this could be seen as a considerable inhibition of Monet's pictorial free will. Alternatively, one can
view the situation as facilitating precisely the kind of experimentation
Monet needed to keep landscape relatively open as a significant and exciting imaging mode, as significant and exciting as the most radical realist figure painting that had occupied the critical foreground of the 1860s.

As a colorist from the start, Monet was eventually to reap enormous
benefits from the availability of a purified musical discourse to herald his
accomplishment in terms that were sufficiently established to be understood clearly *and* positively. In critical discourse, Monet's painting came
increasingly and inseparably to be conceived as refined color and part-
nered with music as refined sound. By the late 1880s and continuing well
into the twentieth century, critics of all sorts seem virtually in competition with one another for the production of the most extended descriptions of the new partnership. Monet's international reputation and
concomitant market successes would likely have been unimaginable
without his "musical" recognition.[23] Additionally it appears doubtful
that Monet could have so confidently pursued the ever more frontal ab-
stractness of his imaging practice had he not been able to count on that

practice being musically understood and respected as an ongoing matter of course.

Obviously it is not difficult to make an argument regarding the circumstantial utility, even the necessity, of Monet's accommodation of his painting practices to a discursive tradition that privileged cross-modeling between landscape imaging and music. What is perhaps more difficult to argue is Monet's enthusiasm regarding this accommodation, particularly at the beginning of his artistic career. As already noted, Monet's voice on the subject is silent, but this is true of most subjects that the historian might like to have seen him address. Intentionality as a category of speaking and writing comes rather late in the primary documentation of Monet. It does not really appear with any frequency or consistency until the artist finds himself in the wordy "intentionalist" ambience of neo-impressionism and symbolism in the 1880s. Only then does Monet theorize in a more or less systematic and self-justifying way, and then it is with more "period specific" attention to science and aesthetic system that he finally speaks.[24]

In the 1860s, however, one must of necessity reconstitute Monet's attitudes and sensitivities by association. His early work was produced in that preeminently music-obsessed decade and one must argue that the work was largely authored by the decade's *mentalité*. Hardly a solitary figure, Monet moved actively in artistic circles where music, along with painting, was *the* subject. While it is impossible to locate Monet physically at evening musical soirées with Manet and his talented pianist wife, he clearly knew of them. Similarly, it is impossible to place Monet next to Fantin-Latour at a particular concert or recital. Yet Fantin-Latour inscribes Monet within a privileged circle of artist-melomanes in his musically allegorical *Studio in the Batignolles* of 1870.[25] And in the same year, in *Bazille's Studio, 9 rue de la Condamine,* Frédéric Bazille locates Monet in his studio where music is being played on the piano. The previous year Monet had worked extensively alongside Pierre-Auguste Renoir at La Grenouillère and it would be most ostrichlike of us to imagine Renoir, himself a trained musician, being mute on the subject of music during their extended time together—a time which, as we have noted, coincided with Monet's most radical chromatic experiments of the decade.

Yet by far the most persistent of Monet's contacts with musical obsession in this period centered around his friend, enthusiastic promoter, protector, and fellow painter, Bazille. Unlike Monet, Bazille left a fairly lengthy body of correspondence to document his short life, which ended tragically in the Franco-Prussian War.[26] Writing routinely to his parents in Montpellier and occasionally to other members of his family, Bazille seemed always eager to share his enthusiasms and to report on his painting ambitions, while always apologizing for his difficulties as a medical student. The family letters are preserved for the most part, but much of his other correspondence to various friends is not. Those letters which Bazille received from some friends, Monet among them, have survived. Monet's letters rarely speak of anything besides financial problems or of his perception that Bazille was not working hard enough as a painter. Rarely is there an expression of personal enthusiasm for anything beyond painting.

Possibly reacting to a diffuse or evasive quality in Bazille's now-lost letters to him, Monet used his correspondence to sustain a high level of artistic authority over Bazille which would justify relatively constant demands for assistance of both a financial and promotional sort. But there was much more to the Monet-Bazille relationship than that which appears in the letters. Monet often shared a studio with Bazille when working in Paris, particularly in the middle years of the decade, and when he wasn't actually in residence he stored a substantial number of paintings with Bazille. The two painters literally surrounded one another in a variety of ways, and to the end of his life Bazille remained firmly convinced that Monet was the strongest painter of his generation, even though Bazille had in the later 1860s turned almost exclusively to figure painting while Monet increasingly concentrated on landscape. Renoir was far closer to Bazille at the end of the decade, if closeness can be defined in terms of pictorial practice and shared studio space, but Monet remained Bazille's most esteemed colleague.

Monet had met Bazille shortly after the latter arrived in Paris in 1863. Over the next seven years the Bazille that Monet knew was increasingly a person of divided aesthetic emphases. On the one hand Bazille was a sincerely ambitious young realist painter; on the other, he was a devoted mélomane. A reasonably accomplished amateur pianist, Bazille had been brought up in Montpellier by a family that seems to have been very active musically. Not long after setting up a Paris studio, Bazille acquired a piano and it combined with ever-increasing concert attendance (some opera and theater as well) to keep him very occupied musically. The new German music of Schumann and then Wagner was the passion of the later 1860s for Bazille—a passion shepherded by Bazille's "musical" friend, the musicologist Edmond Maître, with whom Bazille regularly played four-hand piano transcriptions of the concert music of the day. Maître appears to have been the main force in updating Bazille's musical taste to include Wagner, whose work was becoming a staple of the Pasdeloup popular concerts as the decade developed.[27]One also suspects that it was Maître who arranged for Bazille to obtain a ticket to the production of *Tannhäuser* planned for Brussels in early 1870 and to manage an invitation to a reception with the composer. That production never happened because of the escalating Franco-Prussian tensions that led to war in the same year.

Even though it is impossible to implicate Monet directly in Bazille's musical activities and enthusiasms, it would be equally impossible to imagine that he was not affected by them in some basic way. Here was a fellow painter, the one closest to him, vascillating constantly between music and painting, the passion for one perpetually infiltrating the passion for the other. This was not like the publicly discursive link between Corot's painting and musicality, but a personal experience of a particular artist's absorption in both media at once, like two accents of the same language. Futhermore, as we have noted, Bazille was not to be viewed as eccentric in this regard. Renoir, Manet, Cézanne, and Fantin-Latour were also dedicated melomanes to different degrees. Bazille should be seen as the most persistent focus of Monet's awareness of the pictorial-musical blur of the late 1860s, but hardly his sole informer. In any event, it seems clear that association alone provides sufficient circumstantial evidence to argue that Monet's most experimental years as a landscape painter were the same years in which he was surrounded by the highest degree of aesthetic enthusiasm for music.

But what was even more important to Monet's eventual success in devising landscape images that attracted music-modeled appreciation like Silvestre's is the fact that the melomanes among the younger painters of the 1860s had *not* produced anything like a consistent painting practice modeled on music. Thus, unlike the imaging closure that emanated from Corot criticism, something like absolute openness (or at least a multiplicity) of pictorial options existed in the circle of artists with whom Monet was most intimately involved. Within this circle mania for music was an established component of aesthetic modernity. In a sense, any manner of imaging developing out of the circle could be imagined to be both modern and musically directed in some way or other. Musicality was somehow inherent in modern aesthetic practice across the board, never exclusively tied to a particular type of image. Only some form of immediacy in sensuous presentation was required for the pictorial to be at the same time musical. Realist-based practice of one sort or other guaranteed this immediacy without dictating what as representation might best intensify sensation.

Probably more than any other artist of this circle, Monet believed landscape to be the best vehicle for generating sensuous immediacy. He had tried his hand at monumental figure painting throughout the 1860s, finding invariably that the force of the pictorial sensation he constructed overwhelmed figural presence. Only by removing the figure as focus and concentrating on a wide range of modern landscape motifs did Monet find a sufficiently receptive pictorial matrix with which to work in productively original ways, foregrounding, as we have noted, pure color along with recognizable visual modernity in his choice of subjects. Without any of the complex representational strategies employed by others to destabilize potential viewers' expectations, Monet offered in his landscapes of the early 1870s images of the familiar present in both the city and the country, letting that familiarity anchor his most ambitious chromatic excursions and making them, like the experience of concert music, part of the nervously exciting present described by Haweis and many others. Through his landscape practice Monet saw clearly into both the post-Romantic and pure musical experience and the form of imaging that best accompanied it. Perhaps because he was not a conventional "period" melomane himself, Monet was ideally positioned to invent the most brilliantly conceived strategy of grafting the musical to the pictorial without ever appearing to do so directly.

NOTES

The author's sincerest thanks are extended to Judith E. Tolnick for discussion and editing of this essay and to Michele Verduchi for final typed preparation.

[1]Rev. H. R. Haweis, *Music and Morals* (London: W. H. Allen and Co., 1871), 38.

[2]John Ruskin, *Elements of Drawing* (London: Routledge, 1857). See also William J. Gatens, "John Ruskin and Music," *Victorian Studies* 30 (1986), 77–97. I am indebted as well to Anne Elizabeth Nellis for her seminar paper "The Harmony of Science and Aestheticism," produced at Brown University in 1996.

[3]Laura Hendrickson, "Art Aspiring to the Condition of Music: 1850–1900, English Avant-Gardism and the Case of Wagner," (Ph.D. diss., Brown University, 1998).

[4]Walter Pater, "The School of Giorgione," in *The Renaissance* [1873], in William E. Buckler, ed., *Walter Pater: Three Major Texts* (New York: New York University Press, 1986), 153–169. R.A.M. Stevenson, *Velasquez* (1895; reprint,

London: G. Bell and Sons, 1962). J.A.M. Whistler, *Mr. Whistler's Ten O'Clock* (London: Chatto and Windus, 1888).

[5]Leo Schrade, *Beethoven in France: The Growth of an Idea* (New Haven: Yale University Press, 1942).

[6]Ralph De Sola, ed., *Beethoven By Berlioz* (Boston: Crescendo Publishing Co., 1975). For the most recent discussion of Parisian music commerce see Charlotte Nalle Eyerman, "The Composition of Femininity: The Significance of the 'Woman at the Piano' Motif in 19th-Century French Culture from Daumier to Renoir" (Ph.D. diss., University of California at Berkeley, 1997), Chapter 1.

[7]Eyerman, 12.

[8]Schrade, 57–60.

[9]Ibid., 57.

[10]Charles Baudelaire, *Delacroix, His Life and Work* (New York: Garland, 1979). See also Théophile Gautier, *L'Art Moderne* (Paris: Michel Levy Frères, 1856), and Gautier, *La Musique* (Paris: E. Fasquelle, 1911).

[11]Kermit S. Champa, *The Rise of Landscape Painting in France: Corot to Monet* (Manchester, N.H.: The Currier Gallery of Art, 1991), 32–33.

[12]Ibid., 25–30.

[13]David Ogawa, "Corot's Musical Studios," (Ph.D. diss., Brown University, forthcoming).

[14]Alfred Robaut et Étienne Moreau-Nelaton, *L'Oeuvre de Corot* (Paris: H. Floury, 1905), 196–197, 260, 282, 329. See also André Coquis, *Corot et la Critique Contemporaine* (Paris: Dervy, 1959).

[15]Key texts securing the Corot-music discourse are George Moore, *Modern Painting* (London: W. Scott, Ltd., 1893); John C.Van Dyke, ed., *Modern French Masters* (New York: T. Fisher, 1896); and especially Gustave Geoffrey and Arsène Alexandre, *Corot and Millet* (Paris, New York, and London: "The International Studio," 1902).

[16]Alfred Sensier, *Souvenirs de Théodore Rousseau* (Paris, Léon Techener, 1872), 6, 155, 361–362.

[17]Selected texts conveying the Corot-music discourse through the Corot centennial year of 1975 are Germain Bazin, *Corot* (Paris, Pierre Tisné, 1942), 12–55; François Fosca, *Corot* (Bruxelles, 1968), 121–129; Madeleine Hours, *Corot* (Paris: H. N. Abrams, 1972); and Hélène Toussaint, Genevieve Monnier, and Martine Servot, *Homage à Corot*, exh. cat. Orangerie des Tuileries (Paris, 1975), 83.

[18]Kermit S. Champa, "Concert Music: The Master Model for Radical Painting In France, 1830–1890," *Imago Musicae* (forthcoming).

[19]Deborah Johnson, "Confluence and Influence: Photography and the Japanese Print in 1850," in Champa, *Rise of Landscape Painting in France,* 78–97.

[20]The concept of "facing" is adopted from Michael Fried, *Manet's Modernism,or the Face of Painting in the 1860's* (Chicago: Chicago University Press, 1996).

[21]*Galerie Durand-Ruel Receuil d'Estampes* (Paris: Durand-Ruel, 1873), 21–24; cited and translated in Kermit Swiler Champa, *Studies in Early Impressionism* (New Haven: Yale University Press, 1973), 98–99.

[22]Edmond Duranty, *La Nouvelle Peinture. A propos du groupe d'artistes qui expose dans les Galeries Durand-Ruel* (Paris: E. Dentu, 1876).

[23]Kermit Swiler Champa, *Masterpiece Studies—Manet, Zola, Van Gogh and Monet* (University Park, Penn.: Pennsylvania State University Press, 1994), 119–144. See also Lisa Ann Norris, "The Early Writings of Camille Mauclair: Toward an Understanding of Wagnerism and French Art, 1885–1900," (Ph.D. diss., Brown University, 1993).

[24]Gustave Geffroy, *Claude Monet, sa vie, son temps, son oeuvre* (Paris: G. Crès, 1922) and Lionello Venturi, *Les Archives de l'Impressionisme* (Paris: Durand-Ruel, 1939).

[25]Champa, "Concert Music."

[26]Kermit Swiler Champa, "Monet and Bazille: A Complicated Co-dependence" in High Museum of Art, *Claude Monet and Frédéric Bazille: Early Impressionism and Collaboration in The Studio* (Atlanta: High Museum of Art, 1999).

[27]Ibid.

CHAPTER 6

In the Toils of Queen Omphale
Saint-Saëns's Painterly Refiguration of the Symphonic Poem

CARLO CABALLERO

> *Hercule souriait, penché; la chevelure*
> *D'Omphale frissonnait près de sa gorge pure.*
> *La Lydienne, proie adorable d'Éros,*
> *Languissante, et levant vers les yeux du héros*
> *Ses yeux de violette où flotte une ombre noire,*
> *Lui posa dans les mains sa quenouille d'ivoire.*
>
> —THÉODORE DE BANVILLE,
> "LA REINE OMPHALE" (1861)

The story of Hercules and Omphale enjoyed a particular vogue in French poetry and the visual arts between 1843 and 1866. The trappings of the tale—a debased hero, a powerful queen, slavery, love, and cross-dressing—piqued the interest of a number of poets and artists, including Victor Hugo, Théodore de Banville, Gustave Boulanger, and Charles Gleyre. In music, however, Camille Saint-Saëns's *Rouet d'Omphale (Omphale's Spinning Wheel)* stands apart. Before him, only a few composers had made Omphale the heroine of operas, ballets, or other staged entertainments, and Saint-Saëns was the first to compose a nondramatic musical composition on her story.[1] *Le rouet d'Omphale* is an elegant piece in ternary form lasting seven or eight minutes. It had its premiere at the Salle Erard in an arrangement for two pianos on December 7, 1871; a month later, on January 9, 1872, a performance with full orchestra was given under the auspices of the Société Nationale de Musique.

This essay treats the individual qualities of Saint-Saëns's work in some detail and touches on differences between his conception of the symphonic poem and that of Franz Liszt. But I shall also tug on the strands of *Le rouet d'Omphale* in order to place it, and its mixed genre, in the broad context of arguments about the relations between music, art, and poetry in the period from about 1848 to 1886.

Let us begin with the mythological sources. Apollodorus tells us that Hercules killed Iphitus in a fit of anger. Haunted by nightmares, Hercules went to the Pythoness Xenoclea, who told him that in atonement for this act he must be sold into slavery for one year. Taken to Asia and offered for sale as a nameless slave, Hercules was bought by Omphale, Queen of Lydia. He remained with her three years, and during his servitude he rid her kingdom of bandits, monsters, and scoundrels. Whether Omphale bought Hercules more as a fighter or as a lover is unclear, but she eventually bore him three sons. The details of Hercules's other domestic activities are shadowy but titillating. Ovid tells us that "Hercules discarded his lion pelt and aspen wreath, and instead wore jewelled necklaces, golden bracelets, . . . a purple shawl, and a Maeonian girdle." Surrounded by "wanton Ionian girls," he teased wool from the wool-basket and spun thread at Omphale's feet.[2] Painters thus show a girdled Hercules spinning wool while his mistress Omphale wears the skin of the Nemean lion and wields his club over him.

At the head of the score of *Le rouet d'Omphale* Saint-Saëns placed an explanatory notice. He thus provided his music with a "program," here quoted in its entirety:

> The subject of this symphonic poem is feminine seduction, the triumphant struggle of weakness against strength. The SPINNING WHEEL is a mere pretext, chosen only with a view to the rhythm and general motion of the piece.

> Those interested in details will see, on page 19 (letter J), Hercules groaning in the bonds he cannot break, and on page 32 (letter L), Omphale mocking the hero's vain efforts.[3]

Saint-Saëns makes a special plea for the spinning wheel, for he knew that it was a late medieval invention and thus unknown to the ancient Greeks. He explains its presence as a "pretext" for rhythm and movement, and indeed the turning of the wheel provides the musical figuration that sets the piece in motion. The spinning wheel, or its residual impetus, is present on nearly every page. However, the wheel appears in none of the paintings we shall consider, which restrict themselves to the ancient spindle and distaff. Indeed, I have examined depictions spanning four centuries and have found no painting, drawing, or sculpture in which Omphale and Hercules are shown with a spinning wheel. To the best of my knowledge, there is only one precedent for Saint-Saëns's anachronism: Victor Hugo's poem, "Le rouet d'Omphale," which was written in 1843 and published in 1856 (see appendix). Although Saint-Saëns knew Hugo well, and the titles of the two works are identical, Saint-Saëns never mentioned Hugo's poem in connection with his symphonic work. If one studies this poem carefully, the reason for Saint-Saëns's silence becomes clear: quite simply, the music and the verses, beyond their identical titles, have almost nothing in common.[4]

What we do know of Saint-Saëns's inspiration for the work comes to us from a reliable source, his private secretary Jean Bonnerot, who wrote:

> The idea of the spinning wheel was furnished by a beautiful ebony spinning wheel he had admired in the salon of an attractive woman. The next day, Saint-Saëns was visiting the atelier of the painter Cabanel, who had invited him to see his *Vénus,* still on the easel, and was amazed by the coloring of this picture, by the rendering of the flesh and the sensuality emanating from it. . . . The symphonic poem was subsequently born from the union of these two memories, the harmony of these two visions.[5]

One may wonder whether the ebony spinning wheel mentioned by Bonnerot existed, or whether it was a convenient, if esoteric, biographical fiction. But what reason could he have had to fabricate a reference to a painting that did not even share its subject with Saint-Saëns's symphonic poem? If the painting to which he refers was still on Cabanel's easel, it must have been *Vénus victorieuse (Victorious Venus)* of 1872 (Figure 6–1), not the more famous (or infamous) *Naissance de Vénus (The Birth of Venus)*, painted a decade earlier. In *Vénus victorieuse* we see Venus in her triumph; accompanied by her doves, she holds the golden apple that she won in the Judgement of Paris. The date on the canvas, 1872, allows us to place the completion of *Vénus victorieuse* the year after Saint-Saëns composed *Le rouet d'Omphale*. The link between this painting and Saint-Saëns's work is not only borne out chronologically, but also thematically. We need only look beyond the trappings of the two myths to see the common theme, which is the triumph of voluptuousness, and specifically, feminine voluptuousness.

The symphonic poem has traditionally been more closely associated

Figure 6–1. Alexandre Cabanel, *Vénus victorieuse,* 1872, oil on canvas, 145 × 92 cm. Musée Fabre, Montpellier, France.

with literature than with the visual arts. Yet in uncovering Saint-Saëns's sources, I have set aside a poem that shares with his music both its theme and its title in favor of a painting that shares neither. In order to justify this perverse strategy, it is necessary to explain Saint-Saëns's aesthetic orientation, and even before that, to consider the nature and history of the kind of work he was trying to create.

The symphonic poem was a crossbred genre. Franz Liszt was the inventor of this new kind of orchestral composition, whose first example was *Ce qu'on entend sur la montagne,* a long composition completed around 1850. Liszt intended it as a musical complement to Hugo's poem of the same title, and his starting point in poetry is significant. One of the main reasons Liszt seems to have brought the symphonic poem into being was to test the possibilities of recreating a poetic or intellectual discourse in the "language" of music. Liszt spoke of "directing the listener's attention not only to the web of the music but also to the *ideas* expressed by its contours and successions."[6] In a series of studies written around 1980, Carl Dahlhaus identified the peculiarly linguistic nature of Liszt's aesthetic project in terms of a specific musical technique: motivic transformation, that is, the practice of drawing opposing or seemingly unrelated musical ideas out of a single compact, rudimentary structure of pitch and rhythm (or a small group of such structures).[7] To achieve an intimate union of the musical and the literary, Liszt proposed the use of musical motives that would signify ideas not merely through their pregnant individuality, but through their modes of presentation, transformation, and combination. Most interestingly, Dahlhaus also points out that the very content of Hugo's poem might have helped foster the motivic techniques of Liszt's first symphonic poem. Liszt's programmatic note supports this interpretation, for not only does Liszt fix on Hugo's evocation of the contrasting voices of "Nature" and "Humanity" but he also continues the evocation and imposes on it a more specific image—that of "voices . . . following one another, at first from afar, then drawing nearer, crossing, intermingling." He continues:

> The poet hears two voices: the one immense, magnificent, ineffable, singing the beauty and harmonies of creation; the other swelling with sighs, groans, sobs, cries of revolt and blasphemies:
>
> One said NATURE, the other HUMANITY!
>
> . . . .
> . . . two voices, strange, extraordinary,
> Endlessly reborn, endlessly vanishing,

follow one another, first from afar, then drawing nearer, crossing, intermingling their concords, now strident, now harmonious, to the point
where the poet's contemplation, moved, silently touches the boundaries of prayer.[8]

Liszt's annotation builds on the content of the poem but also draws out of
it a justification for a particular kind of musical discourse.
     Liszt himself claimed that it was precisely "the unlimited alterations
which a motive may undergo" that gave music a means of doing what it
had been unable to do before without the direct assistance of words or of
dramatic action: "to express thoughts."[9] Through motivic work, abstract
music becomes "articulate," like intelligible speech, and is no longer a
mute art. Liszt's contemporaries, whether or not they unravelled his motivic technique, understood the central place of literary expression in his
conception of the symphonic poem. Amédée Boutarel, a French critic
contemporary to Saint-Saëns, noted that one of Liszt's first decisions was
to "replace the thematic development of a musical phrase" with a "system of amplification" whose "infinitely variable procedures" better
suited his aesthetic needs.[10] This is Boutarel's way of describing Liszt's
motivic practice, which Dahlhaus would later find so significant for its
abstraction of musical parameters. Liszt seems at times to begin from el-
ementary, separable structures of pitch and rhythm rather than from
themes and motives in which rhythm and melody are already coeffi-
cient.[11] Boutarel was not nearly so explicit about Liszt's technique, but
he more broadly and importantly described Liszt as seeking "to relax the
forms of instrumental music so as to render it . . . as explicit, as flexible,
as persuasive as a spoken language expressing general ideas."[12] In France,
this was a new vocation for instrumental music. The traditional French
view, stated by Victor Cousin in 1853, was that only poetry "expresses
what is inaccessible to every other art . . . thought in its most sublime
flight, in its most refined abstraction."[13] Liszt's aspirations to a music of
ideas placed him at the forefront of a trend that would overturn the old
aesthetic hierarchy and, by the end of the century, place music in direct
competition with poetry, formerly regarded the loftiest of the arts.[14]
     Saint-Saëns was the first composer in France to follow Liszt's initia-
tive and write symphonic poems, his first being *Le rouet d'Omphale*.
How is it, then, that Saint-Saëns's symphonic poems are so different
from Liszt's? Saint-Saëns admired Liszt deeply and understood his aesthetic intentions, but he seems to have been attracted to the genre for different reasons.[15] Rather than seeking to infuse his music with the powers

of intelligible speech, Saint-Saëns viewed the symphonic poem more as a tableau set into musical motion. He left aside Liszt's fascination with an "articulate" discursive network of motivic ideas in favor of a more traditional, linear, thematic treatment. Liszt's mode of development in *Ce qu'on entend sur la montagne,* especially in the middle sections of the piece, seems like a mute discourse striving for verbal articulation. Saint-Saëns abstained from this discursive approach and instead used more conventional developmental techniques underpinned by a continuous rhythmic pattern or instrumental figuration. His music tends to create a sense of propulsive motion, sometimes almost abstracted in its animation. Indeed, Saint-Saëns's first three symphonic poems are all built upon a strong emblem of physical movement: the spinning of the wheel in *Le rouet d'Omphale,* the gallop of the solar chariot in *Phaéton,* and the spectral waltzing of *Danse macabre.* Hence, above and beyond Saint-Saëns's more traditional developmental techniques, the decisive role of physical motion in these pieces detracts from whatever pretensions to abstract thought one could claim for them. This limited mimesis, sometimes reduced to the rhythmic impetus of background figuration, reminds us of our existence in and among moving bodies, not a detached meditation on the ideal.

Now let us also remember that, so far as Saint-Saëns's *Rouet d'Omphale* is concerned, Hugo's great poem provided nothing more than a title, or at most a fruitful association of the spinning wheel with the mythic figure of Omphale. Saint-Saëns knew that Liszt had been inspired by the romantic poetry of Lamartine, Schiller, and Hugo, putting their poetic language to musical "work" in different ways in *Ce qu'on entend sur la montagne* and in three other symphonic poems.[16] But Saint-Saëns chose *not* to put Hugo's "Rouet d'Omphale" in the service of his music. Perhaps we can explain this choice by considering Saint-Saëns's own aesthetic ideas and the value he assigned to the visual arts.

In his important essay on Liszt, Saint-Saëns discusses the symphonic poem as a genre and defends its aesthetic viability, but his first recourse is to painting, not literature. This orientation is extremely significant:

> The reproach that music expresses nothing on its own, without the aid of the word, applies to painting, too.

> A picture would never represent Adam and Eve to a viewer who did not know the Bible; it can only depict a man and a woman naked in a garden. Nonetheless, the viewer or the listener will fall perfectly into

that deception which consists of adding, to the pleasure of his eyes or
ears, the interest and emotion of a subject. There is no reason to refuse
him this pleasure; there is no reason to accord him it either. This is a
matter of complete freedom: artists make use of it, and they do well.[17]

I have isolated this quotation because here Saint-Saëns grants music and
painting a common privilege: to exist for their own sake, without benefit
of the word and its explicative powers. Programs, titles, or subjects are
for him, in either medium, pendants to an already integral art form. In
glaring contrast to many of his contemporaries, Saint-Saëns insisted that
"music is a *plastic art . . .* composed of *forms,*" though the peculiarity of
these forms, he added, is that they "exist only in the imagination."[18] It is
not surprising, then, to discover that Saint-Saëns, in his classification of
the arts, separates the fine arts, including music, from literature. Music is
"the most mysterious of all the fine arts," but it has, like painting and
sculpture, "line, modeling, and color (this last through instrumentation),"
and in addition to these, "movement."[19]

Saint-Saëns chose his terms, "line, modeling, and color," very carefully, and he repeated them elsewhere in a statement we may take as his
artistic credo: "The artist who does not feel fully satisfied by elegant
lines, harmonious colors, a beautiful succession of chords, does not understand Art."[20] It surely does Saint-Saëns no dishonor to describe him as
a strong formalist. Liszt, however, was a very different thinker, deeply attached to a belief that a programmatic musical work keeps the fullness of
its intellectual and emotional meaning whether or not its program is
made explicit. That is, where Liszt sees the finished programmatic work
as a true synthesis whose meaning is inextricable from its subject, Saint-
Saëns considered the program an accretion which changes the listener's
interpretation of the work but remains separable from it.[21] Parantheti-
cally, let us say that both views have their drawbacks. Liszt is stipulative
in his view of musical expression; he essentializes the synthesis of music
and intellectual meaning. Saint-Saëns's view is more logical but takes little account of the possibility that the sum of an abstract score and its program may be greater than the parts. That is, an act of pure composition
may be radically influenced and shaped by extramusical thoughts, and
the resulting work may have moments of synthesis that cannot be accounted for as separate layers of activity.

Liszt, in short, sought to transcend the abstract beauty of the classical symphony and rival the intellectual power of the literary word, while
Saint-Saëns insisted on the self-sufficient beauty of musical sounds and

was content to leave literature in its place, separate from the fine arts.[22] Thus it seems reasonable to suppose that the visual arts, as much as or more than poetry, could provide symphonic inspiration and an attractive expressive model to a composer in Saint-Saëns's particular aesthetic situation. For other composers, and even some poets, music's annexation of literary qualities sealed its triumph as an intellectual art as opposed to a "merely" sensual and formal one, but Saint-Saëns's conception of the symphonic poem made no such pretenses. On the contrary, he openly celebrated the fundamental sensuality of music.

The aesthetic result of this stance was music that achieved vividness and carefully controlled coloristic nuances within formal perfection. In this limited sense, we might call his conception "painterly" or "plastic."[23] His overall aesthetic strategy would not have pleased Liszt's German advocates, such as Franz Brendel, who promoted Liszt's conception of the symphonic poem as a triumph of Germanic "idealism" over an older "sensuous," plastic model of musical expression, which Brendel associated with France and Italy.[24] In France itself, Boutarel described Liszt's achievement in similar terms, though without any of the nationalistic overtones. "To those who said *art for art's sake*," we learn, "Liszt responded, *art for idea's sake*."[25] Little did Boutarel know that it would be Saint-Saëns, Liszt's first French follower, who would later write an essay entitled precisely, "Art for Art's Sake." It is the most uncompromising defense of aestheticism penned by any major composer at the turn of the century.

Saint-Saëns ignored Victor Hugo's "Rouet d'Omphale" where another composer might have been moved to recreate it in music. He set the poetry of Hugo to music on many occasions, but for this purely orchestral project, the plastic beauty of an antique ebony spinning wheel and the impression of an erotic painting spurred his imagination. His tastes were classical and epicurean, and the musical style of *Le rouet d'Omphale* has the elegance, formal clarity, and delicate coloring of a canvas by one of his academic contemporaries, not the dark grandeur of Hugo's poem. At the same time, Saint-Saëns realized his traditional tastes in an untraditional genre, and he did so without following many of its originator's aesthetic cues. Saint-Saëns's symphonic poems stood in the vanguard of French orchestral music in the 1870s. If he wished to defend the new genre, he could cite only the three most controversial figures in European music: Berlioz, Liszt, and Wagner. Their authority in compositional matters wasn't worth a sou to the French public of 1871.

It seems highly significant that Saint-Saëns chose for the underlying

theme of his first symphonic poem the power of sensuality and its victory, for in a sense *Le rouet d'Omphale* is an allegory of itself: it communicates the values of its own theoretical premises. The triumph of the
sensual is not only the theme of *Le rouet d'Omphale* but also the banner
of Saint-Saëns's refiguration of the Lisztian symphonic poem. Perhaps,
too, it may betoken his spiritual alliance with such painters as Ingres,
Gérôme, Regnault, and Cabanel, all of whom he knew.[26] A fascination
with the sensual, the feminine, and the world of oriental and classical antiquity attracted Saint-Saëns to a particular kind of painting, and his genius allowed him to mirror these fascinations in his music.[27]

In order to understand where Saint-Saëns's work stands in relation
to the kinds of paintings he seemed to admire, let us look to his specific
representation of Hercules and Omphale in music. *Le rouet d'Omphale*
begins with a tonally unstable introduction in which the gradual amalga-
mation of various sixteenth-note patterns is masterfully coordinated with
the harmonic structure. The representation by these means of a spinning
wheel slowly whirled into action is entirely convincing. When the main
theme finally appears, the spinning figures melt into a neutral, fluctuating
background of sixteenth notes. Saint-Saëns develops this theme (Figure
6–2) in the outer sections of the composition. Whether this music represents Omphale spinning or Hercules spinning—or spinning without
actors—is not clear. Spinning, however, is clearly associated with Omphale's triumph, and when this same material returns for the final third of
the work, we are meant to imagine that the vanquished Hercules spins,
alongside his mistress or alone. The middle of the work, a contrasting
section in C-sharp minor, brings in a serious, striving melody on the low
strings, bassoons, and trombone. Saint-Saëns indicates in his program
that this new theme represents "Hercules groaning in the bonds he cannot break" (Figure 6–3). At the end of each phrase of Hercules's com-
plaint, we hear sweeping arpeggios in the harp, which must represent
Omphale's victorious toils. This section ends with an exhaustion of the
masculine struggle, after which an impertinent variation of Hercules's
once-earnest theme appears brightly on the oboe, soon joined by a bas-
soon and two flutes (Figure 6–4). Here is mockery in the strict sense, for
Omphale taunts Hercules by repeating his low theme in her own high,
staccato voice. This is the only "Lisztian" transformation of a musical
idea in the work. Yet even here, the procedure is thematic rather than motivic and owes as much to Berlioz (specifically, the use of the *idée fixe* in
the *Symphonie fantastique*) as to Liszt. The oboe, at first taunting, quietly
disengages itself from this situation in an especially interesting way. It is

Figure 6–2. Saint–Saëns, *Le rouet d'Omphale,* main theme (rehearsal letter B).

as if Omphale does not have the heart to continue her raillery.[28] As an English critic noted, "We are led to suppose that Omphale, conscious of her triumph, after laughing at him relents and finishes by not proving too obdurate."[29] This transition, which leads back to the spinning wheel, is ambivalent and perhaps touched by a trace of pity: pity with a wry smile, to be sure, but even Omphale's mockery of Hercules is coquettish rather than aggressive.

Is this the same mistress and slave we see depicted in Gustave Boulanger's *Hercule aux pieds d'Omphale* (*Hercules at Omphale's Feet*), exhibited at the Salon of 1861 (Figure 6–5)? I think not. Saint-Saëns's characterization of the protagonists was far more discreet, as critics of the symphonic poem were quick to observe. Georges Servières wrote, "We do not take Hercules' rumblings of protest very seriously. This hero is not suffering very deeply from his humiliation."[30] Just before the end of the work, Saint-Saëns subtly suggests another dialogue

Figure 6–3. Saint–Saëns, *Le rouet d'Omphale,* Hercules (rehearsal letter J).

Figure 6–4. Saint–Saëns, *Le rouet d'Omphale,* Omphale's mockery of Hercules (rehearsal letter L).

between Omphale and Hercules.[31] A rising bass line in the cellos and bassoons alternates with a solo oboe. These same instrumental colors painted Hercules and Omphale for us before. But now Hercules no longer struggles and strains for freedom; he is resigned to his lot. And Omphale's melody no longer taunts but rather busies itself confidently in weaving light scalar patterns.

This dialogue soon ceases and the spinning wheel remains as the only "audible" actor on the scene. Saint-Saëns could have stopped here, with the spinning wheel in motion. The piece is, after all, a scherzo and could have ended like so many scherzos, in a flurry and a blink. Instead, the wheel very gradually stops turning and comes to rest. Some listeners will be content to explain this slackening as a formal device of purely musical relaxation. Others will cite the analogous speeding-up of tempo at the start of the piece in order to suggest that the "tableau" set into musical motion with the first notes is frozen back into pictorial stillness at the end. But still others may wonder just what Hercules and Omphale are doing. Why have the spinners left their wheel idle? Perhaps, in another room of the palace, they have found a more stimulating pastime, one that involves no wool. . . . What Saint-Saëns called "the triumphant struggle of weakness against strength" is not only Omphale's triumph, but of course that of Venus—*Vénus victorieuse.*[32]

Uncertainty about the nature of Omphale's emotional hold over Hercules brings us to a third painting, *Hercule aux pieds d'Omphale,* a late work by Charles Gleyre (Figure 6–6). I have no reason to believe that Saint-Saëns saw this work, although it was on exhibit in a Paris gallery for two or three months at the beginning of 1863.[33] Rather, I am interested in it as a parallel representation of the tale. Omphale's physical bearing and facial expression are of central interest here. Although her

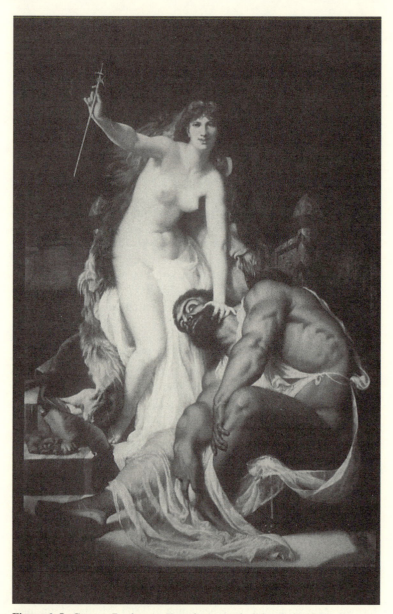

Figure 6–5. Gustave Boulanger, *Hercule aux pieds d'Omphale,* 1861, oil on canvas, 233 × 173 cm., Private Collection.

aspect is ambiguous, the mise-en-scène is not. Let us turn back to Boulanger's painting for comparison. Boulanger's Hercules is unmistakably a slave in abject bondage to Omphale. She throws the lion's skin over her back, and while she holds the beast Hercules at bay, grabbing

Figure 6–6. Charles Gleyre, *Hercule aux pieds d'Omphale,* 1863, oil on canvas, 145 × 111 cm. Musée d'art et d'histoire, Neuchâtel, Switzerland.

his neck and beard with her left hand, she raises the distaff up in triumphant mockery with her right. Here, too, observe the cross-dressing that figures in some versions of the Greek story. Omphale wears the lion's pelt of Hercules, and Hercules has a feminine tunic and sandals.[34] The iconography is not unusual. Many earlier depictions of this myth have Omphale wrest Hercules's weapons and spoils from him.

Gleyre, however, took a less conventional approach. His Omphale neither restrains Hercules nor touches any of his physical emblems; in fact, Hercules keeps his lion's pelt beneath him. It is not Omphale who holds the hero's great club, but Amor, her spiritual double. The peacock perched on the architrave may represent Omphale's pride, but her eyes seem to hesitate between disdain and love. Does she hold her right hand over her heart merely to support an undone tunic? Or is this an expressive gesture? One of surprise . . . or of sympathy? We are in doubt. But Amor, visibly smitten and leaning on her thigh, seems to tell us the true or future nature of her emotions.

Hercules's club is given special prominence. To the right, opposite Hercules and in the same visual plane, it completes the semicircle of figures. Held nearly erect, it undoubtedly alludes to the virility that Hercules will maintain even in his servitude.[35] But this is not just a wooden limb; the club also functions as a symbol of Hercules's dignity. The instrument of his heroism is held by Amor because through the love and intelligence of his mistress, Hercules will ultimately benefit by the punishment the gods prepared for him. Omphale's love, and Hercules's love or faithful service to her, will raise him from his fallen state. He makes no attempt to repossess the club; he has ceded it to Omphale, who has ceded it to Love. Amor, in turn, holds the club in place of his customary bow.[36]

In French academic painting of the middle and later part of the century, voluptuous renderings of the female form play no small role. I think we tend to value most those works among them, like Gleyre's or Saint-Saëns's, that cast some veil of ambiguity over their glimpses into the sex lives of the ancients. Both Gleyre and Saint-Saëns took advantage of loose threads in the fable in order to impart complexity to their depictions, while the Omphale in Boulanger's canvas is a one-dimensional figure; even contemporary viewers found her cruelty banal.[37] Gleyre paints us a more intriguing figure perched on a psychological threshold. Saint-Saëns, too, stimulates our consideration of Omphale's ambivalent feelings and leaves us to wonder about the conclusion of his piece.

Before ending, I would like to ruffle the surface of my own arguments. I pointed out, in passing, that Saint-Saëns did use the theme of Hercules's struggle as an object of thematic transformation. That is, Hercules's theme, transformed by Omphale's voice, becomes an expression of mockery after Hercules fails to escape his mistress's toils. Saint-Saëns's method, I also noted, might owe more to Berlioz than to Liszt. But to balance this appraisal, we must admit that Saint-Saëns, in other symphonic poems, sometimes developed his ideas through processes of thematic variation that at least approach the small-scale, cellular, motivic techniques used by Liszt. Perhaps Dahlhaus's work on Liszt's symphonic poems has even lent too much importance to Liszt's motivic techniques. Dahlhaus is persuasive, but he seems to have formed his views of the motivic complexity of *Ce qu'on entend sur la montagne* less around an examination of the music than around an essay written by Alfred Heuss in 1911. Heuss's is the sort of study of themes and motives that concludes with the statement, "Every measure of this great work is motivic."[38] Liszt's work *is* motivically complex but, as one might guess, Heuss's analyses are often forced.

There are indeed striking differences in thematic and motivic technique between *Le rouet d'Omphale* and *Ce qu'on entend sur la montagne*. But the differences in scale and thematic economy are just as significant. First and most simply, Liszt's symphonic poems are consistently longer than Saint-Saëns's and painted in broader strokes. Second, the two composers take different approaches to what might be called the economy of musical ideas. Where a symphonic poem by Liszt typically musters six distinct ideas—or ten, in the case of *Tasso*—Saint-Saëns makes do with as few as three.[39] In the Lisztian symphonic poem, disparate ideas, whether or not they are ultimately derived from one motive, are brought into mysterious collisions and nudge the listener back toward the program for imaginative corroboration or understanding. Saint-Saëns, for better or worse, tends to eschew the kind of perplexity that takes the listener to a speculative position somewhere outside the bounds of pure music. Indeed, *Le rouet d'Omphale* is completely satisfying as a piece of instrumental music without any program. One might even say that the formal self-sufficiency of Saint-Saëns's symphonic poem renders its program superfluous. The beginning of Liszt's *Ce qu'on entend sur la montagne*, it is true, could pass for the beginning of an ordinary symphony. But the middle sections of the work build to passages of fantastic disorder and contrast—far beyond what anyone would expect of the development section of a symphony in the middle of the nineteenth century. Liszt's translations of the different "voices" of nature and humanity, thundering and colliding, propagate episodes whose sudden, rapid changes of mood and tonality pull the listener back into the composer's literary interpretation of Hugo's poem.

In each case, we may now observe, the aesthetic effect of the music corresponds to the composer's expressed intentions for the genre of the symphonic poem. For Liszt, the interweaving of music and idea is inextricable; for Saint-Saëns, the music stands on its own; the "interest and emotion of a subject" is a pleasurable "deception" that the music can take or leave. As a self-consciously impure genre, the symphonic poem opened up possibilities for the exchange of topics and methods between the arts. Thus, it is curious to observe that this exchange did not always determine the content of a specific work so much as offer certain kinds of theoretical leverage. For Liszt, the crossing voices of Hugo's "Ce qu'on entend sur la montagne" provided an impulse for, or a validation of, a motivic and episodic technique striving for the articulation of ideas. Saint-Saëns, a professing formalist, a lover of perfect rather than sublime beauty, found in his predilection for visual art a warrant for imparting a "plastic" conception of musical expression to a genre born out of Liszt's very different aesthetic intentions. Thus, as so often happens in music, once composers identify what they want and need, they turn it to their own purposes with impunity.

APPENDIX

Victor Hugo, "Le rouet d'Omphale" (1843, first published in 1856). Reprinted from Hugo, *Les contemplations* (Paris: Michel Lévy, 1856), 1:129–30.

Le rouet d'Omphale

Il est dans l'atrium, le beau rouet d'ivoire.
La roue agile est blanche, et la quenouille est noire;
La quenouille est d'ébène incrusté de lapis.
Il est dans l'atrium sur un riche tapis.

Un ouvrier d'Égine a sculpté sur la plinthe
Europe, dont un dieu n'écoute pas la plainte.
Le taureau blanc l'emporte. Europe, sans espoir,
Crie, et baissant les yeux, s'épouvante de voir

L'Océan monstrueux qui baise ses pieds roses.

Des aiguilles, du fil, des boîtes demi-closes,
Les laines de Milet, peintes de pourpre et d'or,
Emplissent un panier près du rouet qui dort.

Cependant, odieux, effroyables, énormes,
Dans le fond du palais, vingt fantômes difformes,
Vingt monstres tout sanglants, qu'on ne voit qu'à demi,
Errent en foule autour du rouet endormi:
Le lion néméen, l'hydre affreuse de Lerne,
Cacus, le noir brigand de la noire caverne,
Le triple Géryon, et les typhons des eaux,
Qui, le soir, à grand bruit, soufflent dans les roseaux;
De la massue au front tous ont l'empreinte horrible
Et tous, sans approcher, rôdant d'un air terrible,
Sur le rouet, où pend un fil souple et lié,
Fixent de loin, dans l'ombre, un oeil humilié.

NOTES

[1]For a useful list of representations of this fable in the arts, including music, see Jane Davidson Reed and Chris Rohmann, *The Oxford Guide to Classical Myth in the Arts, 1300–1990s* (New York: Oxford University Press, 1993), 1:540–544. In French literature and painting, we should note the following nineteenth-century treatments of the theme before Saint-Saëns's symphonic poem: Théophile Gautier, "Omphale," short story (1834); Hugo, "Le rouet d'Omphale," poem (1843, publ. 1856); Banville, three poems,"Omphale" (1857, 1866), "La Reine Omphale" (1861, 1866), and "La Lydienne" (1868); Boulanger, *Hercule aux pieds d'Omphale*, painting (1861); and Gleyre, *Hercule aux pieds d'Omphale,* painting (1863).

[2]Robert Graves, *The Greek Myths* (London: Penguin Books, 1960), 2:165.

[3]Camille Saint-Saëns, *Le rouet d'Omphale: Poëme symphonique* (Paris: Durand Schoenewerk, [1872]), n.p.

[4]Later I shall suggest one implicit "scene" in which they might meet.

[5]Jean Bonnerot, *C. Saint-Saëns: Sa vie et son œuvre* (Paris: A. Durand, 1914), 62.

[6]Franz Liszt, "Berlioz und seine *Harold-Symphonie,*" in *Gesammelte Schriften* (Leipzig: Breitkopf and Härtel, 1882), 4:62 (italics mine).

[7]Carl Dahlhaus, *Nineteenth-Century Music,* trans. J. Bradford Robinson (Berkeley: University of California Press, 1989), 240.

[8]Liszt, *Ce qu'on entend sur la montagne,* in *Symphonische Dichtungen,* vol.1 (Leipzig: Breitkopf and Härtel, n.d.), n.p. The lines quoted by Liszt are from Hugo's poem.

[9]Liszt, "Dornröschen: Genast's Gedicht und Raff's Musik gleichen Namens" [1856], in *Gesammelte Schriften,* 5:172. Quoted in Dahlhaus without documentation, 242.

[10]Amédée Boutarel, *L'œuvre symphonique de Franz Liszt et l'esthétique moderne* (Paris: Heugel, Fischbacher, 1886), 53, 55.

[11]Dahlhaus, 240–241.

[12]Boutarel, 42.

[13]Victor Cousin, *Du Vrai, du Beau, et du Bien* (Paris: Didier, 1853), 216–217; see also 219. Théodore de Banville would still affirm the position in his *Petit traité de poésie française* [1872] (Paris: G. Charpentier, 1881), 9.

[14]One of the most astonishing examples of an early revisionist viewpoint in France may be found in Baudelaire's great essay of 1861 on Wagner, where he grants Wagner's music, *separated from its words,* the status of a poetic work: "Indeed, even without the poetry Wagner's music would be a poetic work, being endowed with all the qualities of a well-made poem, explicative in itself, so well is everything in it unified, joined, reciprocally balanced. . . ." See Baudelaire, "Richard Wagner et *Tannhäuser* à Paris," in *Œuvres complètes,* ed. Y.-G. Le Dantec and Claude Pichois (Paris: Gallimard, 1961), 1232. The use of the term "explicative" is extremely significant, as it refers at once to the conceptual power of language and to "unfolding," as of the pages of a book.

[15]For Saint-Saëns on Liszt, see his long essay, "Liszt," in *Harmonie et mélodie,* 2nd ed. (Paris: Calmann-Lévy, 1885), 153–172.

[16]Considering symphonic music as a vehicle for ideas, Liszt took literary works as the starting point for eleven of his thirteen symphonic poems. In only two, then, was he directly inspired by visual art: *Hunnenschlacht (The Battle of the Huns)* (1857), after a fresco by Wilhelm von Kaulbach; and *Von der Wiege bis zum Grabe (From the Cradle to the Grave)* (1881–1882), after a drawing by Mihály Zichy. In neither case, however, did he change his motivic technique appreciably, and the "transfiguring" symbolism associated with the other, literary, symphonic poems remained central to his musical conception. *Von der Wiege bis zum Grabe* is particularly interesting in this respect. By dividing his work into three "vignettes" or sections, Liszt took a direct structural cue from Zichy's drawing, but this very structure is what makes the visual work explicitly narrative and allegorical, and Liszt's musical reflection of it turns out once again to be a "symphony of ideas."

[17]Saint-Saëns, "Liszt," 160–161.

[18]Saint-Saëns, *Les idées de M. Vincent d'Indy* (Paris: Lafitte, 1919), 7–8.

[19]Saint-Saëns, "L'art pour l'art," in *École buissonière: Notes et souvenirs* (Paris: Lafitte, 1913), 136–137.

[20]Saint-Saëns, *Les idées,* 7.

[21]See Liszt, "Berlioz und seine *Harold-Symphonie,*" in *Gesammelte Schriften,* 4:58–59; also Saint-Saëns, "Liszt," 160.

[22]I should add that Saint-Saëns did not make the division between the arts and literature absolute; he thought that literature "begins to enter art through verse and withdraws from it by prose" ("L'art pour l'art," 138).

[23]It is strange to observe that Saint-Saëns's symphonic poem would go on to inspire a painting. In *Saint-Saëns: Le rouet d'Omphale* (c. 1931), the Swiss "musicalist" painter Charles Blanc-Gatti translated Saint-Saëns's music into an abstract pattern of overlapping circles defined in graduated hues. Philippe Junod kindly acquainted me with this painting, which is reproduced in his book, *La musique vue par les peintres* (Lausanne: Vilo/Edita, 1988), 139.

[24]See Franz Brendel, "F. Liszt's symphonische Dichtungen," *Neue Zeitschrift für Musik* 49 (1858), 98–99, 109–110, 112, 121–122.

[25]Boutarel, 54.

[26]See Saint-Saëns, "Les peintres musiciens," in *École buissonnière,* 349–355.

[27]We may think also of his operas *Samson et Dalila, Phryné* and *Hélène.*

[28]See rehearsal letter M, four bars before the return to the main tempo (page 33).

[29]Arthur Hervey, *Saint-Saëns* (New York: Dodd Mead, 1922), 87.

[30]Georges Servières, *Saint-Saëns* (Paris: Alcan, 1930), 123.

[31]Twelve measures after rehearsal letter O (pages 40–41).

[32]This interpretation of the ending also suggests an isolated point of contact between Saint-Saëns's music and Hugo's poem. Hugo presents an allusive, silent scene. Hercules and Omphale are not present in the text of the poem but only represented by their emblems, the spinning wheel and the club, and the spinning wheel is idle from the start; a thread hangs from it untended. Hugo's deliberate emphasis on absence leads one to the speculation that he, too, may have wished us to infer that the hero and his mistress were enjoying their leisure in another room of the palace. See Cellier's notes in Victor Hugo, *Les contemplations,* ed. Léon Cellier (Paris: Garnier-Frères, 1969), 542. Our initial observation is still true; there are no echoes of Hugo's poem in Saint-Saëns's music. But the symphonic poem may be thought of as a kind of prelude to Hugo's silent scenario— or better yet, a *pre-text* (Latin, *prætexere,* "to weave before").

[33]For the successive sales of Gleyre's painting, see William Hauptman, *Charles Gleyre, 1806–1874* (Zurich: Swiss Institute for Art Research; Princeton: Princeton University Press, 1996), 1:262–263, 2:436–437; and Charles Clément, *Gleyre: Étude biographique et critique* (Paris: Didier, 1878), 419.

³⁴This painting, formerly belonging to the Minnesota Museum of Art, was sold in 1976. See Sotheby Parke Bernet, sale catalogue, *19th-Century European Paintings: Property of Various Owners,* Sale 3873, May 14, 1976, New York, lot 241.

³⁵So far as I can see, there is nothing feminine about Hercules's drapery. Charles Clément, in his extremely detailed description of the painting, treats Hercules's clothing in neutral terms: "Sa draperie est rejetée en arrière." Since Clément is explicitly distressed by Gleyre's choice of a theme that shows Hercules in an unflattering, unmanly state, he would have had every reason to cite any effeminate traits to make his case (see Clément, 419). Clément's interpretation of the painting as a whole is curiously bifocal: he begins, very much in opposition to my interpretation, by despising Omphale for her "disdainful, mocking air" and Amor for his "malicious and perfidious expression" (289). But within a few pages he waxes enthusiastic and ends up asking if "there is not, in the Queen's expression . . . some trace of feeling and goodness?" (294).

³⁶Clément (419) notes that the miniature group atop the Ionian column (in the background between Hercules and Omphale) represents a statue of Astarte and Amor in the "Musée de la Campagne à Rome" (probably the Museo Civico Archeologico at Campagnano di Roma).

³⁷Théodore de Banville was among those who criticized Boulanger's painting in 1861. Some of his remarks have been reprinted, alongside those of Théophile Gautier and Gustave Bertrand, by François Brunet in his critical edition of Banville's *Exilés,* vol. 4 of the *Œuvres poétiques complètes* (Paris: Champion, 1994), 374–375. Brunet suggests that Banville's irritation with a "madrigalesque tradition" behind the painting (Banville's words) was what inspired the composition of "La Reine Omphale" (1861), which depicts Omphale's transformation from haughty mistress to lovestruck companion. Omphale's self-abasement before Hercules in Banville's poem places it very far indeed from Boulanger's canvas. But the poet goes beyond even Gleyre and Saint-Saëns, for neither of the latter went to so far as to put Omphale in a suppliant position: "La grande Omphale avait les yeux baignés de pleurs. . . . Elle s'agenouilla, baisant les pieds d'Hercule. / Elle courbait son front orgueilleux et vaincu, / Et ses lourds cheveux roux couvraient son sein aigu."

³⁸Alfred Heuss, "Eine motivisch-thematische Studie über Liszt's sinfonische Dichtung *Ce qu'on entend sur la montagne,*" *Zeitschrift der internationalen Musikgesellschaft* 13, no.1 (1911): 20.

³⁹The exception is Saint-Saëns's last symphonic poem, *La jeunesse d'Hercule,* the only one of the four that clearly cleaves to the Lisztian model. The extramusical elements behind this music, the struggle between "virtue" and "pleasure" in the life of the Greek hero, have no obvious analogues in physical

movement. That is, the conflict Saint-Saëns sets up as the motivating idea of the piece provides no cues for imitation (such as spinning, galloping, or dancing). Significantly, Saint-Saëns resorts to some ten different musical ideas, in contrast to the thematic parsimony of the preceding symphonic poems, and *La jeunesse d'Hercule* is twice as long as the longest of the other three. Likewise, his formal strategies here are closer to Liszt, and the resulting piece is episodic. The work has long been considered the least successful of Saint-Saëns's symphonic poems and is the least often performed. Could it have failed in some respects because Saint-Saëns abandoned his expressed tendencies as a formalist and thus produced a work that, while breaking the bonds of his self-imposed restraint, also proved too grand for the expressive material he was able to invest in it?

CHAPTER 7

Painting *Around the Piano*
Fantin-Latour, Wagnerism, and the Musical in Art

LISA NORRIS

> *But, of course, the real villain is Wagner. He has*
> *done more than any man in the nineteenth cen-*
> *tury towards the muddling of the arts. . . . Every*
> *now and then in history there do come these*
> *terrible geniuses, like Wagner, who stir up all*
> *the wells of thought at once.*
> —E.M. FORSTER, *HOWARD'S END,* 1910

Emmanuel Chabrier sits at the keyboard in Henri Fantin-Latour's painting *Around the Piano* (Figure 7–1). In the history of Wagnerism in
France, Chabrier is perhaps best known for throwing his head into his
hands and sobbing, "I've waited for ten years to hear that A on the cellos!" when he heard the first notes of Richard Wagner's *Tristan und
Isolde* in Munich in 1879. So tremendous was the work's impact on the
forty-eight-year-old French music lover that he abandoned his career as a
lawyer to become a composer. Wagner's music repeatedly overwhelmed
Chabrier. At a performance of *Parsifal* in 1889, he stammered that at the
end of each act he found himself "bewildered, distraught, with tears run-
ning down my cheeks. It is worse than *Tristan* at Munich. What can I
say? It is sublime from beginning to end."[1]

Perhaps more astonishing than Chabrier's hysteria is the fact that
such strong reactions to Wagner's work were common among French
Wagner enthusiasts, who called the German composer "maître." Such
fervent devotion is more comprehensible when one considers that during
the nineteenth century, music was increasingly perceived as the most in-

Figure 7–1. Henri Fantin-Latour, *Around the Piano,* 1885, oil on canvas, 160 × 222 cm., Musée d'Orsay, Paris. Seated figures include, from left: Emmanuel Chabrier, Edmond Maître, Amédée Pigeon; standing figures, from left: Adolphe Jullien, Arthur Boisseau, Camille Benoît, Antoine Lascoux, Vincent d'Indy.

novative and powerful of the arts.[2] In France especially, profound shifts in musical taste occurred with the introduction of Germanic symphonic music.[3] By the later nineteenth century, the music dramas of Richard Wagner specifically emblematized the enormous potency of music in the culture, and his aesthetic theories were taken by some as a guide for innovation in, and even the salvation of, all the arts. Charles Baudelaire was the first important figure in France to proclaim Wagner as the spearhead of this development in 1861, and his view would be echoed with increasing frequency. As the critic Octave Mirbeau pronounced in 1887, "Wagner is assuredly the most sublime expression of Art in the nineteenth century. . . ."[4] Fantin-Latour himself had long held this opinion, having declared in 1876 that Wagner's work was "certainly the Art of the future."[5]

Fantin's *Around the Piano,* exhibited at the 1885 Salon, heralded the artist's allegiance to Wagnerism, one of the most controversial aesthetic and political phenomena in later nineteenth-century French culture. His involvement with Wagnerism is most evident just when the movement peaked in Paris between 1885–1888. In addition to *Around the Piano,* Fantin also exhibited two lithographs of Wagnerian subjects at the 1885 Salon.[6] That year Fantin made another lithograph, the *Evocation of Erda* (third version) for the new, fanatical *Revue wagnérienne.* During 1886, Fantin produced fourteen new lithographs for a major biography of Wagner as well as a second oil of *Tannhäuser on the Venusberg* and a pastel of *Siegfried and the Rheinmaidens* for the Salon. He exhibited three more Wagnerian lithographs at the 1887 Salon, and the next year he showed his last large-scale Wagnerian work, the oil version of *Das Rheingold: Opening Scene.*[7]

Critics acclaimed Fantin's submissions to the 1885 Salon. The Wagner disciple and aesthetic theorist Téodor de Wyzewa even declared him the supreme Wagnerist artist who paid a double homage to the composer with the subject of *Around the Piano* and the "musical" style of his lithographs.[8] From this time, Fantin's art was increasingly referred to as "painted music,"[9] and his reputation grew as "the painter who made music visible."[10] This essay follows Wyzewa's dual designation for Fantin by exploring how the subject of *Around the Piano* demonstrates his immersion in Wagnerism and by explaining how Fantin's contemporaries understood the "musicality" of his style.

Wagnerism in Paris originated in the early 1860s and, although its history lies outside the focus of this essay, its major events do correspond to the development of Fantin's interest in music. The young artist had shown an unusual penchant for music from the 1850s, when he formed the first of a number of friendships that introduced him to progressive music, such as that with German musician and artist Otto Scholderer and with Edwin and Ruth Edwards in the 1880s.[11] In February 1860 Fantin attended one of three concerts where Wagner's works were performed under the composer's own baton. These were essentially the first performances of his music in Paris, and they aroused a storm of controversy, as did the premier of Wagner's *Tannhäuser* the following year. The furor forced the opera to close after the third performance, enraging Fantin, who had a ticket for the fourth. In response to the scandal he created his first lithograph, *Tannhäuser on the Venusberg,* based on the overture he had heard in concert form. For the 1864 Salon he submitted an oil version of *Tannhäuser on the Venusberg* (Figure 7–2) as well as his first major uncommissioned group portrait, the *Homage to Delacroix* (Figure 7–3).

These two paintings connect in several respects. Through them the

Figure 7–2. Henri Fantin-Latour, *Tannhäuser on the Venusberg,* 1864, oil on canvas, 97.5 130.2 cm., Los Angeles County Museum of Art, Gift of Mr. and Mrs. Charles Boyer.

batailleur Fantin supported Wagner as well as his friends James Whistler and Edouard Manet, who flank Delacroix's portrait in the *Homage.* As Wagner had scandalized Paris, so had these two painters in 1863 with their exhibitions of the *White Girl* and *Luncheon on the Grass* at the *Salon des refusés.* The presence of Baudelaire and Jules Champfleury flanking Manet in the *Homage* tie the two paintings together, since these critics had published two of the earliest and most ardent defenses of the composer in response to the tempests of 1860 and 1861.[12] In fact, Douglas Druick has noted that Fantin possibly intended the *Tannhäuser* lithograph as a visual counterpart to their verbal support of Wagner.[13] Fantin's decision to portray himself in a seated position like Baudelaire and Champfleury reinforces the connection of the three as defenders of avant-garde artists. Furthermore, in his painting of *Tannhäuser* Fantin employed Delacroix's palette, which is also referred to in the *Homage* by the bouquet and by the palette the artist holds.[14] Delacroix himself was a "mélomane" (an extreme music lover) who had stated that color alone, acting independently from the description of objects, had an abstract

Figure 7–3. Henri Fantin–Latour, *Homage to Delacroix,* 1864, oil on canvas, 160 × 250 cm., Musée d'Orsay, Paris. Seated figures include, from left: Edmond Duranty, Henri Fantin–Latour, Jules Champfleury, Charles Baudelaire; standing figures, from left: Louis Cordier, Alphonse Legros, James McNeill Whistler, Édouard Manet, Félix Bracquemond, Albert de Balleroy.

communicative power like that of music.[15] This notion, which Baudelaire promoted in his articles on Delacroix, would become essential to the development of a "musical" aesthetic in the later part of the century.

Throughout the 1860s, Fantin's involvement with music was steady. He attended public concerts with his closest friend, the pianist Edmond Maître (seated prominently in *Around the Piano,* leaning into the instrument), along with Pierre-Auguste Renoir and Frédéric Bazille.[16] It is likely that at these concerts they heard orchestral renderings of portions of Wagner's music dramas, since the works were being performed with growing regularity and acceptance.[17] Yet throughout his life, piano transcriptions were Fantin's primary means of satisfying his craving for music, although he himself did not play. During the 1860s Fantin listened almost nightly to Maître and Bazille play duets of transcribed music by "progressive" composers such as Brahms and Schumann, the latter his favorite.[18] He also heard Mme. Manet and Mme. Meurice play such pieces together. His ever-expanding knowledge of modern—particularly German—music is evidenced by his letters to the Edwardses and others. Fantin's preferences were clear; he stated approvingly: "Schumann and Wagner are the Music of the future."[19]

Fantin struggled in the second half of the 1860s to reconcile the realist orientation of his generation with his own proclivity for fantasy, which he associated with music.[20] He had even remarked cryptically to his parents in 1864, "[T]his music of the future, I would present it. It is what I would like to do if I were a musician, alas!"[21] His support for the notion of the unity of the arts, fueled by his understanding of both Wagner and Baudelaire, may have motivated Fantin's *Toast! Homage to Truth* of 1864–1865. Using friends such as Manet and Whistler to symbolize their respective art forms, Fantin represented the visual arts, music, and literature gathered in solidarity around an allegorical figure of Truth. The juxtaposition of real and allegorical figures was awkward, however, and the painting failed. Fantin attempted to conjoin *réalité* and *rêve* again in his 1869 *Reflets d'Orient*. This time he depicted a "real" figure (Scholderer as Schumann) surrounded by fantastic imagery conjured by the composer's music. The Salon jury rejected the painting and Fantin destroyed it as he had the *Toast!,* conceding that in both cases he had not been able to present the two realms as one. Yet these disappointments did not diminish his rising interest in fantasy to which music irresistibly drew him. In March 1869 he told Edwin Edwards that naturalism would always factor into his art, but he wanted to manifest more of his "self" by depicting what he imagined; he particularly recalled his *Tannhäuser* as a successful example.[22]

As he turned more to fantasy, Fantin preferred the company of musicians and poets to realist-oriented painters.[23] Even in his homage to Manet, *An Atelier in the Batignolles* (Figure 7–4), music's presence is felt, since the image is populated with Fantin's *mélomane* friends: Manet, Maître, Scholderer, Bazille, and Renoir.[24] The painting dates from just before the Franco-Prussian War of 1870–1871, which demonized Wagner in Parisian eyes and halted performances of his work. And although the war took Bazille's life, Maître continued to indulge Fantin's need to hear music with a new duet partner, Adolphe Jullien, the eventual owner of *Around the Piano*.[25] The two musicians provided Fantin with access to Wagner's music at a time when very few heard it in Paris. Later, as war-related hostility subsided in the latter 1870s, Wagner's works were increasingly heard at public concerts. However, anti-German sentiment flared again in the mid-1880s, causing attempts to stage full productions to be thwarted by the small but extremely potent band of *revanchistes*.

Figure 7–4. Henri Fantin–Latour, *An Atelier in the Batignolles,* 1870, oil on canvas, 204 × 273.5 cm., Musée d'Orsay, Paris. Seated figures include, from left: Édouard Manet, Zacharie Astruc; standing figures, from left: Otto Scholderer, Auguste Renoir, Émile Zola, Edmond Maître, Frédéric Bazille, Claude Monet.

The high point of Fantin's experience of Wagner's work occurred in 1876 when he saw the first full production of the *Ring des Nibelungen* at the theater especially constructed for it in Bayreuth, Germany. Fantin's presence is quite remarkable, as there were very few French attendees present at all and, within this small minority, most were professional musicians, composers, or music critics. This event marked the pivotal point in Fantin's career, for it sparked his production of lithographs as an outlet for his interest in fantasy, which he would pursue until about 1889.[26] Indeed, Fantin remarked to Edwards that the experience at Bayreuth "changed [his] ideas,"[27] leading him to develop a unique, "musical" lithographic style that excited much critical attention by the mid-1880s.

The first lithograph he made after Bayreuth was *Das Rheingold: Opening Scene* (Figure 7–5), the first complete scene of any Wagnerian music drama Fantin himself had witnessed. Although the "musicality" of Fantin's style is addressed below, it is worth noting here that even at this

Figure 7–5. Henri Fantin-Latour, *Das Rheingold: Opening Scene,* 1876, lithograph, 51 × 33.7 cm., Courtesy of the Boston Public Library, Print Department, Gift of Albert H. Wiggin.

early date, his singular technique was associated with music. Upon receiving a copy of the lithograph as a gift from Fantin, the Symbolist poet
Stéphane Mallarmé rhapsodised that it was "marvelous . . . . how one
senses that all this is seen through music. . . ."[28]

Originally known as *Souvenir of Bayreuth,* this lithograph was dedicated to Antoine Lascoux, who had enabled Fantin to attend the festival.
Fantin had met Lascoux when, with Maître and Manet, he attended musical soirees given by Lascoux's father in the 1860s.[29] Lascoux, who stands
nobly in *Around the Piano* to the right with hand to chest, was a pivotal
figure for Fantin's exposure to Wagner. In fact, all of the figures in
Around the Piano not only contributed to Fantin's love and knowledge of
music; they were all somehow involved with the Wagnerist "cause." Fantin's choice to depict these Wagnerians together when Wagnerism began
to peak in Paris provides an opportunity to investigate the movement itself and Fantin's involvement with it.

First, what prompted Fantin's painting? The artist's timing was aus-
picious, both for himself and for the Wagnerists. Although Fantin sought
success at the annual Salon exhibitions, his work had not drawn substantial attention since 1878 when he exhibited a group portrait of the
Dubourg family.[30] Fantin's letters indicate that he carefully planned his
Salon entries with an eye to acclaim. He had precedents for success, as
well as *succès de scandale,* in his uncommissioned group portraits. Furthermore, Fantin must already have known that his *Homage to Delacroix*
would feature prominently at the "Portraits of the Century" exhibition,
which was due to run concurrently with the 1885 Salon. He may have
then reasoned that a new group-portrait-cum-homage would draw additional public notice.[31] Thus, an idea dating from 1872 for a tableau of
women gathered around a piano metamorphosed into a group portrait.[32]
The new plan took form sometime between Wagner's death in 1883 and
1884, as the composer became the key figure in heated cultural debates
that would escalate tremendously, especially for political reasons, over
the next few years.[33] Fantin's choice of Wagner *devotés* as the subject for
a group portrait was therefore both shrewd and consistent with his reputation as a *batailleur* for controversial artists and art movements.

Fantin remarked to Ruth Edwards that, as he had done in the past, he
again wanted to depict a meeting of a "group of artists" of which he was
a part.[34] He meant "Petit Bayreuth," which Lascoux had created after his
return from the *Ring* in 1876. Initially this was a group that gathered privately at Lascoux's home to perform portions of Wagner's works (especially *Parsifal* after its premier at Bayreuth in 1882) with a reduced

orchestra. A few select listeners including Fantin were also invited.[35] Hugues Imbert, a musicologist who knew the artist, claimed it was Petit Bayreuth that inspired Fantin to make this "beau tableau."[36]

One could argue that Lascoux was the keystone of the Wagnerist movement in France. He was one of the few who maintained personal ties with Wagner's widow Cosima after the composer's death, informing her about the status of her husband's reception in Paris throughout the 1880s and '90s.[37] In addition to Petit Bayreuth, Lascoux financially supported the radical *Revue wagnérienne,* published between 1885 and 1888, even after its extremism alienated all of its other backers.[38] He was also associated with Charles Lamoureux, the conductor who often played first violin at Petit Bayreuth while Lascoux himself led the musicians. Lascoux also helped Lamoureux with various productions of Wagner's music dramas beginning in 1886.

By virtue of his (in)famous public concerts at the Eden Theater, Lamoureux was the highest profile Wagnerist of the 1880s, and he dedicated himself completely to the promotion of Wagner's art.[39] In January 1885 he even turned down the directorship of the Paris Opéra because he would be prohibited from staging Wagner's music dramas. After some consideration he declined, saying, "I could never deny my gods."[40] From their inception in 1881, Lamoureux's Sunday concerts contributed immeasurably to the public's exposure to Wagner's music, and he also premiered the work of progressive French composers, most of whom had succumbed to Wagner's influence. Such concerts were a rich resource for Fantin's musical education. Yet given the increasingly germanophobic climate, including Lamoureux in *Around the Piano* would have been quite inflammatory.[41] As Jullien pointed out, Fantin excluded Lamoureux precisely because he "was then the most determined champion of the Wagnerian cause. . . ."[42]

Instead of portraying Lamoureux, Fantin foregrounded two other Petit Bayreuth members, Chabrier and Vincent d'Indy, the last of whom stands with the cigarette holder next to Lascoux. Imbert noted that Chabrier often attended Petit Bayreuth in 1884–1885,[43] and d'Indy's devotion to Wagner's ideas was total at this time.[44] Both Chabrier and d'Indy worked with Lamoureux, and their compositions were heard at his concerts.[45] Thus Fantin indicated the importance of the concerts for Wagnerism without actually including the conductor. By their prominent placement in the painting he also hailed these two composers as the primary innovators of their art, as he had done for Manet and Whistler in the *Homage to Delacroix* and Paul Verlaine and Arthur Rimbaud *A Corner of a Table,* Fantin's 1872 group portrait in homage to avant-garde poets.

In truth, the sitters gathered in *Around the Piano* are "all Wagner-ists!" as Fantin exclaimed privately in 1885.[46] In addition to Lascoux, Chabrier, and d'Indy, Fantin included the respected music critic Jullien, who is top-hatted and standing to the left.[47] This prominent cultural figure published a major Wagner biography in 1886. He dedicated it to his close friend Fantin, whose lithographs accompanied the work. Clearly Jullien contributed to Fantin's knowledge of music, as did two of the remaining figures in the painting. The musician Camille Benoît, who turns the pages of music, was a friend of Fantin's from the 1850s, and he translated Wagner's writings. Furthermore, he had accompanied d'Indy to the Bayreuth *Ring* cycle and was a regular at Petit Bayreuth.[48] Amédée Pigeon, seated at the far right, wrote articles on German-related topics for such publications as *Figaro* and the *Gazette des beaux-arts*.[49] The last figure, who stands beside Jullien at the far left of the painting, is violinist Arthur Boisseau, another performer at Petit Bayreuth.[50]

For Fantin personally, *Around the Piano* paid homage to those through whom he enjoyed the most progressive music of the time, in forms ranging from full productions of Wagner's works to piano transcriptions heard in private settings. This exposure gave Fantin a far greater musical education than the average concertgoer in Paris could claim; Pigeon noted that the artist was unusually erudite.[51] For the public, his painting acclaimed major Wagnerists, and a number of critics, not fooled by the generic title, specifically described the subject as such. The pseudonymous "Cesario," for example, stated that the portrait created "the impression of an audition of Wagner," and he remarked that "the well known fanaticism of the Wagnerian painter and the presence of M. Chabrier . . . . quickly baptised the work . . . . [as *The Wagnerians*]" at the Salon.[52]

While Fantin remarked to Ruth Edwards that *Around the Piano* extended his series commemorating "painters, poets, [and] musicians,"[53] the art form of music which unites the figures was also venerated here. Just as the two earlier group portraits celebrate painting and poetry, *Around the Piano* pays tribute to music, the art form that guided his fantasy work. Like the bouquet in the *Homage* composed of the colors in Delacroix's palette, the sheet music in the *Piano* clearly draws the eye. Its brightness, the diagonal slope of the piano's lid and the arrangement of the hands all direct the viewer to the nearly centrally placed music, while its sliver of blue-green provides the image's only note of color aside from some fairly prominent red in the flesh tones. Visually, just as the figures in the *Homage* cup the color of the bouquet, the darkly painted mélomanes cradle the luminous music, as if to offer it to the viewer.

As a celebration of the art form acknowledged to be the most powerful of the age and as a tribute to those Wagnerists most active in championing the composer's work, *Around the Piano* did elicit a great deal of
critical attention, as Fantin must have hoped. Reviews were generally
quite enthusiastic; some even claimed *Around the Piano* as the best
painting of the year. A few, like Gustave Geffroy, grumbled that the work
lacked compositional unity,[54] but a number of others applauded the
shared "sentiment" that united the sitters. Octave Maus described "a collective of men united in a common sentiment, the love of music, and
more especially the admiration of Wagner." Further, "in this superb canvas . . . . one hears the distant resonance of harmonies that unite the
souls, like beautiful chords. A thought hovers, elevating the tableau well
above the material reproduction of known faces and giving the ensemble,
despite the diversity of individuals, the unity of sentiment and expression
that makes a work of art."[55]

In addition to the shared love of music, critics commented upon the
painting's unity of form. André Michel noted a visual unity suggested by
the "voluntarily veiled color" and the atmosphere created by the consistently applied, heavy brushstrokes and closely valued tonalities.[56] Mirbeau concurred; he applauded the "envelope" and "vibration of air" that
synthesized and abstracted the work, leading him to conclude that "no
one is more essentially modern" than Fantin.[57] Roger Marx, who also described "an absolute conformity of tastes, ideas and sentiments" among
the figures, was another who praised *Around the Piano* as "incomparably
original."[58] Such descriptions of Fantin's formal qualities, especially
with regard to atmospheric effects, were usually raised in relation to the
"musical" style of his lithographs, four of which hung in the same Salon.
Indeed, it is in the critical discourse on Fantin's lithographs that a specific language of musicality emerges, beginning in the mid-1880s and escalating until by the time of his death in 1904, the musical essence of
Fantin's work was assumed.[59]

When considering how Fantin's "musical" lithographs were understood, it is important to clarify that critics did not find them to be musical
because they illustrated operatic narratives. Rather, they specifically
stated that Fantin *evoked* the music itself, or equivalents to the emotions
expressed by the music that had inspired them. For example, an American writer insisted that Fantin did not illustrate staged scenes, but instead
"wrapped his soul in music. Then he took his crayons and with wondrous
dexterity drew . . . . the visions he heard."[60] One must recall that although he frequented public concerts regularly, these were essentially or-

chestral performances, and Fantin attended operas only a handful of times. He *saw* very little in the way of staged musical narratives. His everyday experience of music was through transcriptions for piano; indeed, the prominence of the instrument in *Around the Piano* could well commemorate the means through which Fantin most often enjoyed music. Thus, despite the theatrical nature of the subjects, the notion that Fantin attempted to evoke emotional equivalents of what he had *heard* makes sense.[61] And since Fantin's own musical experiences were themselves essentially evocations, his preoccupation with subjects of evocation, conjuring or apparition, such as *The Evocation of Erda* (Figure 7–6) and *Lohengrin: Prelude* (Figure 7–7) seems almost inevitable.[62] There is ample evidence that Fantin became transported to realms of visionary fantasy or sank into reveries upon listening to music; Fantin himself repeatedly noted this in his letters, including those from Bayreuth.[63] Thus, the subjects of his musical images were chosen as a way to capture the emotional intensity of the *rêves* that the music conjured in his imagination,[64] and critics rightly understood that the musicality of the lithographs resided not in their subjects but in their form.

The writer who examined "the musical in art" most thoroughly was Wyzewa, a Wagner fanatic and Symbolist who wrote essays on Wagnerian painting, literature, and music in the *Revue wagnérienne* and elsewhere. His aesthetic derived from extrapolations of Wagner's theory of the *Gesamtkunstwerk,* Baudelaire's theory of Correspondences (which the poet himself had related to Wagner), and Mallarmé's filtering of the two.[65] When Wyzewa first addressed the musical in art in his 1885 Salon review, he cited Fantin's work as the primary example. He stated that two types of painting exist: that which describes physical reality, as seen in paintings like *Around the Piano,* and that which creates a "poem of plastic emotion" through line and tone and therefore more directly "feels" and "expresses" life. The latter is "Wagnerian" and is demonstrated in Fantin's lithographs.[66]

Wyzewa explained this idea more fully when he reviewed a publication of ten platinotypes from Fantin's lithographs in 1887.[67] He, too, stated that it was not the musical subjects that made Fantin's work "Wagnerian." Rather, Fantin "has yet wanted to be, by the processes of drawing and color, a musician: to express special emotions . . . . by means of their combination alone. . . . And in the work of Wagner he has chosen very precise emotions, that he then transposes into pictorial language: [he is] perfectly unconcerned with scenic exactitude, traditions of costumes or decors, completely occupied with the intimate sense of the

Figure 7–6. Henri Fantin-Latour, *The Evocation of Erda* (third version), 1885, lithograph, 20.8 × 12.7 cm., Courtesy of the Boston Public Library, Print Department, Gift of Albert H. Wiggin.

Figure 7–7. Henri Fantin-Latour, *Lohengrin: Prelude* (first version), 1882, lithograph, 48.5 × 34.4 cm., Courtesy of the Boston Public Library, Print Department, Gift of Albert H. Wiggin.

scenes. . . ." Further on Wyzewa praised Fantin's works as "symphonies"
and "sonatas," calling them "original poems, where the harmonious
plays of pale shadows and lascivious whites evoke, without even the aid
of musical memories," the various emotions of the chosen scenes.[68]

A number of critics made similar assertions in language closely resembling that of Wyzewa. Fairly frequently, they invoked Baudelaire's
Correspondences between music and painting in this regard. One of the
first to treat Fantin's lithographs as a synaesthetic endeavor was Geffroy,
writing on *Tannhäuser: The Evening Star* in his review of the 1884 Paris
Salon. Calling upon Baudelaire, he noted that Fantin "has attempted the
union of the two arts; he has sought by means of the vibrations obtained
with the black and white to represent scenes he has glimpsed in the harmonies of the musicians he likes; he can be said to have often succeeded;
some of these sketches create a musical impression. . . . The dream figures appear in the shadows and in the light; they tremble, move, fade
away like the musician's languid phrases; they stand out against brilliant backgrounds and suggest . . . . [sic] an impression of ringing short
notes. . . . They represent an astonishing transposition of art. . . ."[69]

The stylistic qualities noted by Geffroy are seen in *Das Rheingold:
Opening Scene, Lohengrin: Prelude,* and *The Evocation of Erda.* In all
three, line obscures form and creates the sensation of a scintillating atmosphere and light. Geffroy's language here and that of other critics at
times echo descriptions of Wagner's musical style itself, with their emphases on imprecision, lush atmospheres, and dizzying effects. Léonce
Bénédite's sentiments on Fantin's work offer another example. He said
that Fantin's fantasy figures "live and breathe in a fairy world . . . impre-
cise, confused as in a dream, which accompanies them and envelopes
them equally in a savvily orchestrated, truly musical harmony."[70]

Interestingly, the work of Fantin's Impressionist colleagues was also
being discussed in such terms. The most prominent early example of this
is found in Jules Laforgue's essay of 1883, "The Eye and the Poet." Ad-
dressing the landscapes of Camille Pissarro and Claude Monet, he stated
that "everything is obtained by a thousand little dancing strokes in every
direction like straws of colour—all in vital competition for the whole impression. No longer an isolated melody, the whole thing is a symphony
which is living and changing like the 'forest voices' of Wagner . . . . like
the Unconscious, the law of the world, which is the great melodic voice
resulting from the symphony of the consciousness of races and individuals. Such is the principle of the *plein-air* Impressionist school."[71]
Laforgue's views reflect the growing preoccupation with synaesthesia

and musicality among poets and *litterateurs* of the time, most notably Symbolists like Wyzewa, who congregated around Mallarmé. Their primary inspirations in this regard were of course Wagner and Baudelaire, two of Fantin's own idols from the early 1860s.

In fact, Fantin's style was regularly discussed in terms of Baudelaire's notion of synaesthesia. Geffroy referred to the poet a second time when in the 1890s he observed that "one could almost apply in its entirety the verse of Baudelaire in the conceptions of the painter-poet infatuated with the harmonies of lines and colors and the rhythms of music: 'the forms, colors and sounds respond to each other.' "[72] Raymond Bouyer also related Fantin's work to synaesthesia, wherein "by a natural phenomenon of *audition colorée,* the remembered melodies assimilated by the painter's soul are transfigured into vaporously precise decors,"[73] and he concluded in 1903 that Fantin's work itself is "a symphony, a music."[74] Roger Marx was another who called upon Baudelaire's Correspondences as the source for Fantin's endeavor to capture "the fugitive impression of the music," declaring in 1904 that Fantin created "plastic equivalents" for the music rather than illustrations of specific operatic scenes.[75]

By the early twentieth century, one is hard pressed to find statements on Fantin that do not refer to musicality. In 1903, Prosper Dorbec described more precisely than most the musical essence of Fantin's art: "Just as the Wagnerian work has considerably increased the importance of [orchestration], with Fantin-Latour, this melodic theme floats amid a complex ambiance where colored shadows offer a cradling of bluish half-tints, where lights play in multiple prismatic tints. The figure is thus surrounded by sonorous vibrations that exhale on it and wet its contours like waves. In this effect, the Master proceeds by little juxtaposed touches or tangled dashes of the paintbrush, identical to the thousand harmonies of diverse instruments."[76] This language again recalls Laforgue's on the Impressionists, and in fact, Dorbec specifically attributed these "musical" techniques, which Fantin employed so successfully, to them.[77]

Many critics in addition to those cited above referred to Fantin's ability to "orchestrate" his forms and color, to "transpose" the music or create a visual equivalent to the emotions called forth by it.[78] The idea of transposition between music and art had been broached in Wyzewa's "Wagnerist" Salon review of 1886. To demonstrate how this was possible he first explained that humans can be stimulated in three ways: by sensation, notion, and emotion. Each of these corresponds to an art form.

Sensation, an external stimulus, is addressed by the formal elements of painting. When the soul thinks in response to sensations, *notions* are born; these pertain to literature. Gradually, sensations and thoughts accumulate and mix, creating imprecision, confusion, and even a rather drunken state; at this point *emotions,* the highest of the three modes of address, are born. Music alone stimulates emotional responses directly, and as such is the superior art form.[79]

In asserting music's hegemony, Wyzewa upheld an opinion that was rooted in eighteenth-century German Idealist philosophy and voiced with increasing frequency throughout the nineteenth century by such prominent figures as Thomas Carlyle, John Ruskin, and Hippolyte Taine.[80] In the mid-1880s, Wyzewa's Symbolist generation adapted these ideas enthusiastically. They also became enamored of Arthur Schopenhauer's notion of the Will and its direct manifestation in music. The German philosopher's writings became known in France after about 1860, in part through Wagner's own Schopenhauer-inspired views on music.[81] In fact, Wyzewa was especially preoccupied with these ideas. In 1885 he published in the *Revue wagnérienne* both "Le Pessimisme de Richard Wagner" and a translation with analysis of "Beethoven," the primary essay of Wagner's later career in which the influence of Schopenhauer is quite evident.[82]

Wyzewa insisted in his 1886 review of Fantin's work that a musical visual art could exist because it can bypass the intellect altogether, as music did, with sensations evoking feeling immediately through age-old associations between lines, forms, and particular emotions. Therefore a "musical" artist could transpose the emotions that music had directly aroused by using form and color abstractly instead of employing them to describe physical objects. The musical artist, Wyzewa said, "neglect[s] the concern of objects that the colors and lines represent, taking [colors and lines] only as signs of emotions, wedding them in a fashion to produce in us, by their free play, a total impression comparable to a symphony."[83] This is precisely the language in which Fantin's works were being discussed from the mid-1880s until after his death. Roger Marx, for example, said that in Fantin's work, "the sensation provoked by the sounds is spontaneously transformed into an image by passing through the brain of a painter. . . ."[84] Pierre Jobbé-Duval was more detailed in his estimation of Fantin's paintings: "[O]n each canvas the colors respond to each other in magnificent chords and give the sensation of a symphony where the nuances substituted for the notes replace the auditory emotion by the visual impression. Yes, this art . . . . [is] the work of a musician who would paint."[85]

Fantin's own accounts to Maître of the *Ring* at Bayreuth in 1876 contain observations that resonate remarkably with Wyzewa's system as stated ten years later. Concerning the opening to *Das Rheingold,* Fantin exclaimed, "[N]othing is like it. It is a *sensation* not yet proven [or felt]." And "here, as in all the rest, it's about *sensation.* Not the music, the decor, the subject; but the way it grips [one]. . . ." Furthermore, Fantin referred to the suspension of the intellect and his unmediated reception of the work on a primal emotional level: "I saw myself forced to let go sometimes, to remain animal, to submit, to live [or experience] without reflection." Fantin reported of being overwhelmed by his sensations throughout the *Ring* cycle. In *Siegfried,* for example, during the hero's awakening of Brunnhilde (conveyed throughout the act not so much by word or action but "almost only by the orchestra"), Fantin exulted, "I was carried away not just for a moment, but constantly and by ever higher degrees . . . . it is the greatest *sensation* ever *felt.*" By the end of the four performances Fantin could only conclude weakly to Maître, "I cannot express how *transported* I *feel.*"[86] Fantin's descriptions of his experiences echo those by Baudelaire and Champfleury in the early 1860s, as well as by many other Wagnerists.[87] In a manner that fits Wyzewa's theory of modes of address, all are preoccupied with sensation and emotion. There are continual references to revelations, the suspension of the intellect, and states of intoxication and confusion, of being swept away on waves of sound and overwhelmed by the emotions they arouse.

Is the concordance of Fantin's language with that of others coincidence, or did he share the belief in music's hegemony and explore its potential to infuse new life into the other arts? Several facts indicate that the artist was indeed conversant with these ideas. Both his wife and sister-in-law, who was a German teacher, translated German philosophical writings for him,[88] so it is likely that his exposure to these ideas was substantive. Furthermore, Fantin had remarked in the early 1860s that he found the visual arts to be in a state of transition and experimentation, indicating that he maintained an interest in current aesthetic debates. Given these conditions, his early interest in Baudelaire and later contacts with Symbolists, as well as his legendary melomania, it seems probable that he was well aware of these views on music, its dominance of aesthetic discourse, and its potential offerings to the visual arts.

There is also evidence that Fantin went beyond the theoretical and consciously attempted to create a visual equivalent to music. For example, Fantin's musicality was often described in terms of Baudelaire's Correspondences, which the poet had publicized in his article in defense and praise of Wagner's *Tannhäuser* in 1861, just as the young Fantin began his love affair with Wagner's music. At the 1864 Salon Fantin had celebrated both Wagner and Baudelaire, and his *Toast! Homage to Truth* of 1864–1865 had presented the arts as unified. Thus, he seems to have entertained these synaesthetic ideas from early in his career, a possibility that is reinforced by frequent references in Fantin's letters to his reverence for music, his interest in making art from fantasies conjured by music he had heard, and his enigmatic statement that he wanted to "present" music.

The clearest evidence that Fantin deliberately attempted to create a musical visual art is the fact that he turned so resolutely to lithography upon his return from Bayreuth in 1876. The intensity of Fantin's response to the music dramas spurred him to create a lithographic technique that could evoke equivalents for his sensations.[89] In the three lithographs reproduced here, for example, one is engaged more by the formal elements themselves than the subjects they depict. The unique qualities of Fantin's style—the energetic, sharp lines, heavy textures, and dense tonality, Fantin's hand in short—assert themselves aggressively. Fantin even gouged the stone itself to create these effects.[90] In nineteenth-century terms, the forms communicate not by description but by *evocation,* and they affect the viewer in an unmediated manner that was considered equivalent to the way instrumental music worked directly on the emotions of the listener. Such an understanding of the arts stands behind statements like Geffroy's 1884 Salon review, when he discussed the musicality of Fantin's lithographic "sketches." In fact, Fantin himself stated that he preferred to "maintain the freshness of the sketch" because, like music, it did not describe or illustrate, but instead stimulated the viewer's imagination to complete the image. He noted that "the charm of the sketch is . . . in its uncertainty; that each viewer completes according to his taste, those who have the imagination and taste to dream, not people like Fontanelle, who, hearing Sonatas, end by exclaiming, 'Sonata, what do you want of me!' "[91]

That Fantin attempted to make musical equivalents through the signature style of his lithographs is evident. Can the same be said for his paintings, including his nonmusical subjects? In most twentieth-century studies the answer has been no; most scholars have long insisted that Fantin employed different styles for different genres. Yet late nineteenth-century critics used a similar language for all of his oeuvre, especially after 1890 when the idea of musicality in art had become quite firmly established. Fantin himself claimed a "musical" function for color distinctly separate from the description of objects, asserting that it addresses "that region of the imagination which is supposed to be under the exclusive domain of music."[92] And in most of his paintings, whether musical subjects like *Tannhäuser on the Venusberg,* flower pieces such as *Still Life: Roses in a Glass Vase* of 1879 (Figure 7–8),[93] and even portraits like *Around the Piano,* the mimetic representations and smooth, finished surfaces of the academic tradition are not present. Instead, one is struck by the works' thick yet transparent surfaces and their heavy atmospheres because Fantin worked the color energetically, leaving the marks of his presence on the canvases by a combination of scumbling, working wet into wet, and removing paint with the butt end of his brushes, much as one would use the scraper in lithography. Differences of effect from genre to genre and between mediums are evident, but they are due to skilled variations of a singular approach that always foregrounds the artist's presence. It should then not surprise that the musicality of Fantin's still lifes was noted early on,[94] and that Fantin himself related the art of portraiture to music: "What of the interior, the inner life? The soul is like music playing behind the veil of flesh; one cannot paint it, but one can make it heard . . . . [sic] or at least try. . . ."[95]

In 1885 Wyzewa proclaimed that, among artists, Fantin was the supreme Wagnerist, not only because he was a "conscious" Wagnerist, as demonstrated by the homage of *Around the Piano,* but also because he was a consciously musical artist.[96] For his contemporaries, Fantin was a central figure in the triumph of *ut pictura musica,* supplanting the traditional literary paradigm for painting with a musical one. Many considered this to be the primary aesthetic development of the later nineteenth century and largely attributed it to Wagner's colossal impact. Camille Mauclair described this development succinctly in 1900: "The omnipotence of music over the last thirty years has given to painting, to sculpture and to poetry a powerful impulse toward the ideal of the pure symphony, that is, to the production of emotion by combinations of harmonies and not by associations of logical ideas. . . . [E]verything in contemporary art is calculated to create the almost magnetic state of reverie, the excitation of the sensibility."[97] Fantin's aspirations encapsulate this development. In all genres, although most obviously in works inspired by music, he asserted his own "self" by freeing form and color from mimetic description to allow them to sing on their own. Indeed, Fantin

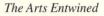

Figure 7–8. Henri Fantin-Latour, *Still Life: Roses in a Glass Vase,* 1879, oil on canvas, 43.9 × 38 cm., ©Manchester City Art Galleries, Manchester, England.

consciously considered himself a Wagnerist painter and lithographer. As he himself admitted in 1892, "I've been trying to translate Wagner pictorially since 1864."[98]

NOTES

[1]Cited in Robert Hartford, *Bayreuth: The Early Years* (London: Victor Gollancz, 1980), 181; 182–183.

[2]For example, Raymond Bouyer observed that "music became part of our existence" and that the Germanic symphony had the strongest impact. Bouyer, "Un Peintre mélomane: Fantin-Latour," *Les Maîtres artistes* (February 28, 1903), 240.

[3]See Jeffrey Cooper, *The Rise of Instrumental Music and Concert Series in Paris, 1828–71* (Ann Arbor: UMI Research Press, 1983); see also Elaine Brody, *Paris: The Musical Kaleidoscope* (New York: Braziller, 1987), and Leo Schrade, *Beethoven in France: The Growth of an Idea* (1942; reprint, New York: Da Capo Press, 1978).

[4]Cited in Edouard Dujardin, "*Lohengrin* à Paris," *Revue wagnérienne* 3 (May 1887), 112.

[5]Fantin to Edmond Maître, August 31, 1876; copy of letter conserved in the Fonds dauphinois, Bibliothèque d'étude et d'information, Grenoble (fascicule IV, 8); hereafter cited as Grenoble. My sincere thanks to Marie-Françoise Bois-Delatte, conservateur of the Fonds dauphinois, for her kind assistance.

[6]Fantin exhibited a total of four lithographs. One, entitled *Vérité*, depicted a muse inscribing the names of Fantin's preferred composers on a tablet. Another, entitled *Italie!,* portrayed a scene from Hector Berlioz's *Les Troyennes*.

[7]Fantin's lithographs caused a sensation when they appeared in 1886 as illustrations for Adolphe Jullien's biography of Wagner. Later, Jullien published a study on Berlioz, for which Fantin again supplied lithographic illustrations.

[8]The terms "Wagnerian" and "Wagnerist" (*wagnérien[ne]* and *wagnériste* in the original French) were both employed in Fantin's time. I have chosen to use "Wagnerist" in most instances in this essay because it is more closely associated with Wagnerism, a movement that extended far beyond music and music dramas. "Wagnerian" tends to have narrower connotations, indicating either a musical style that is modeled upon Wagner's or a person with an extreme passion for his music dramas. Fantin himself used the term "Wagnerist," so it seems fitting to do so here.

[9]Germain Hediard, *Fantin-Latour: Catalogue de l'oeuvre lithographique du Maître* (Paris: Librairie de l'art ancien et moderne, 1906), 24.

[10]Anon., "Modern French Pastellists: Fantin-Latour," *The Studio* (October 1904), 43.

[11]The Edwardses were an English couple with whom Fantin stayed several times in the early 1860s; they eventually became his dealers. During his visits much of their interaction involved music, and Ruth Edwards was one of the early

figures in Fantin's life to educate him about it. They especially shared a passion for Schumann, memorialized by Fantin's 1864 etching, *Un Morceau de Schumann.* Fantin's surviving letters to them show the centrality of music in Fantin's life; they also reveal that over time, he provided the couple access to works by Schumann and others that they had not previously heard, indicating a level of knowledge and engagement that was unusual for a nonmusician.

[12]Champfleury published a laudatory brochure immediately upon the performances of 1860. See his "Richard Wagner," in *Grandes figures d'hier et d'aujourd'hui* (Geneva: Slatkine Reprints, 1968). In response to this concert, Baudelaire sent Wagner a private letter about his own overwhelmed response. After the debacle of *Tannhäuser* in 1861, Baudelaire published his famed essay defending Wagner and articulating his notion of "Correspondences." See Baudelaire's letter in *Critique littéraire et musicale,* ed. Claude Pichois (Paris: Librairie Armand Colin, 1961), and Baudelaire, "Richard Wagner and *Tannhäuser* in Paris," in *The Painter of Modern Life and Other Essays,* trans. and ed. Jonathan Mayne (London: Phaidon, 1964), 111–146.

[13]Douglas Druick and Michel Hoog, *Fantin-Latour* (Ottawa: National Gallery of Canada, 1983), 152; hereafter cited as Ottawa.

[14]On Fantin's palette see Barbara A. Ramsey, "A Note on Fantin's Technique," in Ottawa, 58, 60–61.

[15]Delacroix's journals are liberally peppered with musings on music and aesthetics. See Delacroix, *Journal: 1822–1863* (Paris: Plon, 1980) or *The Journal of Eugene Delacroix,* trans. Walter Pach (1937; reprint, New York: Hacker Art Books, 1980). See also Michele Hannoosh, *Painting and the Journal of Eugene Delacroix* (Princeton: Princeton University Press, 1995). Baudelaire also addressed the relation of Delacroix's art, especially color, to music; see "The Life and Work of Eugene Delacroix," in *The Painter of Modern Life,* 41–68, especially 41, 47, 49. Fantin began sketches for his *Homage* just nine days after the publication of Baudelaire's long article prompted by Delacroix's death. Baudelaire likened Delacroix's palette to a bouquet, perhaps providing the inspiration for Fantin to include both the bouquet and the palette in the *Homage.*

[16]Ottawa, 210. On the importance of the public concert, see Cooper, *The Rise of Instrumental Music.*

[17]For a survey of the history of Wagnerism in Paris, see Gerald D. Turbow, "Art and Politics: Wagnerism in France," in *Wagnerism in European Culture and Politics,* ed. David C. Large and William Weber (Ithaca: Cornell University Press, 1984), 134–166.

[18]Fantin apparently met Maître in about 1865 at the Café de Bade. Ottawa, 14, 275, 99.

[19]Fantin to his parents during a visit with the Edwards, August 23, 1864; Grenoble (cahier 6, 41–42).

[20]The view of Fantin's oeuvre as split between "réalité" and "rêve" began to emerge in his own lifetime, but it became entrenched with the 1906 retrospective exhibition of his work and its accompanying catalog. See *Exposition de l'oeuvre de Fantin-Latour* (Paris: Palais de l'école nationale des beaux-arts, 1906), where the works are divided into sections on "observation" and "fantasy." This view has been perpetuated, most notably by Druick and Hoog's ambitious 1983 Fantin-Latour exhibition and catalog in which they asserted, with justification, that fascination with contemporary reality *and* with escape from it through fantasy were endemic to the age. Their catalog is invaluable to Fantin scholarship. More recently, the Fantin exhibition at the Musée d'Hazebrouck focused on how his work proceeded "from reality to dream," a view which has great merit. See *Fantin-Latour (1836–1904): de la réalité au rêve* (Hazebrouck: Musée d'Hazebrouck, 1991).

[21]Fantin to his parents, September 19, 1864; Grenoble (cahier 7, 47). Fantin's use of "présenter" here is tricky, since it could mean "present" as in "manifest" or even "represent," but in French it also connotes paying tribute or making an offering, which he would do in his homagistic images.

[22]Fantin to Edwin Edwards, March 21, 1869; Grenoble (cahier 27, 153–154). Interestingly, Fantin indicates here that he associates manifestations of his "self" with a sketchy, unfinished technique.

[23]Letters to Edwards from the mid-1860s indicate Fantin's growing impatience and even disgust with the art circles he frequented. Only Manet seems not to have irritated him.

[24]Manet and Maître are the only two persons to appear more than once in Fantin's surviving group portraits. Maître also appears seated at the piano in the music-loving Bazille's *In the Studio* of 1870, along with many of the same figures seen in the *Batignolles*.

[25]Fantin was notoriously apolitical and was not at all involved either in the defense of Paris or the Commune. See letters to Edwin Edwards, July 30, 1870 and June 6, 1871; Grenoble (cahier 29, 168–169; cahier 30, 173). The musical evenings shared with Maître are verified in Jullien's letter of condolence to Victoria Dubourg upon Fantin's death. He reminisced to her on August 29, 1903 about "those evenings on the rue Tarame where Fantin listened to us, Maître and me, make music. . . ." Letter conserved in the Cabinet des estampes, Bibliothèque nationale, Paris; hereafter cited as Estampes). My sincere thanks to M. Claude Bouret of the Cabinet des estampes for his considerable help and support of this project.

[26]Actually in 1875 Fantin had produced the *Commemoration* (dedicated to Manet), an allegorical scene that paid tribute to Berlioz. However, *Das Rheingold: Opening Scene* marks the inaugural work in Fantin's sustained involvement with the making of lithographs on musical subjects. See Hediard, *Catalogue de l'oeuvre lithographique.*

[27]Fantin to Edwin Edwards, September 13, 1876; Grenoble (cahier 33, 199).

[28]Stéphane Mallarmé to Fantin, February 5, 1877. Letter lost; quoted in Ottawa, 283.

[29]Ottawa, 275.

[30]For most of his career, Fantin planned carefully for each Salon, but between circa 1879–1884 his submissions seem substantially less ambitious than those of prior years. In a letter to Ruth Edwards before the 1884 Salon he acknowledged as much, stating that he could afford a rest from success for a while (January 22, 1884; Grenoble [cahier 34, 203]). Fantin exhibited at every Salon until 1899.

[31]The *Homage* was indeed included in the *Portraits of the Century* exhibition and elicited much comment. Octave Maus was one of several who noted the connection between the two portraits. See "Mozart" [Octave Maus], "Le Salon de Paris," *L'Art moderne* (May 24, 1885), 163. The *Homage* had special value for Fantin; he remarked specifically to his parents that he had made the painting for himself (August 10, 1864; Grenoble [Cahier 6, 39]), and the painting hung in his studio for years. Geffroy was among those who recalled seeing it there. See Gustave Geffroy, "Fantin-Latour," *Revue universelle* 121 (November 1, 1904), 589.

[32]Fantin mentions such plans in two letters. One to Edwin Edwards, dated October 3, 1872, includes a drawing with a composition similar to *Around the Piano.* The second, addressed to Ruth Edwards and dated December 20, 1872, refers to a procession of young girls "like muses," decorating Schumann's tomb with flowers; Grenoble (cahier 31, 184–186).

[33]During the 1880s ever larger portions of Wagner's music were being heard, including entire sung acts, leading many Wagnerists to the optimistic but erroneous prognosis that Paris would soon accept Wagner's music dramas in their entirety. See for example Adrian Remacle, "Le Mouvement wagnérienne en France," *Revue Indépendante* 1 (May 1884), 44–57; and 4 (August 1884): 313–321. As the production of *Lohengrin* neared in December 1885, *revanchiste* hostility grew and forced conductor Léon Carvalho to withdraw the work from the Opéra Comique. The *revanchistes* had been fueled by rising tensions with Germany and were probably enflamed by the *Revue wagnérienne*'s untimely publication, in its September-October 1885 issue, of Wagner's *Eine Kapitulation,* a poor satire of the sufferings Parisians endured under siege during the

Franco-Prussian War. The editors of the review were not necessarily enthusiastic about full productions of Wagner's early works such as *Lohengrin,* and it could be that they intended to rankle the *revanchistes.*

[34]Fantin to Ruth Edwards, February 25, 1885; Grenoble (cahier 34, 208). Jullien devoted an entire chapter of his Fantin biography to the making of *Around the Piano,* drawing on several earlier articles he had written on the artist. See Jullien, *"Autour du piano* et le portrait d'un ami," in *Fantin-Latour: sa vie et ses amitiés* (Paris: Lucien Laveur, 1909), 125–136; hereafter cited as Jullien. See also Jullien, "Fantin-Latour: Groupes et portraits d'artistes et d'hommes de lettres," *Les Arts* (May 1906), 30. One of the 1885 reviews of *Around the Piano* is so similar in opinion and language it could very well be by Jullien; see "Histoire d'un tableau," incomplete reference with "Ropartz" and "1885" written by hand, in Album de coupures de presse, vol. I, Estampes; hereafter cited as Album. Jullien's account of the painting's making is usually accepted as accurate, but on one point is rather fishy. He repeatedly stressed that it was mere coincidence that all of these figures shared a love of Wagner, and he denied that there was any conscious reference to "Petit Bayreuth." In light of what is known about these figures, this seems absurd. His insistence was probably a response to the public's hostility towards Wagnerism.

[35]The new public venue for Petit Bayreuth gatherings was noted in the June 1886 issue of the *Revue wagnérienne.* Attendance had escalated greatly and the gatherings had completly lost their private character. Lascoux felt compelled to end them in the wake of the *Lohengrin* scandal, because his association with Wagnerism was threatening his career as a magistrate.

[36]Hugues Imbert, *Profils de musiciens* (Paris: Fischbacher, 1888), 30. Jullien is the source for the notion that Fantin's idea for the work was sparked when he saw Chabrier at Manet's funeral (Jullien, 129). That may have been a factor, but Petit Bayreuth, where Fantin would have seen Chabrier anyway, is logically the more direct inspiration.

[37]Letters from Lascoux to Cosima Wagner are conserved in the Nationalarchiv der Richard-Wagner-Stiftung, Bayreuth, which also houses letters from other French Wagnerists. These, however, are nearly always addressed to Adolf von Gross rather than Cosima herself. Visits with Lascoux are mentioned twice in *Cosima Wagner's Diaries,* ed. Martin Gregor-Dellin and Dietrich Mack, 2 vols. (New York: Harcourt, Brace, Jovanovich, 1978), 2: 363, 719.

[38]Lascoux insisted on anonymity to protect his government position. He is never named, for example, in the *Revue wagnérienne*'s list of financial supporters. Nonetheless, everyone seemed to know who he was! On the history of the *Revue wagnérienne,* see Edouard Dujardin, *"La Revue wagnérienne,"* in *Wagner*

et la France (numéro spéciale de la *Revue musicale* [October 10, 1923]): 141–160; and Isabelle de Wyzewa, *La Revue wagnérienne: Essai sur l'intérprétation esthétique de Wagner en France* (Paris: Perrin, 1934).

[39]Even Cosima Wagner herself was aware of Lamoureux's dedication, as indicated in a letter to Gräfin Mimi von Schleinitz. See Cosima Wagner's correspondence with her, conserved in the Nationalarchiv der Richard-Wagner-Stiftung, Bayreuth.

[40]Lamoureux to Gross, January 14, 1885; Bayreuth (III.B.23.3 [5]).

[41]From the time he inaugurated his concerts in 1881, Lamoureux performed controversial works by Wagner and the young French composers who had been inspired by him. Not surprisingly then, he was a figure of some notoriety despite his renown for extremely high performance standards. His devotion to Wagner was so unshakable that, when death threats were launched at him in an attempt to halt his *Lohengrin* in 1887, he simply took to carrying a pocket revolver to rehearsals! Lascoux reported to Cosima on the rising hostility to *Lohengrin* in Paris in a letter dated April 13, 1887; Bayreuth (III.B.24–2.3).

[42]Jullien, 131. Jullien also insisted here, as he had elsewhere, that Fantin desired to avoid the impression that the painting served as some sort of manifesto (130–131).

[43]Imbert, *Profils de musiciens,* 29–30.

[44]Like Lascoux and others, d'Indy travelled extensively to hear Wagner's work, especially between 1876 and 1887. Fantin noted to Maître that he was one of the few Frenchmen at Bayreuth in 1876. D'Indy also had a personal relationship with Fantin; he was known to visit Fantin's home to play the piano for him. See L. M., "Madame Fantin-Latour," *Colour* (November 1928), 13. A few notes from d'Indy to the Fantins are conserved in Estampes.

[45]Chabrier served as Lamoureux's right arm and was the conductor's choir master from 1880. His *Gwendoline* was first heard in fragments at a Lamoureux concert. D'Indy served as the choral master for Lamoureux's production of *Lohengrin* in 1887. See Imbert, *Profils de musiciens,* 37–56. D'Indy's Wagnerian *Chanson de la cloche* also premiered in 1886 at a Lamoureux concert. Although his first major opera, *Fervaal* (1889–1895), included strong Wagnerian elements, d'Indy became increasingly devoted to a "purely French" music. On this and a general history of French music, see Edward Bulingaine Hill, *Modern French Music* (Westport, Conn.: Greenwood Press, 1970), 64.

[46]Fantin to Ruth Edwards, April 19, 1885; Grenoble (cahier 34, 208–209).

[47]Jullien's letter of condolence to Victoria Dubourg on Fantin's death verifies the depth of their friendship. See also copies of fragments of letters from Fantin to Jullien (1885–1900) conserved in Grenoble (fascicule III), in which the

tone and topics covered, from Jullien's eczema to a musical joke about flatulence, indicate a comfortable intimacy.

[48]Ottawa, 306–307.

[49]Ibid., 307.

[50]Boisseau's participation in Petit Bayreuth is noted in the *Revue wagnérienne* (May 1885; April 1886).

[51]See Amédée Pigeon, "Fantin-Latour: Souvenirs sur l'homme et sur l'oeuvre," *l'Art decoratif* (March 1905), 110. Furthermore, in his obituary, André Michel noted that Fantin would quiz him and the renowned music critic Louis de Fourcaud by writing musical phrases for them to identify. See Michel, "Nécrologie," *Journal des débats* (September 2, 1904), n. p., Estampes.

[52]These included "Cesario," Joris-Karl Huysmans, Mirbeau, Armand Silvestre, and Maus. A reviewer for *L'Indépendance belge* admired Fantin's "magnificent envoy of *Wagnerians,*" while Silvestre noted "the Wagnerian cenacle." See these and other reviews collected in Album, Estampes.

[53]Fantin to Ruth Edwards, February 25, 1885; Grenoble (cahier 34, 207–208).

[54]Geffroy (1885), Album, Estampes.

[55]"Mozart" (Octave Maus), "Le Salon de Paris," *L'Art moderne* (May 24, 1885), 163.

[56]André Michel, "Le Salon de 1885," *Gazette des beaux-arts* (June 1, 1885), 495–496.

[57]Octave Mirbeau, "Le Salon," Album, Estampes.

[58]Roger Marx, Album, Estampes.

[59]Fantin produced about two hundred lithographs; the great majority are of specifically musical subjects, and essentially all of the rest are on bather themes. A handful are homages to various composers and artists.

[60]Anon., "A Painter of Music Poems," *The Sun,* n.d., n.p. Folio Yb3.2749, Estampes.

[61]On the notion of evocation in music's address of the emotions, see R. T. Allen, "The Arousal and Expression of Emotion by Music," *British Journal of Aesthetics* 30, no. 1 (January 1990), 57–61.

[62]Edward Lucie-Smith is one scholar who has noted Fantin's consistent treatment of such subjects. See his *Fantin-Latour* (Oxford: Phaidon, 1977), 34. Wagner's prelude to *Lohengrin* is itself an evocation, in which he attempted to have the music alone conjure the apparition of the Holy Grail in the viewer's mind.

[63]See for example Fantin to Edwin Edwards, November 27, 1864 and December 26, 1864; Grenoble (cahier 13, 41; cahier 14, 50). Copies of Fantin's letters to Maître from Bayreuth are conserved in Grenoble (fascicule IV); they

are quoted extensively in Jullien, 111–119, and Adolphe Jullien, "Un Peintre mélomane: Fantin-Latour et la musique d'après des lettres inédites," *Revue des deux mondes* 35 (September 1906), 365–380.

[64]See Fantin to Edwin Edwards, January 13, 1865, in which Fantin stated emphatically that his goal in painting was to visualize what he had felt; see Grenoble (Cahier 15, 56). F. Templaere noted that at the end of his life, Fantin still would "abandon himself to musical rêverie" as his wife and sister-in-law regularly played the piano; see F. Templaere, "Fantin-Latour à Buré," *L'Echo d'Alençon* (February 7, 1937), 4.

[65]The intricacies between Mallarmé's and Wagner's views on the interrelations of the arts have been examined in Lisa Norris, "The Early Criticism of Camille Mauclair: Toward an Understanding of Wagnerism and French Art, 1885–1900" (Ph.D. diss., Brown University, 1993), specifically in Chapter IV, "Interlude: Points of Confluence and Conflict in the Aesthetics of Mallarmé and the Wagnerists."

[66]Téodor de Wyzewa, "Peinture wagnérienne," *Revue wagnérienne* 1 (June 1885), 155.

[67]By this time Fantin's lithographs had received wide acclaim with their appearance in Jullien's Wagner biography, which was available by November 1886. Copies of the book were sold at the offices of the *Revue wagnérienne,* where Fantin's folio of photo-reproductions was also on sale for fifty francs. Proceeds from the latter were donated by Fantin to the "oeuvre wagnérienne," indicating that he supported the *Revue* despite its radicality.

[68]Téodor de Wyzewa, review of *Les Lithographies de M. Fantin Latour* [sic], *Revue wagnérienne* 3 (February 1887), 25–26. Wyzewa's quite convoluted prose is typically Symbolist.

[69]Gustave Geffroy, Salon review of 1884; cited in Ottawa, 300.

[70]Léonce Bénédite, *Catalogue des lithographies originales de Henri Fantin-Latour* (Paris: Librairies-imprimeries réunies, 1899), 28–29. Bénédite had made a similar assertion in "Artistes contemporains: Fantin-Latour," *La Revue de l'art ancien et moderne* (January 10, 1897), 15.

[71]Jules Laforgue, "The Eye and the Poet," reprinted in *The Post-Impressionists: A Retrospective,* ed. Martha Kapos (London: Beaux-Arts Editions, 1993), 40. The important article of 1883 can be found in Laforgue's *Mélanges posthumes* (Paris: Mercure de France, 1903), 136–138. The relation of Wagnerism to the Impressionists, many of whom were liberally exposed to modern music and to Wagner, is a rich area of scholarship that warrants much more investigation.

[72]Gustave Geffroy, "Les Salons de 94 et 95 [sic]," *Les Maîtres artistes* (February 28, 1903), 229.

[73]Raymond Bouyer, "L'Oeuvre grave de Fantin-Latour," 25–29 and 51–26. Folio DC. 686, Estampes.

[74]Raymond Bouyer, "Un Peintre mélomane: Fantin-Latour," *Les Maîtres artistes* (February 28, 1903), 244.

[75]Roger Marx, "Souvenirs sur Fantin-Latour," *Les Arts,* 34 (October 1904), 6. Marx noted the influence of Corot's style on Fantin, especially his focus on the "envelope" and "harmony," two qualities in Fantin's own work that were associated with the musical. The importance of music for Corot is investigated by Kermit Champa in *The Rise of Landscape Painting in France: Corot to Monet* (Manchester, N.H.: The Currier Gallery of Art, 1991).

[76]Prosper Dorbec, "L'Oeuvre de Fantin-Latour," in *Les Maîtres artistes* (February 28, 1903), 232. Dorbec specifically related Wagner's orchestral innovations to the Impressionists' preoccupation with light and atmosphere. In fact, Wagner's own musical style is quite similar to the language applied here to describe Fantin's "musical" style. For both, writers noted a sea of dense harmonies, out of which leitmotifs or melodies (forms) rise and sink.

[77]Hediard too asserted as much: "[T]he musical impression is everything, with its vague enchantment and fecundity of revery. It condenses itself into visions, and bears forms that float in the air like melodies." And, "as the orchestra accompanies the theme, the landscapes serve as an environment ["séjour"] for these ideal figures." Germaine Hediard, "Lithographie de M. Fantin-Latour," *Les Maîtres artistes* (February 28, 1904), 253–254.

[78]Among them are H.-Ernest Simoni, "Sons et couleurs," *Les Maîtres artistes* (February 28, 1903), 238; and Andrée Myra, who also stated that Fantin led one to understand and admire the musical works that formed the subject, not through details but "by the spirit, the beauty of the color, the depth and amplitude of forms that these luminous shadows take, surrounding flowers and clouds," thus making a "sublime interpretation of the musical genius who created them." See Andrée Myra, "Fantin-Latour," *Le Signal,* n. d., n.p. Folio Yb3.2749, Estampes.

[79]Téodor de Wyzewa, "Notes sur la peinture wagnérienne et le salon de 1886," *Revue wagnérienne* 2 (June 1886), 102–103. This kind of intense emotional turmoil was also noted by Alfred de Lostalot, for example. Upon hearing Lamoureux's performance of the first act of *Tristan,* Lostalot reported a drunkenness of the senses, an absence of precision and clarity, and a confused sensation of abstraction. See Lostalot, "Revue musicale," *Gazette des beaux-arts* (March 1885), 270.

[80]Andrew Kagan has provided a concise summation of the development of the principle *ut pictura musica* during the eighteenth and nineteenth centuries. See Kagan, "*Ut Pictura Musica* to 1860," in *Absolute Art* (St. Louis: Grenart,

1995), 73–99. See also Louis Viardot, "Ut Pictura Musica," *Gazette des beaux-arts* 1 (January 1859), 19–29. Significantly, this was the lead article in the first issue of Charles Blanc's *Gazette.* For Carlyle on music see Thomas Carlyle, *Heroes, Hero-Worship and the Heroic in History* (New York: J. B. Alden, 1892); the essay was translated into French by Hippolyte Taine. The latter's own acknowledgment that music dominated the art of the nineteenth century was put forward in his *Philosophie de l'art,* 1865, relevant excerpts of which are included in Joshua C. Taylor, ed., *Nineteenth-Century Theories of Art* (Berkeley: University of California Press, 1987), 379–382.

[81]On the importance of Schopenhauer's philosophy in France, especially among the Symbolists, see Alexandre Baillot, *L'Influence de la philosophie de Schopenhauer en France, 1860–1900* (Paris: J. Vrin, 1927); and Isabelle de Wyzewa, *La Revue wagnérienne.*

[82]Wyzewa's "Le Pessimisme de Richard Wagner" appeared in the July 1885 issue. His translation and analysis of Wagner's "Beethoven" essay was published monthly in the *Revue wagnérienne* between May and August 1885. In 1923, the *Revue's* cofounder Edouard Dujardin recalled that the journal served as a bridge between the aesthetic of Mallarmé and Wagner, and between Schopenhauer and Symbolism. See Edouard Dujardin, *"La Revue wagnérienne,"* in *Wagner et la France,* 160.

[83]Wyzewa, "Le Salon de 1886," 102, 104–106.

[84]Roger Marx, "Souvenirs sur Fantin-Latour," *Les Arts,* 34 (October 1904), 6.

[85]Pierre Jobbé-Duval, "Notes d'art: Fantin-Latour," n.d., n.p. Folio Yb3.2749, Estampes.

[86]Fantin quoted in Jullien, "Un Peintre mélomane," 374–378. Italics added.

[87]For similar reactions see Champfleury, "Richard Wagner;" and Baudelaire, private letter to Richard Wagner published in *Critique littéraire,* and "Richard Wagner and *Tannhäuser* in Paris." Other similarly worded experiences are recorded by many, including Edouard Schuré, Catulle Mendès, and Edouard Dujardin.

[88]One source that attests to this is L. M., "Mme Fantin-Latour," 13–14.

[89]There are a number of good analyses of Fantin's unusual lithographic techniques, among them three exhibition catalogues: *Henri Fantin-Latour: 1836–1904* (Northampton, Mass.: Smith College Museum of Art, 1966); *Fantin-Latour: Lithographies* (Geneva: Musée d'art et d'histoire, 1981); and *Fantin-Latour: de la réalité au rêve* (1991).

[90]Geffroy, "Salon Review of 1884," cited in Ottawa, 300. Fantin's presence through the marks on the surface call to mind James H. Rubin's notion of the "performative" as discussed in his *Manet's Silence and the Poetics of Bouquets*

(Cambridge, Mass.: Harvard University Press, 1994). Indeed, a number of his ideas are quite compelling, although the reader will understand this writer's view that the paradigm became not the poetics, but the *music,* of bouquets.

[91]Fantin to Edwin Edwards, December 30, 1871; Grenoble (Cahier 31, 180–181).

[92]Quoted, without citation, by Charles Chetham in his introduction to *Fantin-Latour*, Smith College Museum of Art, n.p.

[93]Fantin produced his only lithograph of a still life after this painting.

[94]For example, in a letter of May 1867 to Fantin, Edwards remarked of his still lifes that "each painting is a symphony." Quoted in Ottawa, 132. Whistler even noted to Fantin that the use of color in his still lifes seemed autonomous rather than descriptive (September 30, 1868; letter conserved in the Pennell Collection, Library of Congress, Washington, D.C.); this would come to be associated with the musical. For other references to the musicality of Fantin's still lifes, see Arsène Alexandre, "Les Roses de Fantin-latour," *La Renaissance* (May 1930): n.p.; Michelle Verrier, *Fantin-Latour* (London: Academy Editions, 1977), 13–14; and Elisabeth Hardouin-Fugier, "Fantin-Latour, peintre de fleurs," *Gazette des beaux-arts* 113 (March 1989), 138.

[95]Fantin quoted in Camille Mauclair, *Servitude et grandeur littéraire* (Paris: Ollendorff, 1922), cited in Ottawa, 87.

[96]Wyzewa, "Peinture wagnérienne," 1885, 156.

[97]Camille Mauclair, "Georges Rochegrosse et la peinture d'histoire," *Revue des revues* (October 1900), 163–164.

[98]Cited in *Fantin-Latour: de la réalité au rêve,* 28.

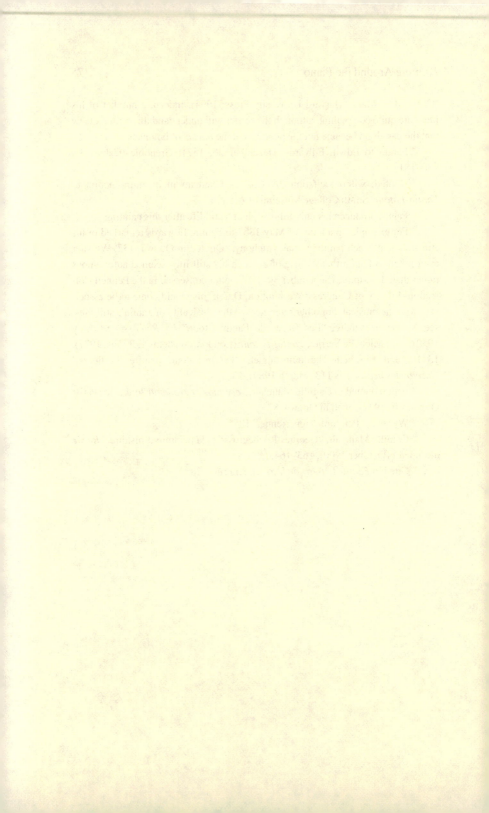

CHAPTER 8

Van Gogh in Nuenen and Paris
The Origins of a Musical Paradigm for Painting

PETER L. SCHMUNK

> *Why am I so little an artist that I always regret*
> *that the statue and the picture are not alive?*
> *Why do I understand the musician better, why*
> *do I see the raison d'etre of his abstractions*
> *better?*
> —VINCENT VAN GOGH, LETTER 522 TO THEO

At the end of the summer of 1888 Vincent van Gogh was thirty-five years old and at the height of his painting career. Living in Arles in the south of France, he was then producing some of his most arresting and enduring works. Earlier that summer he had painted *Harvest at La Crau* (Figure 8–1), a view of "fields yellow and green as far as the eye can reach" that Van Gogh regarded as one of his most successful efforts.[1] He had begun a series of symbolic portraits, having already completed paintings of a twelve-year-old Provençal girl, which he called *La Mousmé,* and a local peasant named Patience Escalier whom he conceived as "a man with a hoe . . . terrible in the furnace of the height of harvest time."[2] At the same time he began the paintings of sunflowers, today among the most popular and widely admired images in Western art. These and other paintings confirm Van Gogh's claim that "ideas for my work are coming in swarms, so that . . . I go on painting like a steam engine. . . . I'm hard at it, painting with the enthusiasm of a Marseillais eating bouilla-baisse. . . ."[3] His correspondence from this period conveys confidence, clarity of thought and, for Van Gogh, relative well-being.

Figure 8–1. Vincent van Gogh, *Harvest at La Crau* (F412), 1888, oil on canvas, 72.5 × 92 cm., Van Gogh Museum (Vincent van Gogh Foundation), Amsterdam.

A letter to his brother Theo from around the beginning of September contains a progress report on the sunflower series, as well as a striking assessment of avant-garde painting in France. "Painting as it is now," he wrote, "promises to become more subtle—more like music and less like sculpture—and above all it promises *color*. If only it keeps this promise."[4] Writing again a few days later, Van Gogh returned to the subject of music, stating that "in a painting I want to say something comforting, as music is comforting. I want to paint men and women with that something of the eternal which the halo used to symbolize, and which we seek to convey by the actual radiance and vibration of our coloring."[5] In these statements and others from the Arles period, Van Gogh gives to music the status of a paradigm for his own art. Seeking to define his artistic aims, he repeatedly invokes music as an artistic ideal—inherently abstract, richly and subtly variable in form, intimate and consoling in expressive affect—to which he aspires in his own painting.

What are the origins of this commitment to a musical approach to painting, articulated with such clarity and conviction soon after the artist's arrival in Arles? As this chapter will establish, Van Gogh's remarks stem from a personal engagement with music that began during his residence in Nuenen in the Dutch province of Brabant between the years 1883–1885 and then was revived in Paris between 1886–1888. It is that background to the Arles period, the prior experiences which informed Van Gogh's epistolary reflections on the model of music, that this chapter explores. I will consider the origins and chronology of the artist's interest in music, the kinds of experiences—literary, auditory, pedagogical, and social—that furthered and shaped that interest, the degree to which he acquired a technical understanding of music, and the ways in which music came to influence his ideas about art as discerned in the things he read and wrote and in the paintings he produced. Admittedly, documentation for such an inquiry is frustratingly scarce. Thus, evidence must often be gleaned from secondhand and chronologically disconnected sources and, in the end, conclusions must remain somewhat speculative. Nonetheless, an informative account may be constructed that at least begins to fill in a significant gap in Van Gogh scholarship and which furthers our understanding of the formation of the artist's commitment to a musical model.

Van Gogh began to develop an awareness of music and its relation to his own art in the late spring or early summer of 1884, when he first copied into a letter to Theo a passage from the collection of biographical essays by Charles Blanc, entitled *Les Artistes de mon Temps,* lent to him by his artist friend Anton van Rappard.[6] Van Gogh was particularly impressed by the essay on Delacroix, copying long passages and recounting anecdotes from it into letters to Theo on several occasions.[7] Blanc's lengthy digression on the "theory of colors that Delacroix commanded thoroughly and scientifically after knowing by instinct" was, perhaps, the most important writing of a theoretical nature that Van Gogh ever encountered, as it explains the "law of simultaneous contrast" and the effects of juxtaposing and combining complementary colors, principles upon which much of his later art was based.[8] In introducing his discussion of color theory, Blanc asserts that people are mistaken when they suppose "that color is a gift of heaven and that it has incommunicable secrets: this is an error; color may be learned like music."[9] He likens the principles of counterpoint to those of color in educating the musician, on the one hand, and the painter, on the other, to become skillful in the practice of their respective arts.[10] Blanc thus suggests a fundamental kinship between the two arts, as both are based on definable, teachable precepts, knowledge of which will produce correct if not necessarily inspired works. In a subsequent passage on "the modulation of colors," he identifies a specific instance of formal equivalence in the character and effect of sounds and colors, stating that "the more intense the color . . . the more the Orientals make it *miroiter,* shade it upon itself, to render it more intense and lessen its dryness and monotony, to produce, in a word, that vibration without which a color is as unsupportable to our eyes as under the same conditions a sound would be to our ears."[11]

Elsewhere in the Delacroix essay, however, Blanc insinuates a deeper correspondence between music and painting through the use of musical metaphors in his descriptions of the techniques and effects of painting. He labels Delacroix's greatest strength as a painter the "orchestration of colors" and likens the effect of white in a dark painting to the sound of a gong within the full orchestra.[12] Analyzing the application of the principles of color in Delacroix's *Women of Algiers*, Blanc observes that the artist employs the effect of whites and blacks variously as contrast, a grace note, and a rest.[13]

In another passage, Blanc promotes a notion of musical painting, though without labeling it as such, by recommending the practice first described by Baudelaire of viewing a painting from a distance or with half-closed eyes, as a means of diverting attention from the subject matter to the general formal design of the work. Then, he says, "one sees only the beauty of the work, and before even knowing the idea of the painter, one is prepared to grasp it from the first view of the picture, or rather a sort of melody which emanates from it like a prelude, a melody heavy or light, melancholy or triumphant, sweet or tragic."[14] Such a practice encourages the association of painting with music by de-emphasizing the imitative and narrative qualities of art, qualities that most of Blanc's readers would have assumed to be primary in painting but which have only a very limited place in instrumental music. Instead Blanc, as with Baudelaire before him, emphasizes the expressive potential of the abstract formal arrangements that are typically foregrounded in works of music, due to an absence of representational subject matter. Early in the Delacroix essay, Blanc condemns David and his followers for "sculptural painting, which is nearly as dangerous as pictorial sculpture," and for this reason, perhaps, he avoids such Baudelairean labels as "melodious" or "quasi-musical" for paintings that have an expressive impact from a distant or partially obscured view.[15] But while Blanc may have evaded the mention of terms that would suggest a blurring of the boundaries that traditionally separated the arts, his use of musical metaphors to describe the general expressive character of a work furthers the association of music and painting in a subtle and even covert way.

A surprising omission in the Delacroix essay, given Blanc's broad treatment of the artist and his own inclination to draw connections between the arts, is any reference to Delacroix's passionate interest in music. Of Delacroix's friendship with Chopin, his frequent presence at concerts and private performances of music, his numerous written statements linking painting to music, and his deliberate choice of narratively ambiguous subjects rendered in a sketchy technique so that "painting triumphs alone, as music does in a symphony," Blanc makes no mention.[16] Had he given some indication of the importance of music in Delacroix's artistic life, then Van Gogh, with his great admiration for Delacroix, might have taken such information to heart and made an effort to gain an understanding of music sooner than he did.

In August of 1884, Van Gogh wrote to Van Rappard, "I have bought myself a book by Blanc, *Grammaire des Arts du Dessin,* on the strength of a passage quoted from it in [*Les*] *Artistes de mon Temps.*"[17] In reading Blanc's influential textbook, Van Gogh would have encountered a consideration of general questions of definition and demarcation of the different arts in the opening pages of the *Grammaire.* Blanc thus has occasion to compare painting to music and to extol music as the most expressive of the arts: "More exact than music, painting defines sentiments and thoughts by visible forms and colors, but it cannot, like music, transport us into the ethereal regions, the impenetrable worlds."[18] Accordingly, the musician is invoked throughout the *Grammaire* as the paradigmatic expressive artist who is unhindered by the obligations and limitations of representation. The painter, says Blanc, may succeed in expressing "the sentiment that animates him" by "imitating the musician who hastens or retards the time according to his own heart-beats."[19] Encountering this discussion at a time when he sought to gain more expressive force in his paintings, even at the expense of "correct" technique, such remarks must have had a considerable impact on the spiritually minded Van Gogh.

It was the chapter on color that Van Gogh found of particular value in the *Grammaire,* and there he encountered essentially a restatement and enlargement of the discussion of color contained in the Delacroix essay. A significant difference between these two presentations of the principles of color, however, is Blanc's insistence in the *Grammaire* upon a phenomenological correspondence between sound and color.

"How do these colors strike the eye," he asks rhetorically, and then answers, "As sounds do the ear. As each sound echoes in modulating itself upon itself and passes, by vibrations of equal length, from fullness to a murmur, and from a murmur to silence, so each color seen in the solar spectrum has its maximum and minimum of intensity."[20] In other words, not only do both colors and sounds come to the sense organs in the form of vibrations, but through incremental modifications to these vibrations both phenomena may be almost infinitely varied. Blanc introduces the section on the vibration of colors, largely recapitulated from the Delacroix essay, by quoting Euler's assertion that, "The parallel between sound and light is so perfect it is sustained even in the least particulars."[21] To this Blanc adds, "As the grave or sharp sounds depend upon the number of vibrations of the stretched cord in a given time; so we may say that each color is restricted to a certain number of vibrations which act upon the organ of sight as sounds do upon the organ of hearing. Not only is vibration a quality inherent in colors, but it is extremely probable that colors themselves are nothing but the different vibrations of light."[22] Even when he presumes to correct the errors of others, as for example Newton's identification of seven primitive colors, "doubtless to find a poetic analogy with the seven notes of music," Blanc makes the reader aware of other points where correspondences between painting and music had been thought to exist and of the prior history of thought on this issue which had involved intellects of the highest reputation.[23]

Cited throughout the chapter on color as the expressive colorist par excellence, Delacroix is noted for his orchestration of colors, compared to a singer endowed with the whole register of the human voice, and likened to a musician who tunes his lyre to the tone of his thought. Blanc fairly wears out the use of musical metaphor in his references to Delacroix, thus characterizing one of the artists Van Gogh would admire above all others as a musical painter. Blanc's linking of Delacroix's color with the expressive force of music would lead Van Gogh in later years to associate the artist with Berlioz and Wagner, composers renowned for the rich orchestral color and profound expressivity of their music.[24]

At a time when Van Gogh was struggling to gain some confidence and control in the handling of color, Blanc's clear exposition of a set of basic principles was an invaluable discovery. They provided a rational basis for the choice, combination, and arrangement of colors as well as some expectation of the affects that would result. In testing these principles through application, as Van Gogh did again and again, he could confirm their validity. And therefore, he came to ascribe to them a truth value, calling them "unutterably beautiful, just because they were *not accidental*" and likening them, "in their connection and completeness for general use," to the scientific laws that Newton had formulated for gravitation and Stephenson for steam.[25] As he read, reread, and pondered the Blanc texts between the summer of 1884 and the fall of 1885, and sought to assimilate the principles set forth there into his own painting practice, Van Gogh would have been reminded repeatedly of the affinities between music and painting, of the correspondences in their physical behavior, and of the reputed expressive primacy of music, to which some examples of painting, most notably those by Delacroix, might be compared. As a result, he might easily have concluded that he could penetrate more deeply into the secrets of color by gaining some knowledge of the behavior of sound and the rudiments of music theory.

In the letters written during the Nuenen period Van Gogh never directly acknowledges an engagement with music or the influence of the painting-music analogy on his thinking about art; however, two kinds of evidence make such an influence clear. The first is a new and distinctly Blancian use of musical metaphor in his discussion of painters and painting. For example, championing the art of Jules Dupré in reaction to Theo's less enthusiastic response, Van Gogh wrote in August of 1884, "But in Dupré's color there is something of a splendid symphony, *complete, studied, manly.* I imagine Beethoven must be something like that. . . . That symphony is *enormously* calculated, and yet simple, and infinitely deep as nature itself. That is what I think of Dupré."[26] Revealing in several ways, this statement indicates that, while Van Gogh's high estimation of Dupré was based on direct experience of his work, his impression of Beethoven's music was apparently formed only from general cultural discourse, from those things he had read and heard in conversation about the composer and imagined of the music, and not by any direct experience of the music itself. By the late nineteenth century Beethoven's music was well established in the concert repertory across Europe, so that if Van Gogh had any history of concert attendance he would likely have had some familiarity with the symphonies of Beethoven. Given his poverty, his social and geographical isolation, and his single-minded concentration on the development of his artistic skills, it is easy to find reasons why he did not then have an acquaintance with concert music. However, the practice of invoking the names of composers whose music he had never heard would persist in his correspondence, especially when he came to regard modern orchestral music as a model for his own painting.

Van Gogh's endorsement of Dupré also reveals a vivid and useful notion of "symphonic color," clarified and amplified by explanatory discussion, rather than a merely casual inclusion of musical metaphor. His elaboration of the phrase conveys a clear idea of what symphonic color looks like in a painting by another artist and what Van Gogh might aspire to realize in his own art. For Van Gogh, symphonic color has a rational basis; it is grounded in sound principles and is carefully calculated in realization, and yet may not at first appear so because its harmony and completeness yield an outer simplicity. Gendered masculine, symphonic color is characterized by wholeness, freedom from the passive imitation of nature, and potent expressivity. This musical conception of color, fundamental to Van Gogh's later art, dates from a surprisingly early time in his career, early in the Nuenen period and well before the painting of *The Potato Eaters*.

A year later, "completely absorbed in the laws of colors," Van Gogh returned to the concept of symphonic color in a letter to Theo of late October or early November 1885, this time comparing Dupré as a colorist to Delacroix: "Jules Dupré is in landscape, rather like Delacroix, for what enormous variety of mood did he express in symphonies of color."[27] He goes on, in this letter of great importance, to apply the lessons gleaned from Blanc to his own painting practice:

> Of nature I retain a certain sequence and a certain correctness in placing the tones, I study nature, so as not to do foolish things, to remain reasonable; however, I don't care so much whether my color is exactly the same, as long as it looks beautiful on my canvas, as beautiful as it looks in nature. . . .
>
> Always intelligently making use of the beautiful tones which the colors form of their own accord when one breaks them on the palette, I repeat—starting from one's palette, from one's knowledge of the harmony of colors is quite different from following nature mechanically and servilely.
>
> Here is another example: suppose I have to paint an autumn landscape, trees with yellow leaves. All right—when I conceive it as a symphony in yellow, what does it matter if the fundamental of yellow is the same as that of the leaves or not?[28]

Music is thus closely implicated with Van Gogh's new thinking about the relation of art to nature, his increased reliance on imagination and willingness to depart from the model, his belief that "color expresses something in itself."[29] Following Blanc's assertion that "nobody would define painting as imitation, and confound thus the means with the end, the dictionary with eloquence," Van Gogh professes to seek a beauty derived, in part, from the very materials of his art and the abstract principles which govern their harmonious combination, a beauty analogous to but not slavishly dependent on nature.[30]

Van Gogh's notion of the correspondence of painting to music was restricted essentially to the element of color. While he might logically have extended such analogical thinking to other elements of visual form—for example, to conceive of lines or shapes in musical arrangements—his thinking remained close to that of Blanc, his source for the kinship of painting to music. And yet, while the conservative Blanc concluded his chapter on color in the *Grammaire* with a warning that the "predominance of color at the expense of drawing is a usurpation of the relative over the absolute,"[31] Van Gogh would eventually ignore such restraints in his mature works, giving primary emphasis to the element of color as the means with which to "express [him]self forcibly."[32]

That Van Gogh took the analogy between music and painting very seriously while residing in Nuenen is evident in a rather humorous reminiscence by Anton Kerssemakers, a tanner in nearby Eindhoven who befriended the artist in November 1884.[33] About Van Gogh, Kerssemakers remembered: "He was always drawing comparisons between the art of painting and music, and in order to get an even better understanding of the values and the various nuances of the tones, he started taking piano lessons with an old music teacher who was at the same time an organist in Eindhoven. This, however, did not last long, for seeing that during the lessons Van Gogh was continually comparing the notes of the piano with Prussian blue and dark green and dark ocher, and so on, all the way to bright cadmium-yellow, the good man thought that he had to do with a madman, in consequence of which he became so afraid of him that he discontinued the lessons."[34] This account is confirmed and Van Gogh's music teacher identified in a reminiscence of largely secondhand information by D. Gestel, another acquaintance from the Nuenen period: "Vincent also occasionally visited other inhabitants of Eindhoven, among others the goldsmith Driek van Gardinghe, and Van der Sande, organist of St. Catherine's Church. Toon Kers [Anton Kerssemakers] and Van de Wakker had already told me how conscientiously Vincent studied the theory of colors in books by Delacroix and others, who also tried to demonstrate a connection between colors and music. I was told that Vincent attached much importance to this, and that he wanted to convince himself personally of the connection there might exist between colors and musical tones, for which reason he went and took piano lessons from Van der Sande."[35]

Van Gogh at least partially verified these reminiscences when he wrote to Theo from Arles in September 1888: "I have got back to where I was in Nuenen, when I made a vain attempt to learn music, so much did I already feel the relation between our color and Wagner's music."[36] While this statement confirms his involvement in a study of music during the Nuenen period, Van Gogh must surely be mistaken in claiming a knowledge of Wagner's music before going to Paris in 1886. He may have been familiar with Wagner's name, but there is no mention in his correspondence before 1888 of any reading or thinking about Wagner. Van Gogh may have unintentionally confused his later enthusiasm for Wagner with his initial engagement with music. Perhaps because he wished to stress the longevity of his own interest in painting-music correspondences, about which he likely heard much discussion later in Paris, he described its beginning in terms that were not entirely accurate. He may also have intended the Wagner reference not in a literal sense, but synecdochically, with Wagner's name standing for modern concert music in general.[37]

Having dealt with Theo's "suspicions" in highly conflicted correspondence during the months of November and December 1884, Van Gogh may have felt it unwise to inform his brother of a decision to begin music lessons, especially as they would have involved some expenditure of Vincent's usually depleted financial resources, which came from Theo. Perhaps Vincent thought that an announcement of his study of music would arouse new suspicions and lead to arguments that he was eager to avoid. At any rate, he made no mention in his letters of this activity until approximately three years later, recalling his "vain attempt to learn music" when he was once again absorbed with arrangements of color and conscious of painting's emulation of music. As a result, one can only hypothesize a date and length of time during which Van Gogh met with Van der Sande in Eindhoven for the study of music. This must have occurred after November of 1884, when Van Gogh became acquainted with Kerssemakers, and most likely during the first half of 1885. Kerssemakers's vivid account suggests that the incident was one he learned of firsthand through reports from both teacher and student. The lessons were, most likely, only a few in number, extending perhaps over a period of a month or two at most. And they were probably not "piano lessons" in the conventional sense. Van Gogh's focus must have been on theoretical rather than performance aspects of music. I imagine him not as a beginning piano student, who plays scales, arpeggios, and simple compositions with the aim of acquiring performance skills, but as a student of music theory, who seeks to understand basic elements of music composition such as chord structures and harmonic relationships, that is, the relations between sounds such as might provide a guide to his efforts to arrange colors on canvas. Predictably, Van Gogh's teacher was incapable of comprehending the rationale behind the artist's desire to learn music. To one of conventional musical background and outlook, the comparison of a particular sonority to cadmium yellow or Prussian blue would have seemed peculiar, if not ludicrous. This anecdotal detail suggests that Van Gogh's attempt to learn music may have foundered upon an overly literal search for equivalents between music and painting, an effort that has been attempted again and again without ever yielding definitive results. He may also have felt defeated by the difficulty of separating the harmonic and timbrel qualities of sound from the temporal elements of music that govern its unfolding in time.

Scattered remarks in his subsequent correspondence suggest that Van Gogh was familiar with a variety of terms and topics specific to the art of music but that his knowledge stopped short of genuine theoretical understanding. As when he invoked the name of Beethoven, apparently without having had any experience of that composer's music, Van Gogh could employ musical terminology adroitly on occasion to enrich an observation and to affect a breadth of cultural expertise.[38] But his "study" of music was clearly too brief and quixotic to lead to knowledge at any depth of the principles of music theory.[39]

While Van Gogh's later paintings from Nuenen show a growing control of color, there is no clear evidence, as yet, of music as a determining influence on his painting practice. An awareness of music's nonrepresentational nature may have encouraged his willingness to depart from the model, to seek a harmony of pictorial form derived in part from the materials of painting. He may have been guided by a notion of "orchestration" in the selection and combination of colors in such late-Nuenen paintings as *Autumn Landscape with Four Trees* (Figure 8–2). Music may have informed the making of the work, yet the result does not appear dependent on the example of music as it does on such pictorial models as the landscapes of Theodore Rousseau and Jules Dupré. While he certainly gave serious thought to the example of music during his years in Nuenen, this interest was probably not continuous. One suspects that Van Gogh was still too preoccupied with basic representational problems to possess the freedom that would have allowed for wide-ranging experiment and the incorporation of remote influences.[40]

After a brief sojourn in Antwerp between November 1885 and the

Figure 8–2. Vincent van Gogh, *Autumn Landscape with Four Trees* (F44), 1885, oil on canvas, 64 × 89 cm., Collection Kröller–Müller, Otterlo, The Netherlands.

end of February of the following year, Van Gogh arrived in Paris in March 1886. During a stay of almost two years, he studied drawing of the human figure in the studio of Félix Cormon, gained a firsthand knowledge of Impressionism after wondering in Nuenen what the new style might be like, and established important friendships with artists of the post-Impressionist avant-garde, such as Bernard, Signac, and Gauguin. He encountered there a cultural milieu in which musical entertainment figured significantly in social life and in which innovative concert music, especially that of Wagner, held a central place in critical and aesthetic discourse. Van Gogh's sojourn in Paris occurred precisely during the time of a highly politicized debate over the merits of Wagner's art, a debate that finally gave way in the 1890s to belated general acceptance of his art in France and to triumphant presentations of his operas.

Three developments in French Wagnerism during the late 1880s stand out with particular prominence: the publication of the *Revue wagnérienne* between 1885–1888, with its application by various writers of

Wagnerian principles to the other arts; the performance of orchestral excerpts from Wagner's operas with increasing frequency by a number of
conductors who championed his music; and the controversial and ultimately abortive attempt to present ten performances of *Lohengrin* in
May 1887. Essentially for political reasons, the latter event provoked
ideological battles in the press, scuffles in the street outside the Eden
Theater, and a withdrawal of the production after only two performances.
Van Gogh made no reference in subsequent correspondence to this sen-
sationalized event, the sole opportunity to experience a fully staged Wagnerian opera in Paris during the 1880s, so it may be safely assumed that
he did not attend a performance. However, the accompanying controversy
may have brought Wagner's name and music to the artist's attention.

Not only did Van Gogh almost certainly never attend a production of
a Wagnerian opera, but his letters give no indication of any awareness of
the mythic literary components of Wagner's art. Given Van Gogh's profound and life-long interest in literature, the literary dimensions of opera,
not to mention the visual ones, would likely have prompted some comment had he experienced a presentation firsthand. Such a lack of commentary may also indicate an absence of contact with the *Revue wagnérienne*
or other literary journals of the time, which published translations and
analyses of the texts of Wagner's operas.

Van Gogh's letters do, however, contain statements that establish his
familiarity with the character of Wagner's orchestral music and thus suggest his presence at one or more of the concert performances of symphonic excerpts from the operas, which took place regularly in Paris
during the late 1880s. Documentation for Van Gogh's activities in Paris
is scanty because his cohabitation with Theo eliminated the need for the
frequent and detailed correspondence that took place between the two
brothers at other times. On March 14, 1888, however, about three weeks
after Vincent had departed Paris for the south of France, Theo remarked
in a letter to his sister Wilhelmina that "[b]efore he left, I went to listen to
a Wagner concert with him a few times. We both thought it was very
beautiful."[41] Vincent may have attended other concerts, but no record of
such activity survives. A likely scenario is that he became aware of the
impact of Wagner on French culture as his stay in Paris unfolded and as
he entered into discussions with the musically engaged artists with
whom he formed friendships. Presumably Van Gogh then sought to gain
a firsthand experience of this celebrated new music, perhaps not until the
winter of 1887–1888 when he was anticipating his departure from Paris
for a provincial destination where such opportunities would not exist.

Theo's label "a Wagner concert" suggests that the brothers thought of these musical experiences primarily as opportunities to hear the music of Wagner, although such concerts almost always included a selection of works by a variety of composers, with the relatively short orchestral pieces by Wagner comprising only a small part of the program's total time. By the late 1880s there were four performance organizations in Paris that presented regular concerts of orchestral music, normally on Sunday afternoons. Three of the conductors involved—Charles Lamoureux, Jules Pasdeloup, and Édouard Colonne—were especially active in their programming and promotion of Wagner's music.[42] The Pasdeloup concerts were modestly priced, at a half franc up to two francs for the best seats, making them accessible to a broad audience of cultural consumers. A sketch by A. Gérardin, published in April 1883 in *L'Art moderne,* portrays a segment of the audience at a Lamoureux concert (Figure 8–3).[43] Variously sitting and standing on the periphery of the concert hall, they are individuals of varied social position, ranging from stolid, top-hatted gentlemen to the solitary working-class figure in wooden shoes and rough clothing leaning against the outer wall of the

Figure 8–3. A. Gérardin, "Sketch after Life at the Concert Lamoureux," *L'Art moderne,* April 1883.

surrounding walkway. Such concerts clearly took place in circumstances that were socially and economically accessible to the Dutch painter, who depicted himself in numerous self-portraits during the time of his Paris sojourn as a rather elegantly attired bourgeois in velvet-trimmed jacket and tie.[44] Van Gogh would likely have been fascinated by the variety of figural types gathered in the concert hall, by the beauty of the women and the heads of the men, not to mention the orchestral music that he had come to hear.[45]

Taking Theo's statement of having attended a few "Wagner" concerts with Vincent "before he left [for Arles]" as a basis for conjecture, one may draw some tentative conclusions about what music they heard. There were nine different concerts between January 15 and February 12 that included music by Wagner.[46] If one interprets Van Gogh's fragmentary remark of January 1889 in a letter to Gauguin—"Not knowing the music of Berlioz"—to mean that he had never heard a performance of the music of Berlioz, then one may further narrow down the concerts the brothers could have attended to seven events between January 22 and February 12.[47] The concerts that took place during that time included performances of seven different compositions by Wagner:

> Overture, from *Tannhäuser,* on January 22 (Colonne).
>
> March, from *Tannhäuser,* on January 22 (Conservatoire) and 29 (Conservatoire).
>
> "The Murmurs of the Forest," from *Siegfried,* on January 22 (Lamoureux).
>
> Idyll, from *Siegfried,* on February 5 (Lamoureux).
>
> Funeral March, from *Götterdämmerung,* on January 22 (Lamoureux) and February 12 (Lamoureux).
>
> Fragments, from *Tristan und Isolde,* on January 29 (Lamoureux).
>
> "The Ride of the Valkyries," from *Die Walküre,* on February 12 (Lamoureux).

All but two of these concert programs also included works by Beethoven, whose music had long been one of the staples of the orchestral repertoire in France. Thus, Van Gogh may have finally experienced the music of Beethoven, along with that of Wagner, after merely imagining in 1884 what this music might be like in his comparison of the symphonies of Beethoven to the landscapes of Dupré. Another noteworthy item on the concert programs between January 22 and February 12 is Bizet's *L'Arlésienne Suite,* which was presented on three different occasions within this three-week period by two different conductors. Scholars have long speculated on the reasons for Van Gogh's choice of Arles as the place to establish himself in the south of France, but no one has yet suggested that the musical experience of hearing a performance of *L'Arlésienne,* Bizet's suite of incidental music for a play by Alphonse Daudet, one of Van Gogh favorite authors, may have contributed to his decision.[48]

Of course, any of the compositions by Wagner listed here may have made a powerful impression on the painter, as a response to music is largely determined by the expectations, the musical literacy, and the openness to emotional and aesthetic experience that one brings to the act of listening. The Funeral March from *Götterdämmerung* and the Fragments (presumably the Prelude and *Liebestod*) from *Tristan und Isolde* are the longest of these compositions at about thirteen and nineteen minutes each, respectively. They are also, perhaps, the most dramatic and powerful in expressive impact, with their enormous contrasts in volume, timbre, tessitura, and mood. "The Murmurs of the Forest" may have had particular appeal to one with Van Gogh's deep feeling for nature. This stunning example of tone painting, shimmering and tremulous, had been likened in an article of 1883 by Jules Laforgue to Impressionist painting, both constituted of "a thousand tiny touches dancing in every direction."[49]

Van Gogh's letters from Arles contain few extended statements indicating what he thought of the music he had heard before leaving Paris and what lessons he might have drawn from the experience that could be applied to the making of paintings. From this time on, however, he cites Wagner in his correspondence as a model artist, a hero figure, for his creation of a deeply expressive art that offered consolation.[50] Van Gogh's association of Wagner and Berlioz (whose music he apparently knew something about secondhand) with Delacroix indicates that he regarded these composers as exemplary for their virtuosic handling and expressive use of sound color, as he regarded Delacroix from the time of his study of the writings of Blanc to be the supreme colorist among painters. This conclusion is confirmed by an observation contained in a letter to Wilhelmina of March or April 1888, where, in trying to describe the colorfulness of the South, Van Gogh articulated the most substantial and analytical statement about the music of Wagner found in all of his extant writings: "But by intensifying all the colors one arrives once again at quietude and harmony. There occurs in nature something similar to what happens in Wagner's music, which, though played by a big orchestra, is nonetheless intimate."[51] Still fresh in Van Gogh's mind about six weeks after his experience in the concert hall, the music of Wagner provided confirmation for his propensity to see and feel the South in vivid hues. He was then painting the blossoming orchards in the countryside around Arles, working on five or six canvases at once, seeking to harmonize the palette (his own and that of the landscape) which he described as "distinctly colorful."[52] Wagner's music offered a model for his efforts, encouraging, on the one hand, Van Gogh's simplification and exaggeration of colors and, on the other, the symphonic orchestration of these strong hues such as might in the end yield expressive effects of "quietude and harmony."[53]

Van Gogh's enthusiastic response to the example of Wagner and to modern concert music in general, though his own actual experience of this music was apparently very limited, suggests that his thinking was significantly influenced by the aesthetic discourse then current in Paris, which held music to be the paradigmatic art for its ideal union of form and content, its expressive force without reliance on imitation or narrative. A number of periodicals—for example, *La Revue wagnérienne, La Revue indépendante,* and *Le Symboliste*—could have provided access to such ideas, but it is impossible to draw any conclusions about Van Gogh's reading habits during his stay in Paris. It is certain, however, that he developed friendships with a number of artists and critics keenly interested in ways that painting might draw on the example of music.[54] Among the artists Van Gogh came to know in Paris, Gauguin, Bernard, and Signac, along with the critics Félix Fénéon and Gustave Kahn, stand out as the most likely contributors to his development of a musical approach to painting. Discussions with these individuals may have reawakened Van Gogh's earlier belief in the relevance of music to painting and provided the very encouragement and critical discussion of music-painting correspondences that he had doubtless found missing in Nuenen.

The chronology of these relationships remains highly uncertain due to the poverty of documentation for this period of Van Gogh's life. It is clear, however, that his friendships with other artists increased in number during his Paris sojourn and were most significant during the latter half of his two-year stay, especially in the final months.[55] Any significant contact between Van Gogh and Gauguin most likely began after the latter's return from Panama and Martinique in November 1887, just a few months prior to Vincent's own departure from Paris. An amateur cellist, Gauguin had begun thinking by the mid-1880s about the relative strengths and weaknesses of the different arts and the correspondences between them. In the manuscript entitled "Notes Synthétiques," variously dated between 1884 and 1888, he asserts that "harmonious colors correspond to the harmonies of sounds" and then briefly describes the analogous means by which both sounds and colors are derived from basic units.[56] Gauguin and Bernard were at least occasional concertgoers as their presence is documented at a Colonne concert "around 1889."[57] Van Gogh's association with Bernard was of longer duration, dating from the winter of 1886–1887 with a break between May and July 1887 when Bernard was in Brittany.

Bernard remembered Signac's working relationship with Van Gogh as having predated his own.[58] During the spring of 1887, Signac and Van Gogh painted out of doors together on a number of occasions in the Parisian suburbs of Asnières and Saint-Ouen. At the same time, Signac frequently played host in his studio to gatherings of an avant-garde coterie that included Seurat, Camille Pissarro, Charles Angrand, and Maximilien Luce, the writers Paul Adam, Jean Ajalbert, Henri de Régnier, and Paul Alexis, the critics Kahn and Fénéon, and the musician Jean-Baptiste Fauré. No account of these gatherings mentions the presence of Van Gogh. However, something of the content of the discussions that took place there, with their inevitable consideration of music and its paradigmatic value for the other arts, must have been passed on to him by Signac. Likewise, while Van Gogh's direct contact with Seurat seems to have been minimal, perhaps limited to as few as two encounters during the winter of 1887–1888, Signac was likely a conduit for the "musical" aesthetic being developed by Seurat, his close associate at the time.[59] Seurat was then embarking on a series of paintings of entertainment subjects which include musicians (for example, *La Parade* of 1887–1888), and which thematize music as the embodiment of, and means of access to, a higher reality.[60] In an 1891 obituary article on the artist, Kahn noted that Seurat "spoke . . . in a very literary and articulate fashion, seeking to compare the progress of his art with the evolution of the arts of sound, very preoccupied with finding a unity at the heart of his efforts and those of poets and musicians."[61]

The artists mentioned here have long been cited as significant influences on Van Gogh's rapid development as a painter while in Paris. What has not been recognized is that contact with members of the Parisian avant-garde almost certainly reawakened Van Gogh's earlier belief in the relevance of music to painting. That Van Gogh sought to attend concerts of Wagner's music during the same period of time lends support to the conclusion that his relationships with Signac, Gauguin, Bernard, and perhaps others included some discussion of music and its paradigmatic value for painting.

A number of statements in Van Gogh's writings from Arles indicate a familiarity with themes prevalent in the avant-garde aesthetic discourse specific to Paris in the late 1880s. Beginning in the spring of 1888, Van Gogh compared the act of painting to a musical performance on several occasions, writing, for example, of the difficulty of getting "one's brush-work firm and interwoven with feeling, like a piece of music played with emotion."[62] Subsequently, he wondered whether he had "really sang a lullaby in colors" in the painting of *La Berceuse* and likened his interpretive copying of the works of Millet and other painters while at Saint-Rémy to what a musician does in performing the work of a composer.[63] The trope of painter as musician is, thus, a recurrent motif in the post-Paris writings of Van Gogh, employed in a variety of contexts to signify the artist's own identity, the manual practice of his art, and his expressive aims.

Another idea that found wide currency in avant-garde circles during the late 1880s is the belief that art in general, and music especially, embodied a superior level of existence, which was revealed to the general public by the artist-musician endowed with the visionary capacity to discern a higher and truer reality. Van Gogh adumbrated this concept as early as 1882, when he claimed to perceive "pictures in the poorest huts, in the dirtiest corner" because the "music" of his artistic imagination enabled him to see to the essence of things, in places where the mundane mentality would see nothing of value or interest.[64] A few months after leaving Paris for Arles, he invoked the idea of music as metaphor for the "better life" with particular clarity, when he wrote: "In the end we shall have had enough of cynicism and skepticism and humbug, and we shall want to live more musically."[65] In the rambling speculative context of this letter, music and art are also cited as the very means to the attainment of the higher "musical" life, for "you cannot study Japanese art . . . without becoming much gayer and happier."[66]

Van Gogh's late-Paris paintings and post-Paris writings also reveal a significant shift in his handling of visual form, especially the element of color, which is consistent with the Wagnerian critic Téodor de Wyzewa's recommendation of an "expressive and musical" approach over an inferior "sensuous and descriptive" one.[67] Numerous letters, most particularly those cited at the beginning of this essay from the summer of 1888, testify to the artist's more subjective and abstract treatment of visual form, his intentional exaggeration, simplification, and "orchestration" of color. In seeking effects of an emotional and spiritual nature such as "quietude," "rest," and "consolation," Van Gogh's painting was practiced, at least intermittently, in conscious emulation of music.

The *Still-Life with Fruit* (Figure 8–4), from the end of 1887, illustrates the considerable extent to which Van Gogh's painting had deviated from a descriptive and impressionist character even before his departure from Paris.[68] The painting's dedication *à mon frère Theo* (indicated below the artist's signature and date), along with its color-coordinated frame, suggests that the work held unusual importance for the artist.[69] It must be regarded as one of Van Gogh's most daring paintings to date, its dense mesh of broken brushstrokes in arching rhythms signifying an autumn landscape almost as plausibly as fruit recumbent on mounds of drapery. Both spatial definition and local color have been sacrificed to the goal of formal harmony. Large areas of the drapery ground adhere emphatically to the painting's surface, just as the lobes of fruit, modeled in color and outlined along many contours, resist the illusion of mass.

Figure 8–4. Vincent van Gogh, *Still Life with Fruit* (F383), 1887, oil on canvas, 49 × 65 cm., Van Gogh Museum (Vincent van Gogh Foundation), Amsterdam.

The golden color of the frame accentuates the unity of surface by fusing the image with its border instead of setting it into relief.

Most striking of all the painting's features is its brilliant mono-chromatic coloring. This is clearly a painting conceived in a specific color key, the ubiquitous yellow made more intense, made to mirror itself, as Blanc recommended, through variation across a spectrum ranging from deep ochre to a paleness approaching white. Complementary hues are subtly worked into the details of the fruit: the orange-gold hue of the lemons intensified by blue cast shadows, and red and green brush-strokes placed in vibrating juxtaposition across the swelling planes of the larger fruit. The frame manifests further modulation of the dominant yellow, its broad main surface of orange-yellow subtly shifting to a greenish cast on the inner beveled edge. Intense subjective color, summarily defined forms, depth-denying space, and rhythmic broken brushstrokes all function to minimize the descriptive character of the work and heighten its "musicality" and expressivity.

As a result, the content of this bold work has little to do with the conventional meanings of mundane experience or the traditions of still-life painting and almost everything to do with the feelings engendered by the painting's pervasive yellow color, its harmony of form and lively brushwork. Functioning like the "emotional signs" prescribed by Wyzewa, these formal features convey ideas of luminosity and warmth, the unity and abundance of nature, harmony and concord. The breadth of meaning evoked by the still life is analogous to the wide range of subjective response that a work of instrumental music might provoke, a virtue for which works of music were prized. Any of the meanings suggested here might engender the consolation that Van Gogh associated with music and that he sought to convey with his own painting "by the actual radiance and vibration of [their] coloring."[70]

By the time Van Gogh left Paris for Arles, music figured significantly among the several models he drew upon to guide and inspire his own artistic efforts. His letters mention music as often and with an emphasis roughly equal to that accorded the Japanese print and the French realist novel. He had come to regard German concert music, along with the French novel and Greek sculpture, as the highest of artistic accomplishments, offering discernable lessons for the painter.[71] These lessons had been gleaned from a variety of experiences which, though disparate in nature and limited in number, nonetheless complemented one another in a meaningful fashion. Though Van Gogh's self-made and independently pursued discovery of the relevance of music to painting in Nuenen produced little immediate result, that introduction prepared him to be receptive and even somewhat knowledgeable when he encountered critical discourse in Paris championing the music of Wagner and linking the arts. There, his interest in music renewed, he availed himself of opportunities for firsthand experience of music and apparently found the stimulating debate and encouragement of musical painting that were missing from his experience in Nuenen.

Arles provided the necessary distance for reflection on these experiences and for the assimilation of Van Gogh's musical paradigm. He had come to realize that a quest for specific formal equivalents between music and painting was futile, but that music, if considered more generally and conceptually, might indeed be a useful model. He perceived the promising future of painting to lie in its increasing emulation of music's nonrepresentational nature, its intense though carefully coordinated sonorities, its subtlety, and its consoling affect. Sometimes identifying himself as a painter with the making of music, Van Gogh cultivated the vivid color harmonies that distinguish his mature work, striving for the comforting sentiments that he associated with music and that would allow one "to live more musically."

NOTES

I wish to acknowledge, with gratitude, the assistance provided by Robert Stanton, Roger Niles, Erika Scavillo, Marsha Morton, and Stephen Michelman with various aspects of this project. I thank Dan Maultsby and Wofford College for funds to support research, travel, and the acquisition of photographs.

[1]This painting, numbered 412 in the 1970 *catalogue raisonné* compiled by Jean-Baptiste de la Faille, is also known as *The Harvest Landscape* and *The Harvest (Blue Cart)*. Van Gogh's description of the subject is from his letter to Theo 496, in *The Complete Letters of Vincent van Gogh,* 2nd ed., 3 vols. (Greenwich, Conn.: New York Graphic Society, 1959), II, 582; hereafter cited by letter, volume, and page number only. In L498, II, 585, Van Gogh mentions *Harvest at La Crau* again, stating: "it isn't at all finished, but it kills everything else I have. . . ."

[2]*La Mousmé,* F431; *The Old Peasant,* F443; L520, II, 6.

[3]L535, III, 33; and L526, III, 18.

[4]L528, III, 21.

[5]L531, III, 25.

[6]L370, II, 292–294. Van Gogh doesn't explain the means of his awareness of the Blanc text or how he gained access to it in letter 370. This is apparent from a letter to Rappard (R48, III, 407), editorially dated September, in which he indi-

cates that he is returning the book and expresses his thanks for the use of it. Both Rappard and Theo had visited Nuenen in May 1884. Presumably, at that time Rappard lent the book to Vincent, who then told Theo about it verbally and so did not need to provide an explanation of his discovery of the book in a subsequent letter.

[7]Blanc's essay on Delacroix was first published in 1864, a year after the artist's death, as an article in two parts in the January and February issues of the *Gazette des Beaux-Arts,* and reprinted within *Les Artistes de mon Temps* in 1876. Van Gogh copied the anecdotal opening paragraphs of the essay on Delacroix in L370, II, 293. Here Delacroix affirms the opinion that "great colorists don't paint local color" with the assertion that "if one said to Paul Veronese: Paint me a beautiful blonde woman whose flesh would have that [dirty gray] tone, he would paint her, and the woman *would be a blonde in his picture.*" Van Gogh made subsequent references to this anecdote in L371, 379, 401, 403, 404, 405, 408, 424, 425, 428, 429, and to Van Rappard in R47, R48, R58. For a comprehensive inventory of the references in the artist's correspondence to this essay as well as a vast number of other texts, see Fieke Pabst and Evert van Uitert, "A literary life, with a list of books and periodicals read by Van Gogh," *Rijksmuseum Vincent van Gogh,* ed. Evert van Uitert (Amsterdam: Rijksmuseum Vincent van Gogh, 1987), 68–90.

[8]Blanc, *Les Artistes de mon Temps,* 64; translation by the author. Van Gogh copied a lengthy passage dealing with basic principles of color from the Delacroix essay into L401. This passage is editorially labeled erroneously in the *Collected Letters* as a "translation of the French pages by Delacroix" when, in fact, the source is Blanc's essay on Delacroix.

[9]Blanc, *Les Artistes de mon Temps,* 62.

[10]Ibid.

[11]Ibid., 72–73. Blanc here quotes Adalbert de Beaumont. This translation is taken from Blanc, *The Grammar of Painting and Engraving,* trans. Kate Newell Doggett (New York: Hurd and Houghton, 1874), 165, where the discussion of the "modulation of colors" reappears.

[12]Blanc, *Les Artistes de mon Temps,* 28, 71.

[13]Ibid., 69.

[14]Ibid., 59; translation by the author.

[15]Perhaps Blanc also wanted to avoid revealing his reliance on Baudelaire for this idea, though he quotes other writers at length within the Delacroix essay and clearly acknowledges his debt to them. The recommendation that a painting be viewed from a distance is a recurrent idea in Baudelaire's writings on art, appearing first, to my knowledge, in his review of "The Salon of 1846": "The right way of knowing whether a picture is melodious is to look at it from far enough

away to make it impossible for us to see what it is about or appreciate its lines. If it is melodious, it already has a meaning, and has already taken a place in our collection of memories." He repeated this advice at least twice, in "The Salon of 1859" and "The Life and Work of Eugène Delacroix," published serially in 1863. The first and last of these instances can be found in Charles Baudelaire, *Selected Writings on Art and Literature,* trans. P. E. Charvet (London: Penguin, 1972), 57, 370.

[16]Eugène Delacroix, *Oeuvres littéraire,* ed. Elie Faure, 2 vols. (Paris: G. Crès, 1923), II, 138. Published only in 1893 and thus apparently unknown to Blanc, Delacroix's journals contain numerous judgments on composers and compositions, accounts of performances attended, and ruminations on the similarities and differences, strengths and weaknesses, of the various arts, providing plentiful evidence of his passion for music. "Superiority of music; absence of reasoning (not of logic)," wrote Delacroix in a journal entry for October 16, 1857. "I was thinking of this when I listened to the simple piece for organ and cello which Batta played for us this evening, after having played it over dinner. The intense delight which music gives me—it seems that the intellect has no share in the pleasure. That is why pedants class music as a lower form of art." See *The Journal of Eugene Delacroix,* ed. Hubert Wellington and trans. Lucy Norton (London: Phaidon, 1995), 395–396. For analysis of the place of music in the thought and art of Delacroix, see Thomas Regelski, "Music and Painting in the Paragon of Eugene Delacroix" (Ph.D. diss., Ohio University, 1970). As founder of the *Gazette des Beaux-Arts* in 1859, Blanc would have known and was presumably sympathetic to the ideas contained in Louis Viardot's essay, *"Ut pictura musica,"* published in its inaugural issue. Viardot is primarily concerned with what he perceives to be parallels in the histories of the arts of painting and music, based, in part, on assumed correspondences between the elements of melody and design, harmony and color. See *Gazette des Beaux-Arts* 1 (1859): 19–29.

[17]R47, III, 406. Van Gogh repeats this announcement, along with an offer to lend the book to Van Rappard, in R48, III, 407. He sent the *Grammaire* to Theo some time later, as indicated in L430, II, 430, editorially dated November 1885.

[18]Blanc, *The Grammar of Painting and Engraving,* 12.

[19]Ibid., 117.

[20]Ibid., 148.

[21]Leonard Euler, *Briefe an eine deutsche Prinzessinn über verschiederne Gegenstünd aus der Physik und Philosophie,* (Leipzig, 1773–1774), cited by Blanc, *The Grammar of Painting and Engraving,* 164.

[22]Blanc, *The Grammar of Painting and Engraving,* 164.

[23]Ibid., 148. By the "seven notes of music," Blanc presumably means the seven different notes of the diatonic scale, for example, C-D-E-F-G-A-B. John

Gage, in *Color and Culture* (Boston: Bulfinch, 1993), 232, notes that: "Newton had argued for a 'musical' division of the spectrum of white light" as early as 1669 and that, as his ideas on the structure of color developed, he persisted in his search for agreement between the divisions and proportions of a fundamental color series and those of musical scales. The diagram of the color wheel contained in the *Opticks,* as published in 1704, was based on Descartes's circular diagram of the tempered diatonic scale found in his *Compendium Musicae,* written in 1618 and published in 1650.

[24]L574, III, 132.

[25]L371, II, 297, and L430, II, 429.

[26]L371, II, 298. Italics here indicate underlines in the original correspondence. This is the same letter in which Van Gogh describes the "laws of color" as "unutterably beautiful" and then refers to Blanc, his source for these "laws," in citing the exemplary use of black by Velazquez.

[27]L430, II, 429; L429, II, 426.

[28]L429, II, 427.

[29]L429, II, 428.

[30]Blanc, *The Grammar of Painting and Engraving,* 5.

[31]Ibid., 169.

[32]L520 III, 6.

[33]Van Gogh describes the beginning of his friendship with Kerssemakers in L386, II, 327–329. Wanting to learn to paint, Kerssemakers received some instruction from Van Gogh and worked with him on numerous occasions in the studio of one or the other as well as in the countryside surrounding Nuenen. Kerssemakers accompanied Van Gogh to visit the newly opened Rijksmuseum and to see other collections of painting in Amsterdam in October 1885. He gives a vivid account of the experience; in his reminiscence included in *Collected Letters,* II, 443–449.

[34]Ibid., II, 447.

[35]Ibid., II, 442.

[36]L539, III, 44.

[37]This latter possibility is consistent with a number of statements made later in the artist's career, for example, when he writes Theo from the hospital in Arles in January 1889: "Perhaps someday everyone will have neurosis, St. Vitus' dance, or something else. But doesn't the antidote exist? In Delacroix, in Berlioz, and Wagner?" (L574, III, 132). My conclusions about the beginnings of Van Gogh's interest in music differ on a number of points from those of Roland Dorn, one of the very few scholars to give serious thought to the topic, in "Van Gogh, Gauguin und Richard Wagner, eine Etude auf das Jahr 1888," *Les Symbolistes et Richard Wagner/Die Symbolisten und Richard Wagner,* ed. Wolfgang Storch

(Berlin: Edition Hentrich, 1991), 67. I thank Professor Erika Scavillo for her invaluable help with the translation of this study. Dorn states that "remarks by Delacroix about the musicality of color caused Van Gogh to study piano" (67). As I have shown, I believe it was remarks by Blanc about Delacroix and about the correspondences between color and music that prompted Van Gogh to study music, not piano in the sense of musical performance.

[38]In this vein, Van Gogh compared Margot Begemann, who had taken poison when her family objected to her liaison with the artist, to "a Cremona violin spoiled by bad, bungling repairs. And the condition she was in when I met her proved to be rather too damaged. But originally it was a rare specimen of great value. . . ." (L377, II, 307)

Writing to John Russell shortly after his arrival in Arles, Van Gogh complements the Australian artist for his ability to paint both "scherzos" and more serious works. His use of metaphor seems to betray a superficial knowledge of music, however, when he says "you are at the same time able to give a Scherzo, the adagio con expressione, the gay note, in one word together with more manly conceptions of a higher order." (L477a, II, 547) The phrase *adagio con expressione,* which Van Gogh appears to use parenthetically to scherzo, would be appropriate to a slow, lyrical musical movement and not a gay and lively one, as is a scherzo.

[39]Van Gogh's persistent naivete, in spite of his growing interest in music, is revealed in a remark of January 1889 when, in describing to Theo his portrait of Augustine Roulin entitled *La Berceuse,* he wrote: "A woman in orange hair standing out against a background of green with pink flowers. Now these discordant sharps of crude pink, crude orange, and crude green are softened by flats of red and green." (L574, III, 129) While this painting was, perhaps, Van Gogh's most important and intentional effort to create a musical image, his explanatory use of musical terminology betrays a misunderstanding of music theory. Sharps are not balanced against flats in a musical composition; their presence depends upon the tonal center(s) and degree of chromatic inflection chosen by the composer. A composition written in a key of many flats, even one of considerable length and harmonic fluctuation, may contain no sharps at all. Nor are sharps inherently "crude" in contrast to the "softness" of flats. A musical work does, however, contain a balance between consonant harmonies and dissonant ones. Interpreted loosely in this way, as a comparison of chordal structures in music and chromatic design in painting, Van Gogh's statement makes a meaningful point in vivid terms which may well have guided the making of the Madame Roulin portrait. For an interpretation of this portrait as an essay in "musical" composition, see Kermit S. Champa, "*La Berceuse*—Authored by Music?" in

"Masterpiece" Studies: Manet, Zola, Van Gogh, and Monet (University Park, Penn.: Pennsylvania State University Press, 1994), 91–118.

[40]Of course, the difficulty Van Gogh faced in trying to find useful parallels between painting and music is similar to that confronted by the interpreter who attempts to discern evidence of nonvisual influences in his paintings. In the absence of musical subject matter and established formal equivalents, the influence (if present at all) may be purely conceptual in nature and clearly signaled only by verbal explanations of the artist's interests and intentions.

[41]Letter from Theo to Wilhelmina van Gogh, March 14, 1888: "Vóór hij wegging, ging ik een paar maal een Wagnerconcert met hem horen, wij vonden het beiden zeer mooi"; cited in Dorn, "Van Gogh, Gauguin und Richard Wagner," 211.

[42]In 1881, Lamoureux founded the Nouveaux Concerts, which subsequently became known as the Concerts Lamoureux. First held at the Théâtre du Chateau-d'Eau, these concerts were moved to the Eden Theater in 1885 and to the Cirque d'Été on the Champs-Élysées in October 1887. Pasdeloup led the series established in 1861 and formally named the Concerts Populaire de Musique Classique, but generally referred to as the Concerts Pasdeloup. They were housed in the Cirque d'Hiver, a "round" structure of twenty sides originally called the Cirque Napoléon in the eleventh arrondisement. The Concert National formed in 1873 under Édouard Colonne, with the Concerts Colonne presented initially at the Odéon Theater and then moved in 1874 to the Châtelet. The Société des Concerts du Conservatoire were begun in 1828 by François Habeneck and conducted in the late 1880s by Jules Auguste Garcin, who promoted a broad range of German choral and orchestral music from Bach to Wagner and Brahms.

[43]For other images depicting the circumstances of these orchestral concerts, see John Singer Sargent's *Sketch: Rehearsal of the Pasdeloup Orchestra at the Cirque d'Hiver,* 1876, Boston Museum of Fine Arts; and Félix Vallotton, *The Third Gallery at the Théâtre du Châtelet,* 1895, Musée d'Orsay, Paris.

[44]Carol Zemel counts seventeen self-portraits from the Paris period, out of twenty-eight total, in which Van Gogh presents himself in the attire proper to the social sphere of "bourgeois society and art commerce." See the chapter "Self-Portraits: The Construction of Professional Identity" in *Van Gogh's Progress* (Berkeley: University of California Press, 1997), especially pp. 147–149.

[45]Van Gogh acknowledged the distraction of visual stimuli in the concert hall when he remarked in a letter to Theo, editorially dated to February 3, 1889: "But have you *heard* [*La Mireille* by Mistral] yet, for you know perhaps that Gounod has set it to music, at least I think so. Naturally I do not know the music, and even if I heard it I should be watching the musicians rather than listening"

(L575, III, 133). Van Gogh produced a few images of musicians and the environment of the dance hall while in Antwerp and Paris (F1350v, 1350a, 1350b, 1244cv, 1244a, 1244b, 1244av, 1244c, 1244d, 1244dv, 1714), but these were merely quick sketches of small size that led to nothing more finished or ambitious in scale. These sketches locate Van Gogh, most likely, in the environment of a café-concert, a setting that would have allowed him the close view of the musicians and the freedom of movement that the sketches imply. There, he reported, "one can amuse oneself a whole evening" (L442, II, 465). Though finding the musical entertainment "very dull" and "insipid," the beauty of the women, the heads of the sailors and soldiers, and their lively activity engaged him fully (L438, II, 455). His interest, thus, may be attributed less to the appeal of the music than to the fact that the café-concert provided an opportunity to observe and record a variety of figural types absorbed in watching, dancing, and music-making.

[46]The early issues of *La Revue wagnérienne,* beginning in 1885, provide a chronicle of the performance of musical works by Wagner, but this feature is missing from the periodical's later issues. The *Revue* was published monthly until July 1887 when it was continued on a bimonthly basis until December 1887, with a final issue appearing in July 1888. Thus, its coverage skips the very period during which the Van Goghs attended concerts of Wagner's music. Martine Kahane and Nicole Wild, in *Wagner et la France* (Paris: Éditions Herscher, 1983), 158–173, include a record of Wagnerian works performed in Paris between 1841 and 1914, but this inventory is woefully incomplete. Both reviews of recent concerts and announcements of upcoming performances may be found in *Le Ménestrel* (Paris, 1833–1940), upon which I rely heavily for the information on concert programs presented here. I thank Stephen Michelman and Marsha Morton for their kind assistance in securing this information.

[47]Known only fragmentarily until recently, this letter appears in Douglas Cooper, *Paul Gauguin: 45 Lettres à Vincent, Théo et Jo van Gogh* ('s Gravenhage: Staatsuitgeverij, 1983), 264–271. The letter is translated by Pickvance in *Vincent van Gogh Exhibition* (Tokyo: National Museum of Western Art, 1985), 257–260.

[48]Ronald Pickvance raises the question, "Why Arles?" and considers a number of possible explanations in *Van Gogh in Arles* (New York: 1984), 11–12.

[49]*Mélanges Posthumes* (Paris, 1919), 137–138, cited in Paul Smith, *Seurat and the Avant-garde,* (New Haven: Yale University Press, 1997), 155.

[50]In June 1888 (L494, II, 578), a few months after leaving Paris, Van Gogh reported of reading a book on Wagner and commented briefly: "What an artist— one like that in painting would be something. It *will come.*" In January 1889 (L574, III, 132), after his first breakdown, Van Gogh wrote: "Perhaps someday

everyone will have neurosis, St. Vitus' dance, or something else. But doesn't the antidote exist? In Delacroix, in Berlioz, and Wagner?" At the same time he wrote to Gauguin: "Ah! my dear friend to make painting like that which is already before us the music of Berlioz and Wagner [*sic*] . . . a consoling art for broken hearts! As yet there are only a few of us like you and me who feel!!!" See Pickvance, *Vincent van Gogh Exhibition,* 260.

[51]W3, III, 431. Pickvance, in *Van Gogh in Arles,* 262, dates this letter to March 30, 1888. The letter provides a particularly interesting example of Van Gogh's fluid thinking in the assimilation of highly varied sources, for, in trying to explain his own efforts to achieve a gaily colorful but deeply expressive style of painting, he cites, in rapid succession and with equal emphasis, models in recent French literature, the music of Wagner, and Japanese prints. While the literary and visual examples in this group have been previously studied in some detail, in keeping with the tendencies of past scholarship, the musical model has not.

[52]W3, III, 431.

[53]Ibid.

[54]Mark Roskill, in *Van Gogh, Gauguin, and the Impressionist Circle* (Greenwich, Conn.: New York Graphic Society, 1970), 91–92, provides a concise summary of the contacts Van Gogh made in Paris which may have contributed to the development of a musical approach to the organization of color in his paintings.

[55]I rely on the analysis of Bogomila Welsh-Ovcharov in *Vincent van Gogh: His Paris Period 1886–88* (Utrecht: Editions Victorine, 1976), 19–40, for the chronology of Van Gogh's relations with other artists in Paris.

[56]This text is reprinted in Herschel B. Chipp, *Theories of Modern Art* (Berkeley: University of California Press, 1968), 60–64, where a date of circa 1888 is given. Daniel Guerin proposes a date of 1884–1885 in *Paul Gauguin: The Writings of a Savage,* trans. Eleanor Levieux (New York: Viking, 1978), 8–11. In his later writings Gauguin frequently draws analogies between music and the formal and decorative aspects of painting: "In [decorative] art, color becomes essentially musical. In the cathedral we like to hear the orderly, auditory translation of our thoughts; to the same extent, color is music, polyphony, symphony, whatever you want to call it." See "Decorative Art," in ibid., 12.

[57]Emile Schuffenecker introduced Bernard at this time to Odilon Redon, who was also in attendance. See Roseline Bacou and Arï Redon, *Lettres de Gauguin, Gide, Huysmans, Jammes, Mallarmé, Verhaeren . . . à Odilon Redon* (Paris: Librairie José Corti, 1960), 203.

[58]Welsh-Ovcharov, *Vincent van Gogh: His Paris Period,* 30. In 1883, Signac christened his first sailboat "Manet-Zola-Wagner." While this may have been primarily a youthful gesture of bourgeois provocation, as Cachin suggests, the

act nonetheless indicates Signac's awareness of Wagner's prominence in cultural politics and even a kind of hero-worship of him. See Françoise Cachin, *Paul Signac,* trans. Michael Bullock (Greenwich, Conn.: New York Graphic Society, 1971), 15. Probably under the influence of Charles Henry's "scientific aesthetics," Signac later assigned descriptive-musical titles to a few paintings, for example, *Setting Sun, Sardine Fishing, Adagio,* 1891.

⁵⁹Welsh-Ovcharov, in *Vincent van Gogh: His Paris Period,* 28, states that Van Gogh met Seurat during the fall or winter of 1887–1888 at the exhibition organized by Van Gogh at the *Du Chalet* restaurant. Vincent later paid a visit to Seurat's studio just prior to his departure from Paris for Arles. She mentions also the possibility that Seurat visited Van Gogh at his rue Lepic apartment on one occasion (57, n. 38).

⁶⁰Seurat's pursuit of "Wagnerian painting" has only recently been explored in depth by Paul Smith, who convincingly establishes Seurat's interest in French Wagnerist theory and identifies its place in his later paintings, in *Seurat and the Avant-garde,* 105–156.

⁶¹Gustave Kahn, "Seurat," *L'Art moderne,*" April 5, 1891, 107–110, cited in Smith, *Seurat and the Avant-garde,* 107.

⁶²L543, III, 57.

⁶³L571a, III, 124; L607, III, 216. Writing to Wilhelmina in the summer of 1888 (W4, III, 435), he asserted that a painter, like a musician, would be able to amuse and impress an audience with the skills required "within a few hours . . . to paint that wheat field, and the sky above it, in perspective, in the distance." Champa, in *Masterpiece Studies,* 114–118, discusses Van Gogh's musical approach to the practice of "copying" in connection with *La Berceuse,* which exists in five different versions.

⁶⁴L218, I, 416.

⁶⁵L542, III, 55.

⁶⁶L542, III, 55.

⁶⁷"Notes sur la peinture wagnérienne et le Salon de 1886," *La Revue wagnérienne* 2 (May 8, 1886): 100–113. The pertinent passages are translated by Henri Dorra, in *Symbolist Art Theories* (Berkeley: University of California Press, 1994), 148–149.

⁶⁸F383; the still life goes by a number of slightly varying titles, for example, *White Grapes, Apples, Pears and Lemons,* in Ronald de Leeuw, *Van Gogh at the Van Gogh Museum* (Zwolle: Waanders, 1995), 89; *Lemons, Pears, Apples, Grapes and an Orange,* in Melissa McQuillan, *Van Gogh* (London: Thames and Hudson, 1989), 161–162; and *White Grapes, Apples, Pears, Lemons, and Orange,* in Hulsker, *The Complete Van Gogh,* 302.

[69]The importance of the painting for Van Gogh is confirmed by an apparent fragmentary reference to the still life within the background of one of the Tanguy portraits (F364) painted just prior to the artist's departure for Arles. There, the inner edge of the frame is painted red, as was the still life's painted frame in an earlier state. Traces of red can be detected through the greenish-gold applied later. On this point see Evert van Uitert, Louis van Tilborgh, and Sjraar van Heugten, *Vincent van Gogh* (Amsterdam: Rijksmuseum Vincent van Gogh, 1990), 86–87.

[70]L531, III, 25. The still life's novel frame and emphatic color key, based on a dominant hue, indicate a strong resemblance to elements of Seurat's "Wagnerian" painting. The handling of these features by the painters, however, differs considerably. Seurat adopted a dark pointillist treatment of the frame, in imitation of the darkened Wagnerian theater which focused attention on the illuminated drama on stage. On this point, see Smith, *Seurat and the Avant-Garde,* 132. While Seurat's paintings were conceived in terms of dominant colors and specific color keys, they were perhaps never as boldly monochromatic as the Van Gogh still life.

[71]B6, III, 485.

CHAPTER 9

Music to Our Ears?
Munch's *Scream* and Romantic Music Theory

ELIZABETH PRELINGER

> *The world sounds. It is a cosmos of spiritually*
> *active beings. Even dead matter is living spirit.*
> —WASSILY KANDINSKY, C.1910
> "ÜBER DIE FORMFRAGE,"
> *DER BLAUE REITER ALMANACH*

This chapter examines the relationship between music and one specific image, *The Scream,* which the Norwegian artist Edvard Munch painted in 1893 (Figure 9–1) and made into a black-and-white lithograph in 1895 (Figure 9–2). Although the image has become so well integrated into the popular culture of the late twentieth century that it may seem difficult to look at afresh, it nevertheless is rich enough in meaning to sustain further scrutiny. Like many landscape images of the nineteenth century, *The Scream* is deeply implicated with music. Students of music history today find *The Scream* in their textbooks used as a visual corollary to the dissonance and atonality of the Expressionist music of Arnold Schoenberg and Alban Berg.[1] The image has always been interpreted as a synesthetic representation of sound, with the swirling lines and acid colors representing visual correspondences to the scream of unknown origin, which pierces nature and which traumatizes the distorted figure in the foreground. This interpretation makes sense both in terms of Munch's oeuvre and in terms of fin de siècle aesthetics.

However, I propose that in *The Scream,* and especially in the black-and-white lithographed version, Munch addressed the notion of music in a way that was far more intricate, one that transcended the ideal of synes-

Figure 9–1. Edvard Munch, *The Scream,* 1893, tempera and oil pastel on cardboard, 91 × 73.5 cm., Nasjonalgalleriet, Oslo.

thesia so popular at the end of the century. In fact, though *The Scream* draws upon the decorative motif of the arabesque, it simultaneously engages complex theories of the relationship between visual art and music formulated by German idealist philosophers and artists at the beginning of the nineteenth century and assimilated at the fin de siècle by the French Symbolists. This paper thus explores how Munch invested a dec-

Figure 9–2. Edvard Munch, *The Scream,* 1895, lithograph with tusche on heavy cream wove paper, 51.3 × 38.5 cm. The Vivian and David Campbell Collection; photograph courtesy of the Art Gallery of Ontario, Toronto.

orative motif with the weight of a century's worth of artistic and philosophical debate regarding music and the visual arts. In its brilliant synthesis of formal and philosophical content, *The Scream* simultaneously signalled the end of nineteenth-century Romanticism and the beginning of twentieth-century modernism.

Like many of his avant-garde contemporaries at the end of the nine-teenth century, Edvard Munch was steeped in the *paragone,* the idea of correspondences among the arts. The ancient concept was still vital in the fin-de-siècle period among Munch's friends and acquaintances, in-cluding the writers Stanislaw Przybyszewski, Charles Baudelaire, and Stéphane Mallarmé, whose Tuesday evening salons Munch attended while in Paris in the 1890s, and among such artists as Max Klinger, Paul Gauguin, and Maurice Denis, all of whom wrote extensively about the relationship between music and painting.[2] In the intellectual and artistic circles of Christiania (Oslo), Paris, and Berlin, all of which Munch fre-quented, synesthetic correspondences among the arts were virtually taken for granted, finding expression both in poetry and in such works of visual art as Gauguin's *Whence Come We? What Are We? Where Are We Going?* of 1897, which the artist claimed Mallarmé had described as a "musical poem that needs no libretto."[3]

Romantic theory regarding the relationship between music and the visual arts was chanelled to Munch and his contemporaries through con-duits as varied and as international as the canvases of the Norwegian romantic painter Johann Christian Clausen Dahl, the writings of Baude-laire, and the German philosopher Friedrich Nietzsche, the last of whom, along with the composer Richard Wagner, Munch considered the great-est figure of German culture, and in whose work he and his friends were deeply immersed, in particular during Munch's sojourn in Berlin in the early 1890s. In France, as well as Germany, much attention was focused on the music of Wagner, the fulcrum of a wide-ranging discussion about the correspondences between music and color that had been a matter of active debate since the time of Goethe. As Gerard Vaughan has observed in his seminal article on the Nabi artist Maurice Denis and music, the French theorist and composer Edouard Dujardin, cofounder with Théodore de Wyzéwa of *La Revue wagnérienne,* also linked Charles Baudelaire's notion of the "inherent musicality of colour" directly to German idealist philosophers such as Arthur Schopenhauer, whose works, though translated into French in the 1880s, had been well-known before then.[4] Aspects of German idealist thought, some of which will be discussed below, were further summarized in Denis's famous treatise of 1890, *Définition du néo-traditionnisme,* at the end of which he af-firmed his argument about the music/color analogy, writing: "The blue arabesques of the ground—a marvelous accompaniment to the engulfing and persuasive rhythm of the orange motif, like the seduction of the vio-lins in the overture to *Tannhäuser!*"[5] However, Denis's arabesque, an ornamental, rhythmic configuration of sinuous line and color, essentially remained a formal device, however eloquent; by contrast, Munch's deployment of the arabesque was ultimately more affective, a conflation of French decorativeness with Germanic *Empfindung*.[6] Indeed, Munch's art had always been perceived as intensely "nordic," related more to northern Romanticism and neo-Romanticism than to their later derivative, Symbolism, especially in its more cerebral French version.[7]

Munch himself was involved with music in a variety of ways, including a close friendship with the English composer Frederick Delius. Most importantly, he was deeply attuned to synesthetic experiences, both how visual impressions can evoke sound and, by contrast, how sound can affect visual impressions, function by association, and occasion mood changes. There are many musical observations scattered throughout Munch's manuscripts; in 1890, for example, he wrote of hearing a performance of Rumanian singers, where the "soft music melted the colours together."[8]

Contemporaries of Munch recognized Munch's tendency to compose his paintings in musical terms. In an article of 1891, the painter Christian Krogh wrote of the painting *Evening,* or *Jealousy,* of 1891, observing that:

> The latest motto is "resonant colour." Has anyone experienced such resonance in colour as in this picture? . . . Perhaps this borders on music rather than painting, but as such it is brilliant. Munch deserves a civil list grant as a composer.[9]

But synesthesia represents only one aspect of the relationship of Munch's work to music. Early on, he invoked music in other ways. For example, the artist himself perceived the great series of paintings that he called *The Frieze of Life* in explicitly musical terms; he called it a symphony. In a letter written later in life, Munch observed that when he hung the canvases of love, death, jealousy, and anxiety together, he found that "various paintings had connections to each other through their content. When they were placed together, suddenly a single musical tone passed through them and they became totally different from what they had previously been. A symphony resulted. It was in this way that I began to paint friezes."[10]

The need to read the paintings successively and experience their sensations progressively demonstrates Munch's acknowledgment of the importance of an issue that would be crucial to the evocation of music in

The Scream: the presence of the fourth dimension, time. Temporality, or sequentiality, which Munch had explored through the *Frieze of Life* series, became one feature among several that create musicality in Munch's single image of *The Scream*. The additional characteristics that relate musicality to the visual arts according to Romantic thought and which are addressed in *The Scream* include the use of landscape as subject, the tendency towards abstraction in visual notation, and the consequent distance from mimesis in representation—all of which combine to produce the profound degree of subjectivity associated with music.

These strategies to create musicality in painting were developed in the early nineteenth century as Romantic theorists began to devise responses to Gottfried Lessing's treatise of 1766, the *Laokoön*. As discussed more completely by Philippe Junod elsewhere in this volume, in this treatise, the Enlightenment writer challenged Horace's notion of *ut pictura poesis,* maintaining that the sister arts of poetry and painting were in fact distinguished by different aesthetic criteria, and that the boundaries of each medium should not be transgressed. In particular, he stressed, poetry was the art of time, painting the art of space. Lessing was concerned about what Rensselaer Lee has called the "serious confusion of the arts" prevailing at the time, and attempted to restore proper delimitations on each medium.[11]

At the same time, the efflorescence of music in Germany and Austria in the eighteenth century, with the work of composers such as Bach, Haydn, Mozart, and Beethoven, resulted in the gradual dominance of a *musical* rather than a literary paradigm for painting, a concept that would make its way to France during the course of the nineteenth century.[12] In their pursuit of individuality, spontaneity, emotivity, and spirituality, the generation of Romantic philosophers and painters, including Hegel, Schopenhauer, Schiller, the Schlegel brothers, Schelling, Adam Müller, and Wackenroder, as well as Philipp Otto Runge and Caspar David Friedrich, were not at all troubled by the blurring of the boundaries of the arts, especially since, to them, music was the highest of the arts and the art to which all others should aspire. Music was valued as such because it seemed to be universal, acting directly upon the senses without relying on material mediation and without dependence upon an arbitrary system such as language; as Schopenhauer observed, "music, if regarded as an expression of the world, is in the highest degree a universal language that is related to the universality of concepts much as these are related to the particular things."[13] In its immediacy of apprehension, music purportedly restored a missing—mythical—original unity of the arts, dating from "primitive times," when, supposedly, as Charles Rosen and Henri Zerner have observed, "there were no distinctions among the different languages or even between music, poetry, dance, and verbal expression; sign and meaning were not then related by arbitrary convention, but the sign was a natural and immediately understandable representation of sentiment and idea."[14] Furthermore, music was primary because the abstraction of its structure and notation represented for the Romantics an ideal, multivalent, symbolic expression that permitted evocation of feelings, and ultimately the attainment of the spiritual, for Nietzsche the mythic. To use Schopenhauer's words, "music is the language of feeling and of passion, just as words are the language of reason."[15] Indeed, the philosopher rejected the role of mimesis for music, arguing that:

> music is as *immediate* an objectification and copy of the whole *will* as the world itself is, indeed as the Ideas are, the multiplied phenomenon of which constitutes the world of individual things. Therefore music is by no means like the other arts, namely a copy of the Ideas, but a *copy of the will itself,* the objectivity of which are the Ideas. For this reason the effect of music is so very much more powerful and penetrating than is that of the other arts, for these others speak only of the shadow, but music of the essence.[16]

If, as Friedrich Schlegel observed, "music [was] the art of the century," and the Romantic artists wished to realize its goals in painting, the question then was what visual strategies could be deployed to realize those goals. The first was the choice of subject matter. In rebellion against the history painting valued by the previous century, the Romantics prized landscape painting above all.

This was no coincidence, because for the Romantics, landscape, which had become subject to new means of being experienced at the end of the eighteenth century and which was implicated with the philosophical notion of the sublime, acquired a privileged status among the arts precisely because of its connection with music. In their rejection of classical landscape painting of the seventeenth century and the frivolity of the eighteenth century, Romantic thinkers elevated the genre by imbuing landscape with both sentiment and with ideas.[17] As Runge asked, "Is there not surely in this new art—landscapery, if you like—a higher point to be reached? Which will be even more beautiful than before?"[18] Linking music to landscape, the Romantics held that both were concerned more with formal composition than with conceptual thought, and that, in contradistinction to language, both forms were suggestive and emotive rather than descriptive. In his essay of 1794 on the poetry of Matthisson, a minor figure, Friedrich Schiller explored this idea, contending that, in Kuzniar's words, "both the composer and the landscape painter" addressed feelings "by arousing indefinite sensations through formal devices and abstraction."[19] Thus, the true subject of the romantic landscape was not nature itself, but the feelings aroused in the viewer by means of the formal devices used to depict the scene. And, as Kuzniar notes, Schiller argued that the landscape painter could appeal not only to the aesthetic sense through the "harmony of the structural arrangement" of the picture, but could also engage the moral sense, "the incessantly active symbolic imagination, that sees significance everywhere."[20]

Some five years later, in 1801, Friedrich Schlegel's brother August Wilhelm built upon Schiller's ideas. Pursuing farther the analogy between landscape painting and music, Schlegel maintained that landscape painting evokes a "series of impressions" that create a successive reaction to the landscape rather than the simultaneous one that Lessing considered the essence of the art of painting.[21] Finally, in his essay of 1808, "Etwas über Landschaftmalerei," the theorist Adam Müller also called landscape painting musical because of its sequentiality. The landscape painting unfolded in what Müller called *Raummomenten*—that is, a series of spatial moments, with the viewer reading detail after detail over time. For Müller too then, landscape, in its temporality and sequentiality, was inherently musical.[22]

As Rosen and Zerner have written, the issue of what such a Romantic, musical landscape would look like introduces the problem of creating visual strategies necessary to "endow landscape with profundity, loftiness of sentiment, an expression not only of appearance but of the reality hidden behind things, of the mystery, the infinity of Nature, and even the drama of the self facing the universe."[23] In other words, how could the artist indicate to the viewer that the image before him was not a mere imitation of nature but instead the material instantiation of larger ideas? Among the approaches suggested by the Romantic theorists, the one most relevant to Munch's choice in *The Scream* is the use of a more abstracted style and pictorial elements intended to refer to "primitive," original forms of expression, or what the Romantics called "hieroglyphic" imagery.

In simplified terms, for Runge and the Romantic philosophers, "hieroglyph" represented a mysterious sign that refers to a profound, even divine, idea, but whose original meaning has been lost so that it remains indecipherable for us. Many Romantics believed that nature itself was the hieroglyph of God. As Frances Connolly has explained, Novalis contended that in the "childhood of humanity the language of nature was understood and re-created through hieroglyphs," although he maintained that "[t]he hieroglyphic of nature has an emblematic character only as long as man is separated from nature."[24] So for Runge, the very choice of landscape as a subject was the choice of a hieroglyph, a material symbol of God.

The arabesque, a term sometimes used interchangeably with "hieroglyph," referred more specifically to the formal visual device, a playful ornamental, decorative, linear flourish, that would be used to give form to the hieroglyph. First used as a critical term for art and music by the German Romantics at this time, the term "arabesque" referred back to the framing devices completing a wall design with a picture in the middle, as in Pompeian wall decoration. Arabesques were often assemblages of fanciful patterns of sinuous vegetal forms or strange creatures. Runge used them in his *Tageszeiten* series (see, for example, *Night*), and Munch employed them in images such as his color lithograph *Madonna* of 1896, where the border of sperm surrounding the central depiction of the woman is an arabesque.[25]

Friedrich Schlegel adopted the term for literary purposes as well. He considered arabesques to be elements introduced in a text which were often "humorous, witty, or sentimental digressions that intentionally disturb the chronological flow of a narrative."[26] Scholars have further linked Schlegel's notion of the arabesque with examples of Romantic music, such as Schumann's C-Major Fantasy for Piano.[27] For the present purpose, though, the arabesque may be understood as a formal device, a kind of abstract notation, or script, intended, through line and color, to capture and to communicate the notion that an idea, especially a "primitive," "original" one, is being referred to rather than an imitation of visible nature. From the combination of hieroglyphs and arabesques, Runge believed, a true landscape painting, able to embody divine mysteries, would emerge.

At this point, I would like to turn back to Munch and *The Scream*. The image is, of course, first and foremost a landscape, in keeping with Munch's neo-Romantic subject matter, and it plays the essential role in the image despite the shock value of the ghostly figure. Indeed, Munch's work has been explicitly related to that of the German Romantic painter Caspar David Friedrich, and in particular his famous painting entitled *Wanderer above the Sea of Fog*, from circa 1818 (Figure 9–3). Elsewhere

Figure 9–3. Caspar David Friedrich, *Wanderer above the Sea of Fog,* c. 1818, oil on canvas, 94.8 × 74.8 cm., ©Elke Walford, Fotowerkstatt Hamburger Kunsthalle

I have discussed how *The Scream* and Friedrich's painting are closely related in that both illustrate the so-called halted traveller, a trope operative in much early nineteenth-century Romantic painting and poetry, in particular Wordsworth's, in which a solitary figure experiences an epiphany in the midst of nature.[28] Both Friedrich and Munch emphasized the importance of the revelation in these images by rejecting traditional horizontal landscape format in favor of a vertical orientation, thus asserting the upright presence and point of view of the protagonist.

However, while deploying the ideas of Romanticism Munch literally "turned away" from it in *The Scream,* subverting essential principles of such archetypal examples as Friedrich's *Wanderer.* First, and most importantly, he swiveled his figure around to face us (the "trope" literally turns around). Unlike Friedrich's *Rückenfigur,* who mediates our experience of the landscape scene, Munch's figure confronts us directly, forcing our engagement and undermining the issue of vicariousness that was so crucial to the apprehension of the Romantic sublime. Second, vastly different landscapes surround the figures. Rather than representing an environment that somehow embraces the spiritual aspirant, as seen in Friedrich's work, Munch twisted the recognizable scene of the Oslo fjord into a horrifying projection of mood. Munch's accompanying prose poem, which he recorded many times, in Norwegian, German, and French versions, restates the experience verbally:

> I was walking along the road with two friends. The sun set. I felt a tinge of melancholy. Suddenly the sky became a bloody red. I stopped, leaned against the railing, dead tired (my friends looked at me and walked on) and I looked at the flaming clouds that hung like blood and a sword . . . over the blue-black fjord and city. My friends walked on. I stood there, trembling with fright. And I felt a loud, unending scream piercing nature.[29]

This evocation of the hostile landscape and the terrifying *sound* that animates it represents the opposite side of the coin of the ecstatic apprehension by Romantics of the link between humankind and godly nature. Munch's experience of the world in *The Scream* could not be more different from this parallel account by Runge of his perception of landscape as the Divine:

> When the sky above me abounds with countless stars, when the wind rushes through the wide space and the wave breaks roaring in the far night, when above the woods the sky turns red; the valley steams and I fling myself upon the grass under the glittering drops of dew, each leaf and each blade of grass teems with life, the earth lives and stirs beneath me, all resounds together in a single chord, then the soul jubilates

aloud and soars into the boundless space around me, and there is no
below and no above, no time, no beginning and no end, I hear and feel
the living breath of God who holds and carries the world, in whom all
lives and works: here is the highest that we divine—God![30]

The Scream of course refers to music, but it is hardly music to our ears.
This is not an image of lyrical harmony, a "single chord," but rather a
shriek, a discordant, atonal *noise,* which subverts the meditative calm of
Romantic landscapes.

Munch further subverted Romantic procedure in his choice of a visual language for creating his landscape hieroglyph. He appropriated the
notation of the arabesque—that ornamental, virtually calligraphic line—
to configure an abstracted scene, pressing his point even more forcefully
in the lithograph than in the painting. This recalls Runge's prophesy that
modern landscape would be "hieroglyphic in character."[31] Stylistically,
of course, *The Scream* IS an arabesque and the whole arabesque screams.
And the psychological rather than descriptive color seen in the painting,
a projection of the figure's emotions, fulfills Runge's "ultimate aim . . .
an ideal of pure expressionism through color . . . an entirely 'musical'
art." It may even be argued that Munch's abstract notation did not just realize the ideal of the arabesque and the hieroglyph, the signs of primitive
and essential meanings, but that his lines literally refer to the language of
musical notation, beyond their obvious synesthetic correspondence to
sound waves. This notion seems even more plausible when, in looking
through Wassily Kandinsky and Franz Marc's *Blaue Reiter Almanach*
from 1911, which abounds with essays on music and abstraction, one
finds a suggestive double spread of pages. Viewed on its side, the
arabesque lines of Kandinsky's semiabstract study for *Composition IV*
echo Scriabin's musical notation on the staves to which they are juxtaposed (Figure 9–4). One can imagine Munch's receding railing, that crucial reference to temporality, as evocative of a musical staff with one
unruly note, a humanoid hieroglyph, escaping its confines.

With regard to temporality, crucial both to the narrative aspect of
the image as well as to its literal instantiation of music, the poetic version
of Munch's experience, quoted above, is obviously able to communicate the notion of temporality or sequentiality. But in the visual version,
too, Munch so cleverly succeeded in alluding to time that his image
captures that aspect of music as well. By inserting into a completely two-
dimensional pattern of arabesques a sharply receding, disjunctive diagonal that subverts decoration once again and creates the third dimension

Study for *Composition No. 4* by Kandinsky [In color in the original edition]

Figure 9–4. Wassily Kandinsky, Composition IV, and A. N. Scriabin, Prometheus, reproduction from *The Blaue Reiter Almanac,* eds. Wassily Kandinsky and Franz Marc (1912; reprint, ed. Klaus Lankheit, New York: Viking Press, 1974), 138–139.

of space, Munch's strategy draws upon allusion to "implied movement," suggesting an identification of "time with space-depth" in order "to overcome the narrative deficiency in naturalistic painting. . . ."[32] He thus invoked Adam Müller's notion of *Raummomenten,* his "spatial moments." As Alice Kuzniar has stated, in a passage that could describe *The Scream,* Müller's

> claim that landscape painting is temporal seems radically new in its reversal of Lessing's categories . . . According to Müller [landscape painting] approaches the verbal and musical arts because it portrays eternity not in the pregnant moment, as does sculpture, but in a *series* of spatial moments, registered as the viewer attends to one detail after the next, reading the painting over time. Müller thus links the key concepts of landscape as musical, allegorical, and sequential. . . . Indeed, for Müller landscape painting does not just suggest a particular atmosphere, recall a pleasant setting, nor arouse sentimental feelings. Landscape painting does much more, for in its innermost essence it is

somehow religious, seemingly oracular. It casts the eye out into distances where horizons seem to merge and boundaries become indistinct. . . .[33]

As I have tried to show, Munch sucessfully subverted Romantic ideals even as he posed the problem in Romantic terms. In fact, his emotional outlook, though a negative twist on Runge's viewpoint, remains far closer to Romanticism than to Gauguin's symbolist formulation of the issue of music and art. Gauguin's cerebral statement, published in *L'Echo de Paris* in June 1895, relates more to Mallarmé's picture poem of 1897, *Un Coup de Dés,* with its abstract musical notation, than to Munch's effusions (Figure 9–5). Gauguin wrote:

> It's music if you like! I borrow some subject or other from life or from nature, and, using it as a pretext, I arrange lines and colors so as to obtain symphonies, harmonies that do not represent a thing that is real in the vulgar sense of the word, and do not directly express any idea, but

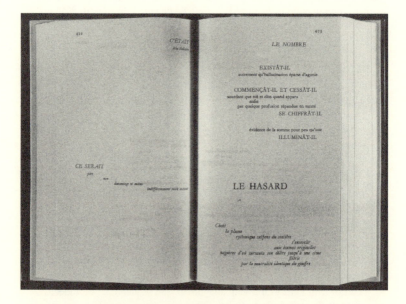

Figure 9–5. Stéphane Mallarmé, two pages from "Un Coup de Dés jamais n'abolira le hasard," (1897; reprint Stéphane Mallarmé, *Oeuvres complètes,* eds. Henri Mondor and G. Jean-Aubry, Paris: editions de la Pléiade, 1945), 472–473.

are supposed to make you think the way music is supposed to make
you think, unaided by ideas or images, simply through the mysterious
affinities that exist between our brains and such arrangements of colors
and lines.[34]

In *The Scream,* then, Munch directly engaged music as notation, as
well as philosophical hieroglyph, trading on romantic principles. But
neither a simplistic synesthetic correspondence to sound nor an abstracted musical model of the mind, *The Scream* undermined these principles as music turned discordant, and the *Rückenfigur* turned around.
For Munch, finally, music was not a unifying metaphor of the divine, as it
was for the Romantics, nor a more abstract model, as it was for the
French Symbolists; rather, Munch exploited music as a kind of performative gesture, when other modes failed,[35] to bid farewell to the
harmonies—both literal and figurative—of an earlier time and, Cassan-
dra-like, to foretell the fate of the individual in the modern era of harsh
cacophony. To paraphrase Nietzsche, what is man if not an "incarnation
of dissonance?"[36] In this sense, *The Scream* was so modern that one
must look forward to the twentieth-century composer Arnold Schoenberg,
master of dissonance, who in 1910 captured some of Munch's intention
when he wrote, "Art is the cry of despair of those who experience in
themselves the fate of all Mankind. . . . The world revolves within—inside them: what bursts out is merely the echo—the work of art! "[37]

NOTES

[1]See for example, Craig Wright, *Listening to Music,* second edition (St. Paul
and Minneapolis, Minn.: West Publishing Company, 1996), 354–356; Robert
Weiss, *Music and Expression* (Dubuque, Iowa: Wm. C. Brown Publishers, 1991),
chap. 16; Bennet Reimer, *Developing the Experience of Music,* second ed. (En-
glewood Cliffs, N.J.: Prentice-Hall, Inc.,1985), 164–174; and Donald H. Van
Ess, *The Heritage of Musical Style* (New York: Holt, Rinehart and Winston, Inc.,
1970), 316–319. I thank Professor Beth Bullard for these references and for her
interest in this project.

[2]See Gerard Vaughan, "Maurice Denis and the Sense of Music," *The Oxford
Art Journal* 7, no. 1 (1984): 38–48.

[3]Paul Gauguin to André Fontainas, March 1899; cited in Herschel Chipp,
Theories of Modern Art (Berkeley: University of California Press, 1968), 75

[4]Ibid., 39. Vaughan's article provides a good summary of the evolution of
the concept of the relationship between music and art in France, especially the

phenomenon of "Wagnerism." For more information, see Martine Kahane and Nicole Wild, *Wagner et la France,* exh. cat. (Paris: Bibliothèque nationale et Théâtre nationale de l'Opéra de France, 1983). Also noteworthy is the fact that in 1874 Théophile Ribot published *La Philosophie de Schopenhauer,* which introduced a generation to the philosopher's ideas.

[5]Maurice Denis, "Définition du néo-traditionnisme," section 25, *Art et Critique,* vol. 2, no. 66 (August 30, 1890), 558; translated in Jean-Paul Bouillon, "Arabesques," in *Lost Paradise: Symbolist Europe,* exh. cat. (Montreal: The Montreal Museum of Fine Arts, 1995), 376; see also Vaughan, 38.

[6]See Bouillon, 376, note 5.

[7]See for example Reinhold Heller, *Edvard Munch: The Scream* (New York: The Viking Press, 1978), 23ff. Also, Elizabeth Prelinger, "When the Halted Traveller Hears the Scream in Nature: Some Preliminary Thoughts on the Transformation of a Romantic Motif," in *Shop Talk: Studies in Honor of Seymour Slive* (Cambridge, Mass.: Harvard University Art Museums, 1995), 198–203.

[8]Arne Eggum, "Munch and Music," in *Frederick Delius og Edvard Munch,* exh. cat. (Oslo: Munch-museet, 1979), 38. Also, Sverre Krüger, "Maleri og Musikk," (thesis, Universitet i Bergen, Høsten, 1985); my thanks to Sissel Biornstad of the Munch-museet, Oslo, for her generous gift of a partial copy of this important thesis.

[9]Eggum, 40.

[10]Edvard Munch, translation adapted from Heller, 30.

[11]Rensselaer W. Lee, "Ut Pictura Poesis: The Humanistic Theory of Painting," *The Art Bulletin* XXII (1940), 202.

[12]See Kermit S. Champa, *The Rise of Landscape Painting in France. Corot to Monet,* exh. cat. (Manchester, N.H.: The Currier Gallery of Art, 1991), 35; also Andrew Kagan, "Ut Pictura Musica, I: to 1860," *Arts Magazine* 60, no. 9 (May 1986), 86–91.

[13]Arthur Schopenhauer, *The World as Will and Representation,* vol. I, section 52, trans. E.F.J. Payne (1819; reprint, New York: Dover Publications, 1969), 262.

[14]Charles Rosen and Henri Zerner, *Romanticism and Realism: The Mythology of Nineteenth-Century Art* (New York and London: W.W. Norton and Company, 1984), 60.

[15]Schopenhauer, 259.

[16]Ibid., 257.

[17]Rosen and Zerner, 52.

[18]Philipp Otto Runge; cited in Rosen and Zerner, 52.

[19]Friedrich Schiller, quoted in Alice Kuzniar, "The Vanishing Canvas: Notes on German Romantic Landscape Aesthetics," *German Studies Review* XI, no. 3 (October 1988), 361.

[20]Schiller, *Werke,* Nationalausgabe (Weimar: Böhlau, 1958), XXII: 273; cited in Kuzniar, 361.

[21]August Wilhelm Schlegel, *Die Kunstlehre* (reprint; ed. Edgar Lohner, Stuttgart: Kohlhemmer, 1963), 176; cited in Kuzniar, 361.

[22]Adam Müller, "Etwas über Landschaftsmalerei," *Ein Journal für die Kunst* (April/May 1808), 71–73; cited in Kuzniar, 361–362.

[23]Rosen and Zerner, 60.

[24]Novalis, quoted in Liselotte Dieckmann, *Hieroglyphics: The History of a Literary Symbol* (Saint Louis: Washington University Press, 1970), 181. This reference is cited with commentary in Frances S. Connelly, "Poetic Monsters and Nature Hieroglyphics: The Precocious Primitivism of Philipp Otto Runge," *Art Journal* 52, no. 2 (Summer 1993), 34.

[25]See Bouillon; and Connelly, 31–39.

[26]John Daverio, "Schumann's 'Im Legendenton' and Friedrich Schlegel's *Arabeske,*" *19th-Century Music* 11, no. 2 (Fall 1987), 151.

[27]Ibid, 150–163; also Daverio, "Symmetry and Chaos: Friedrich Schlegel's Views on Music," *19th-Century Music* 11, no. 1 (Spring 1987), 51–62.

[28]See Prelinger, 1995.

[29]As stated, Munch penned many versions of his experience. They appear in venues as varied as diary entries and inscriptions on the verso of prints and on paintings. The sources are listed in Heller, 65 and 103–109.

[30]Runge to Daniel Runge, March 9, 1802; cited in Rudolf M. Bisanz, *German Romanticism and Philipp Otto Runge: A Study in Nineteenth-Century Art Theory and Iconography* (De Kalb: Northern Illinois University Press, 1970), 49–50.

[31]Runge to Ludwig Tieck, December 1802; cited in Connelly, 35.

[32]David Loshak, "Space, Time and Edvard Munch," *Burlington Magazine* 131 (April 1989), 274, 282.

[33]Alice A. Kuzniar, "The Temporality of Landscape: Romantic Allegory and C. D. Friedrich," *Studies in Romanticism* 28, no. 1 (Spring 1989), 75.

[34]Paul Gauguin; originally published in French in *L'Echo de Paris,* June 13, 1895; translated in "Interview with Paul Gauguin," by Eugène Tardieu, in *The Writings of a Savage,* ed. Daniel Guérin, trans. Eleanor Levieux (New York: Viking Press, 1978), 109; cited in Bouillon, 377, note 8.

[35]I thank Professor Jeffrey Kallberg, Department of Music, University of Pennsylvania, for this idea.

[36]Friedrich Nietzsche, *The Birth of Tragedy and The Genealogy of Morals,* trans. Francis Golffing (New York: Doubleday, 1956), 145.

[37]Arnold Schoenberg, "Problem des Unterrichtes," in *Musikalisches Taschenbuch,* II (Vienna, 1910); cited in Willi Reich, *Schoenberg: A Critical Biography* (New York: Praeger, 1971), 56–57. Translation of the first sentence from Craig Wright, 355.

Contributors

Carlo Caballero received his Ph.D. from the University of Pennsylvania in 1996 with a wide-ranging dissertation on Gabriel Fauré and French musical aesthetics. He has published articles in *Victorian Studies* and *19th Century Music,* and most recently an essay on Fauré's religious beliefs in *Regarding Fauré* (1999). He is currently Research Associate on the faculty of the University of Colorado at Boulder, where he has finished a book on Fauré and is now pursuing new projects on Dukas and Mallarmé.

Kermit Swiler Champa is Andrea V. Rosenthal Professor in the History of Art at Brown University, where he has taught since 1969. His many books and exhibition catalogues include *Studies in Early Impressionism* (1972), wherein his interest in exchange between the arts is broadly apparent, and *The Rise of Landscape Painting in France* (1990), where he examines nineteenth-century landscape painting from the perspective of the rising importance and influence of concert music. His most recent book is *"Masterpiece" Studies: Manet, Zola, Van Gogh, and Monet* (1994).

Stephanie Campbell recently completed her dissertation, "Carl Friedrich Zelter and Text Setting: A Comparison of Goethe Settings by Zelter, Beethoven and Schubert," at Washington University. She has lectured on both Carl Friedrich and Juliane Zelter, published an article on Kurt Weill, and is currently working on an essay about musical structure in Virginia Woolf's *The Waves*. Professor Campbell teachs at Point Loma

Nazarene University in California and is also active as a professional singer.

Thomas Grey, Associate Professor at Stanford University, is the author of *Wagner's Musical Prose: Texts and Contexts* (1995) and editor of *Richard Wagner:"Der fliegende Holländer"* and *The Cambridge Companion to Wagner* (forthcoming). He has published numerous articles and reviews in *19th-Century Music, Cambridge Opera Journal, Opera Quarterly, Current Musicology,* and *Beethoven Forum.* He has previously collaborated with art historians by contributing an essay on opera to the interdisciplinary exhibition catalogue *Romance and Chivalry in Early 19th-Century French Painting* (1996).

Philippe Junod studied art history at the Kunsthistorisches Institute and the Sorbonne, piano and musicology under Nadia Boulanger and others, and was a member of the Swiss Institute in Rome. Since 1971 he has taught art history at the University of Lausanne, Switzerland. His publications include interdisciplinary studies on a variety of topics: *Transparence et opacité: essai sur les fondements théoriques de l'art modern* (1976), "Synthesthésies, correspondances et convergences des arts" (1985), and *La musique vue par les peintres* (1988), and, most recently, "Bach vu par les peintres" (1997).

Marsha L. Morton, Associate Professor at Pratt Institute, has lectured and published articles on topics in nineteenth-century German art ranging from Biedermeier painting to Max Klinger in the *Zeitschrift für Kunstgeschichte, Burlington Magazine, Source,* and *Art Journal.* She contributed an essay to the catalogue *Visions of Antiquity: Neoclassical Figure Drawings* (1993) and was the exhibition curator and author of *Pratt and Its Gallery: The Arts and Crafts Years* (1998).

Lisa Norris is Associate Professor of Art History at Kutztown University of the Pennsylvania State System of High Education. Her interest in the relations between art forms guided her dissertation, "The Early Writings of Camille Mauclair: Towards an Understanding of Wagnerism and French Art, 1885–1990," which she is reworking as a monograph. A planned study of Fantin-Latour's group portraits will investigate further the monumental impact of Wagner and Wagnerism upon the artist and his contemporaries in the visual arts and literature.

Elizabeth Prelinger is Associate Professor and Chair of the Department of Art, Music & Theatre at Georgetown University. She is the author and exhibition curator of *Prints by Edvard Munch from the Vivian and David Campbell Collection* (1997), *Käthe Kollwitz* (1992), and *Edvard Munch: Master Printmaker* (1983). Dr. Prelinger has lectured widely and published many articles and essays on Symbolist printmakers including the Nabis, Charles Dulac, and James Tissot.

Peter L. Schmunk is Associate Professor of Fine Arts at Wofford College in Spartanburg, South Carolina. His wide-ranging interest in the arts led him to pursue graduate studies in both musicology and art history and to earn a doctorate in comparative arts from Ohio University. He has a published article forthcoming from *SECAC Review* on the influence of music on the art of Corot and is preparing a book-length investigation of the impact of music across the nineteenth century on painters in France.

Index